Refinancing the College Dream

THE JOHNS HOPKINS UNIVERSITY PRESS

Refinancing the College Dream

Access, Equal Opportunity, and Justice for Taxpayers

Edward P. St. John

In collaboration with Eric H. Asker

The Johns Hopkins University Press
Baltimore and London

© 2003 The Johns Hopkins University Press
All rights reserved. Published 2003
Printed in the United States of America on acid-free paper

9 8 7 6 5 4 3 2 1

The Johns Hopkins University Press
2715 North Charles Street
Baltimore, Maryland 21218-4363
www.press.jhu.edu

LIBRARY OF CONGRESS CATALOGING-IN-PUBLICATION DATA
St. John, Edward P.
    Refinancing the college dream : access, equal opportunity, and justice for
taxpayers / Edward P. St. John in collaboration with Eric H. Asker.
        p.   cm.
    ISBN 0-8018-7265-0 (hardcover : alk. paper)
    1. Education, Higher—United States—Finance.   2. Educational
equalization—United States.   I. Asker, Eric H., 1950–   II. Title.
    LB2342 .S8754 2003
    378.1′06′0973—dc21   2002011067

A catalog record for this book is available from the British Library.

George Keller, Consulting Editor

CONTENTS

ACKNOWLEDGMENTS

Refinancing the College Dream addresses complex social and policy issues related to public financing of college students and institutions of higher education. While current thought and research on the economics of education has informed this project, my focus extends substantially beyond economic theory and research. To address the issues facing students, taxpayers, researchers, and policymakers who are concerned about access to higher and other postsecondary education, I turned to Rawls's theory of justice (1971) as the foundation for broadening the framework for addressing the access challenge. Many people have helped me with this project over more than six years, and I would like to acknowledge their help.

Writing this book proved far more complicated than I had anticipated, but Jacqueline Wehmueller at the Johns Hopkins University Press and George Keller, consulting editor, were unwavering in their support of the project. I would have dropped the *Dream* on several occasions had it not been for their comments and reflections.

William Goggin and Brian Fitzgerald, staff of the Congressional Advisory Committee on Student Financial Assistance, were extraordinarily helpful through the later stages of the writing process, although our conversations seldom focused on this project. The three of us had worked together on several projects in the early 1980s, when we were employed in the private sector. At the time, we shared a concern that equity issues were being overlooked in new federal policy reports on access. In the past two years, Brian and Bill worked with the Advisory Committee on the report *Access Denied* (Advisory Committee 2001a), which addresses the financial aspect of access more directly than almost any other federally sponsored reports released over the past two decades. Conversations with Bill and Brian about the issues addressed by the Advisory Committee helped me rethink my intent while preparing the final version of the book.

Staff members in the Indiana Education Policy Center also contributed to this project. Ada B. Simmons, associate director of the Policy Center, has done an exceptional job in coordinating the center's many and varied funded research projects, which has given me a modest amount of time to work on this and other writing endeavors. She is also an exceptional copyeditor and willingly reviewed the final draft of this text. Leigh Kupersmith provided support for the production of two earlier drafts and the editing of this final version. Without Leigh's support I would not have been able to complete this writing project. Others in the Policy Center who have helped with this project through assistance in closely related studies include Osman Cekic, Ontario Wooden, and Glenda Musoba.

Refinancing the College Dream would not have been written without the friendship and collaboration of Eric H. Asker. I met Eric in 1967, while serving as a member of the state cabinet for the California Association of Student Councils. At the time, we both dreamed about collaborating on a book that would deal with policy issues in education. When Eric arrived at the University of Dayton as a doctoral student in the fall of 1996, I invited him to collaborate on this book; he transferred to Indiana University when I started here, in January 1998. As the book went through its many revisions his role declined, because he chose to concentrate on completing his doctoral courses and dissertation. He was supportive of the project and completed the trend analyses that were central to this study of financial and academic access.

Finally, I extend a special thank-you to Jim Hearn, Don Hossler, and Mike Paulsen. For more than a decade, Jim and I have been engaged in a dialogue about the issues discussed here. These conversations have helped me refine my arguments. Don reviewed an earlier draft of the manuscript and helped me rethink aspects of my argument. Mike and I have collaborated on several papers on topics related to those addressed here. He helped me refine my thinking about the role of finances in promoting educational opportunity. The friendship and support of all three are gratefully acknowledged.

ACKNOWLEDGMENTS

Introduction

Attaining at least some postsecondary education is essential for rewarding employment in American society (Council for Aid to Education 1997;
Grubb 1996a).[1] The percentage of the population receiving a college education increased during the late twentieth century, but still further expansion is needed in the new century (Boesel and Fredland 1999; Council for Aid to Education 1997; Grubb 1996a,b; National Center for Public
Policy 2000). If educational opportunity were to be expanded with the
current level of public subsidy,[2] taxpayer costs would also expand. And
given public concern about tax rates, we can expect further reductions
in total public funding per student, a pattern that has been evident for
two decades (Zumeta forthcoming). The shift in the burden of paying
for college from the government to students, a trend over the past twenty
years (Toutkoushian 2001), has eroded equal opportunity for low-income
students (Advisory Committee 2001a,b, 2002; Kane 2001; McPherson and
Schapiro 1991, 1997). Thus, to expand access further, we need to reconsider how government funds education, whether funding is adequate,
and how financing strategies should be changed to expand access and
equalize opportunity.

   Some analysts doubt the need to expand access to higher education
(e.g., Finn 2001). However, if large numbers of academically prepared
students cannot enroll in college due to finances, then there is still a need
to reconsider how government finances colleges and college students. It
is crucial to ensure financial access for students who are prepared for col-

---

[1] In this book, the term *postsecondary education* refers to all post–high school education, from technical education to traditional colleges and universities. *Higher education* refers to colleges and universities that offer a two-year, four-year, or advanced
degree. *Other postsecondary education* refers to technical education and other
post–high school education of less than two years' duration.

[2] Public subsidies to higher education include direct funding for colleges (which reduces tuition charges and covers educational expenses) and subsidies to students
with financial need (i.e., student grants, interest and other subsidies for loans, com-
pensation for work-study), provided by states and the federal government.

lege and plan to attend. Only this minimum threshold of financial access can promote economic productivity within states. As illustrated in the pages that follow, this minimum threshold of financial access was not evident in the 1980s and 1990s.

Refinancing the College Dream examines trends in public funding of higher education and analyzes research on the impact of finances and educational reform on access (part I), then evaluates alternative approaches to financing higher education in the period ahead (part II). Theory and research on the economics of education provide a foundation for this inquiry, but I have developed a new framework to illuminate the social justice issues that underlie the debates about public finance and access to higher education. As general background, this introduction summarizes the government's role in financing higher education, identifies commonly accepted understandings about the economics of education, and provides an overview of the current debate about access.

Government Funding

Public colleges, like public schools, were historically funded primarily by states. For most of the twentieth century, states provided a college education at low tuition for their citizens. In the late 1960s, for example, states subsidized more than 80 percent of educational costs (Bowen 1980; Carnegie Commission 1973). But by the late 1990s, about 33 percent of educational costs in public colleges (tuition plus fees) were paid by students and their families (table A.3).[3] And while tuition charges at public colleges were still substantially lower than at private colleges (College Board 2001a,b), the cost of attending public colleges grew substantially in the last two decades of the twentieth century. Thus there is a well-documented trend over the 1980s and 1990s of an erosion of the state role in providing direct subsidies to public colleges and universities (Toutkoushian 2001). Of course, the United States also has a large national system of private colleges, and tuition in these colleges also continued to increase in the late twentieth century (College Board 2000). States generally do not subsidize tuition in private colleges, and the large price differential between public and private colleges remains (Breneman, Finn, and Nelson 1978; College Board 2000). States now provide some financial support directly to college students. This role solidified in the 1970s, after federal student aid programs were developed. We can bet-

[3] Tables including data from several periods, and thus referred to in several different chapters, are in the appendix (tables A.1–A.9). Tables covering a single period and thus applicable to a single chapter are integrated into that chapter.

ter understand the state role in financing access by considering it within a national context.

After World War II, the federal government provided subsidies to returning veterans, both as a reward for their service to the country and as a strategy to promote economic adjustment. Known as the GI Bill, these federal subsidies stimulated gains in educational attainment and economic development (Becker 1964; Finn 1978). The apparent success of this federal aid program informed subsequent policy development. In the late 1950s, the National Defense Education Act included a major new loan program for college students attending both public and private colleges. In 1964, the federal government created a new program through Social Security that provided grants for children of deceased parents who had paid into the Social Security program. These programs, along with a growing body of economic research, provided a foundation for the expansion of federal student financial aid in the 1960s and 1970s (Finn 1978; Gladieux and Wolanin 1976).

The Higher Education Act of 1965 (HEA), passed as one of President Johnson's Great Society programs, created generally available grant and loan programs for students with financial need. Between 1965 and 1978, these programs were expanded in efforts to promote access and equalize educational opportunity. Arguments made by economists about the efficiency of student aid (e.g., Becker 1964; Hansen and Weisbrod 1969) provided one of the rationales for expanding these programs. The federal student aid programs were reorganized to explicitly address the goal of equal educational opportunity in the 1972 reauthorization of HEA (Gladieux and Wolanin 1976). The 1972 HEA reauthorization also included financial incentives for states to develop grant programs through the State Student Incentive Grant (SSIG) program, and state grant programs expanded substantially after 1972.

The Middle Income Student Assistance Act, passed in 1978, broadened the eligibility criteria for federal need-based student grants. However, total federal funding for student grants declined in the late 1970s (St. John 1994). With the expansion in eligibility and decline in total federal grant aid, substantially less grant aid was available for low-income students (chapters 6 and 7).

Ronald Reagan's election as president in 1980 accelerated the decline in federal grant aid for low-income students. While economic rationales were taken seriously in the development of federal student grant programs, public officials argued that this public investment was excessive (Bennett 1987; Carnes 1987; Finn 1988a,b) and educational researchers were asked to build new rationales for restructuring federal student aid programs (St. John 1994). Researchers began to focus on high school math courses as an explanation for college enrollment (Adelman 1999; Pelavin and Kane 1988, 1990). Then a new generation of federal studies, by the National Center for Education Statistics (NCES) (1996a, 1997a, 2000a),[4] used an "academic pipeline" model to study access, an approach that overlooked the role of financial aid in ensuring equal opportunity.

After 1980, substantial changes occurred in the public financing of higher education. Not only did students' share of the educational costs at public colleges increase (St. John 1994; Toutkoushian 2001), but federal investment in grants, especially the need-based grants for low-income students, declined substantially (Advisory Committee 2001a; College Board 2000). Economic rationales ceased to have much influence on government policy, as concerns about taxpayer costs and academic preparation replaced equity as the basis for educational policy, especially at the federal level.

Economics of Education

It is more than a bit ironic that as economic research became more sophisticated and mathematical, its influence on policymaking in higher education declined. As background for this study, we need to consider theory and evidence in the economics of higher education, along with the ways in which this research has been translated into numeric measures that could be used by policymakers, policy analysts, and the media.

THEORY AND RESEARCH EVIDENCE

Three areas of theory and research on the economics of education can potentially inform the debates about higher education finance and access: (1) economics of *human capital*, (2) theory and research on *efficiency and productivity*, and (3) economics of *public finance* (Paulsen and Smart 2001). I briefly summarize each area of research.

Human Capital

The theory of human capital hypothesizes that individuals and governments make educational decisions based on expected costs and benefits (Becker 1964). For individuals, the costs of attending college include both direct expenses, including educational charges (tuition, other edu-

---

[4] Throughout this book I give NCES as the author of NCES publications (e.g., NCES 1996) when this reference method is recommended on the publication's inside cover; the authors of the publications are noted in the reference list. I assume this referencing method is recommended when NCES prefers to be identified as author. When no such recommendation is made, I refer directly to the author(s) of the NCES publication (e.g., Adelman 1999).

REFINANCING THE COLLEGE DREAM

cational fees, and books) and living costs, and forgone income while enrolled in college. Individuals' benefits include increased future earning and gains in quality of life. Research consistently confirms that postsecondary education results in increased earnings (Cohn and Geske 1990; Grubb 1996a,b; Leslie and Brinkman 1988). Human capital theory is also central to the rationale for federal and state student financial aid, as it may have been to the more recent change in state finance.

By providing subsidies to individuals who have financial need, government can reduce barriers on the cost side of the calculus for students from low-income families who cannot afford the direct costs of attending. Further, loans provide a way of delaying payment on the direct cost for low-income and middle-income families (Becker 1964). The economic research consistently confirms that student grants enable low-income students to enroll (Kane 1995, 1999; McPherson and Schapiro 1991, 1997).

Applied to the role of government, the human capital calculus involves considering the ratio of the costs of subsidies (to individuals and institutions) to the economic gains that result from this investment. In other words, states can expect a better economy to result from increased subsidies, a claim confirmed by economic research that compares states (Paulsen 1996a,b, 1998, 2001a). However, state support for higher education underwent a general decline during the last two decades of the twentieth century (chapters 6 and 7), although the economy in general improved. Until the middle 1970s, general concepts of economic development were considered a sufficient rationale for public spending on higher education (Halstead 1974), but with the recent improvement in the economy there is reason to reconsider this simple assumption. Thus, translating human capital research into public policy involves many complexities (Paulsen 2001a).

Given that individuals receive returns (i.e., higher incomes) from their investments in education, it is easier for states to reduce their subsidies to public higher education, especially if sufficient federal loans are available for middle-income families that must pay a substantially larger share of current income for education. While few policy analysts argue that loans are "effective" in promoting educational opportunity, the availability of loans has made it easier for states to reduce their subsidies to institutions, allowing tuition to rise. Further, policy analysts working for NCES (2001d) and the American Council on Education (King 1999) generally accept the status quo, assuming the high-loan environment is equitable, without testing the assumption. As tuition charges have risen, too little attention has been paid to the role of financial aid in maintaining equal opportunity to enroll across income groups.

Efficiency and Productivity

Current theories of efficiency and productivity are difficult to apply to higher education. Economists who study productivity tend to focus on research productivity (i.e., faculty publications) as a stimulus to the economy (Lewis and Dunbar 2001). Efficiency in the costs of educating students receives less attention. Productivity studies in the 1970s focused on efficiency of instruction (e.g., Bowen and Douglass 1971; Carlson, Farmer, and Weathersby 1974; Weathersby et al. 1977), but these studies had little influence on policy or practice. Rather, there was a clear incentive for institutions to maximize revenues rather than to achieve efficiency of operations (Kane 2001; Bowen 1980; St. John 1994). Researchers thus find it easier to focus on research productivity, an outcome associated with faculty salaries (Lewis and Dunbar 2001; St. John 1994). Many critics of higher education focus on the inefficiency of colleges as an explanation for the rising costs of attending (Finn 1988a, 1998b; Finn and Manno 1996). The tendency to avoid the topic of efficiency of services has fueled these criticisms and complicated efforts to craft public policies that promote access.

An issue once central to the policy debates about student financial aid was whether the availability of federal student aid influenced colleges to increase tuition, a claim made by education officials in President Reagan's administration (Bennett 1987; Carnes 1987). NCES's recent publication *Study of College Costs and Prices, 1988–89 to 1997–98* (2001d) should lay this issue to rest. "Regarding the relationship between financial aid and tuition," NCES states, "the models found no associations between most of the aid variables (federal grants, state grants, and student loans) and change in tuition in either the public or private not-for-profit sectors. The single exception is institutional aid, which was found to have a positive association with tuition increases for public comprehensive and private not-for-profit institutions" (x). This finding is consistent with prior research and essentially supports the conclusion that the decline in federal aid influenced private colleges to raise tuition as a means of generating revenue (McPherson and Schapiro 1991, 1997; St. John 1994). However, the debate about institutions' finances, tuition charges, and student aid raises a number of questions about public finance.

Public Finance

Theories of public sector finance are appropriately discussed within the economic theory of supply and demand (Paulsen 2001b; St. John and Paulsen 2001). In addition to subsidizing the price that colleges charge students, public funding of institutions expands the supply of higher education opportunity. In the 1960s and 1970s, expansion of the supply of opportunity was a major issue in many states, given the growth in the traditional college-age populations (Halstead 1974), but forecasters predicted enrollment declines in the 1980s and 1990s (e.g., Carnegie Commission 1973; Cartter 1976; NCES 1980). While states maintained a stable rate of investment in institutions as enrollment expanded in the 1970s (chapter 5), this practice did not continue (chapters 6 and 7). The older arguments (e.g., Honeyman, Wattenbarger, and Westbrook 1996) have not held up well in the past two decades. Some analysts argue that using student aid subsidies to expand private college enrollment is a more economical way to expand supply of opportunity (e.g., Hearn and Longanecker 1985; Zumeta 2001). But ambiguities in research on students' response to college prices (price response) further complicate efforts to build rational models of public finance.

A review of the research (Paulsen 2001a; St. John and Paulsen 2001) points to the following concepts and principles about the financing of the public sector:

(1) [P]rices (e.g., tuition) are influenced by demand-side and supply-side (cost-related) factors; (2) prices of services in nonprofit organizations such as colleges and universities depend on a combination of increases in costs of providing services and the subsidies received from government or private sources; (3) increases in the supply-side factors related to subsidies to institutions (e.g., state appropriations and endowment income) reduce upward pressure on prices; (4) increases in institutional costs or expenditures (e.g., for instruction, administration, student services) put upward pressure on prices; (5) increases in productivity in the use of resources (e.g., a higher student-faculty ratio) can reduce unit costs [e.g., expenditures per student], but often at the expense of reductions in quality of services provided; (6) prices of services are directly related to the benefits consumers expect from purchase of the product (e.g., future earnings), demographic factors that affect the number of consumers in the market (e.g., larger numbers of students of traditional age), increases in the price of substitutes (e.g., prices of tuition charged by other institutions), and decreases in price of complements (e.g., room and board, books, transportation, living expenses) (St. John and Paulsen 2001, 550–51).

As these conclusions illustrate, issues related to the level of public subsidy to students and institutions, as well as the tuition that institutions charge for their services, cannot be reduced to a simple set of ratios. Rather, complex sets of policies and market forces influence the ways in which prices are set by institutions. There are recursive relationships between student and institutional subsidies that influence prices (i.e., tuition) and price response.

USING ECONOMIC RESEARCH IN POLICY

One problem associated with using economic research to inform public policy on access and finance relates to the concepts and measures of net prices and price response used in policy research and policy development. The research on student price response has consistently shown that low-income students are more responsive to tuition and student aid than are the middle-income majority (e.g., Manski and Wise 1983; Kane 1995, 1999; McPherson and Schapiro 1991, 1993, 1997; St. John 1990a). In attempts to translate this research for policymakers, it has been common practice to generate measures of student price response, an estimate of the percentage change in enrollment attributable to a $100 change in price (Heller 1997; Jackson and Weathersby 1975; McPherson 1978; McPherson and Schapiro 1993; Leslie and Brinkman 1988). Most reviewers who develop these standardized measures adjust for inflation, expressing the ratios indexed in a constant dollar amount, although this is not always the case. Inflation adjustments are not the biggest problem with the use of price response measures in policy models. However, the assumption of a standardized and linear price response ratio had many limitations that constrained the direct application of price response measures, including:

—The price response ratios were more applicable to low-income students than to all students (Heller 1997; St. John 1990a).
—Changes in student aid policy (e.g., the increasing emphasis on loans) could change the ways in which students responded to prices and subsidies over time (Dresch 1975; St. John 1990a,b; St. John and Starkey 1995a).
—Changes in family incomes over time or across settings could limit the applicability of generalized ratios (Kane 2001; McPherson and Schapiro 1993).
—Changes in the labor market could induce more students to enroll than would be predicted from price measures alone (Kane 1995, 1999; McPherson and Schapiro 1998).
—Student price response in the area of enrollment differs from price response in persistence (Dresch 1975; St. John and Starkey 1995a).

The ambiguities for policymakers in interpreting price response research have not been resolved. States and the federal government have ignored economic rationales, along with most economic research, when developing annual budgets for higher education. Indeed, many analysts in the debates about access have ignored the role of finances (e.g., Pelavin and Kane 1998; NCES 1997a), an issue that obfuscates the equity concerns raised by economists. While economists and educational researchers have debated different ways of measuring price response and how these measures predict the effects of price changes, the policy community has overlooked the role of finances, especially at the federal level.

The New Conflict over Access

While the federal student aid programs, initiated in 1965 and expanded through 1978, were designed to equalize the opportunity to enroll and persist in college, since 1980 the focus of policy research on access has shifted away from the role of finances. Numerous federally funded studies have concluded that disparities in academic preparation, especially differences in enrolling in high school math courses and applying in advance for college, were the primary causes of the access gap between minorities and the White majority (e.g., NCES 1996a, 1997a,b, 1998b, 2000a, 2001a,c; Pelavin and Kane 1988). Economists have pointed out that during this same period the decline in federal grants caused the gap in opportunity (e.g., Kane 1994, 1999; McPherson and Schapiro 1991, 1997), but their research has done little to restore the federal investment in need-based grants. Throughout this period, the purchasing power of federal grants declined and tuition charges grew much faster than inflation (College Board 2001a,b), increasing the net price of attending college much more substantially for low-income students than for middle-income and upper-income students.

During the 1980s, national groups began the process of redefining access, but the task remains incomplete. For example, the National Post-secondary Education Cooperative (NPEC) and the American Council on Education convened a panel to reconceptualize access (NPEC 1998). They focused on the finding that greater numbers of women and minorities were attending college, but recognized the gap in opportunity for minorities (Ruppert 1998). However, NPEC largely overlooked that this opportunity gap between minorities and Whites had widened after 1980 (Kane 1994; St. John 1994). It pointed to "inadequacies of current concepts of access" (Ruppert 1998, 9), but did not suggest a definition that distinguished between the roles of academic preparation and financial resources in promoting equal opportunity.

More recently, a few groups have begun to focus on the opportunity gap as an increasingly critical social and economic problem. The Advisory Committee on Student Financial Assistance, in its report *Access Denied*, focused attention on a crucial aspect of access that is too frequently overlooked:

> Three decades ago, there was a unanimous agreement on the nation's access goal: low-income students who were academically prepared must have the same educational opportunity as their middle- and upper-income peers. Today, that opportunity—to pursue a bachelor's degree whether through full-time enrollment at a four-year institution directly upon graduation from high school or as a transfer from a two-year institution—is all but ruled out for increasing numbers of low-income students by record levels of unmet need. The rate at which academically qualified, low-income students attend four-year institutions provides one of the most sobering views of America's educational and economic future (2001a, vi).

Given the conflicted terrain of policy studies on college access, it is crucial not only to reexamine the evidence used to make arguments about access, but to do so in a way that integrates and tests the newer claims about academic preparation and the older claims about equal opportunity. Two conceptual models have been widely used to examine how public policy influences access to higher education.

The older model focused on financial access but did not adequately consider the role of academic preparation. For decades, researchers have examined the effect of student aid on enrollment (Jackson 1978, 1988; Manski and Wise 1983; McPherson and Schapiro 1991; St. John 1990a). Although these studies indicate that student aid promotes access for low-income students (Heller 1997), they have had little or no influence on public finance policy after 1980.

The new model focuses on the role of academic preparation. The National Education Longitudinal Study: 1988–94 (NELS:88) provides a database that tracks a national cohort of students from eighth grade into college, an appropriate database for studying access to higher education (NCES 1996a). NCES has made substantial use of the database to study the role of academic preparation in college enrollment. The NCES model (1997b), the "pipeline to college," defines the following steps:

—Step 1: Aspirations
—Step 2: Academic preparation
—Step 3: Entrance exams
—Step 4: College application
—Step 5: Enrollment

The analyses using this model (NCES 1997a,b, 2000b, 2001a,c) systematically overlook the idea that finances could influence enrollment behavior, even when the studies report statistics on financial aid (e.g., NCES 1997a). The following conclusion illustrates the interpretive position typically taken in these federal reports: "Although there are differences by income and race-ethnicity in the four-year college enrollment rates of college-qualified high school graduates, the difference between college-qualified low-income and middle-income students, as well as differences among college-qualified black, Hispanic, Asian, and white students, are eliminated among those students who have taken the college entrance examinations and completed an application for admission, the two steps necessary to attend a four-year college" (NCES 1997a, iii). This statement clearly argues that by taking college entrance tests and applying in advance to four-year colleges,[5] minority students could gain access to four-year colleges. Ironically, this report presented information related to the role of finances, controlling for academic preparation, but failed to consider the possibility that financial aid influenced college enrollment.[6] The report, like many of NCES's other studies (e.g., 1996a, 1997b, 2001c) that analyzed NELS:88, ignored the possibility that the decline in federal student aid after 1980 could have influenced the opportunity gap. The extreme nature of these claims about academic access necessitates a rethinking of the logical models used in federal access studies, especially since the expressed intent of NCES's studies (e.g., 1997a) was to assess the causes of financial disparities in access.

When assessing the impact of finances on access of low-income students to college, it is arbitrary and illogical to exclude the impact of finances at any stage of the access pipeline, from middle school through degree completion. By focusing only on those low-income high school graduates who are college-qualified and who both take tests and apply for college, the impact of finances on expectations, plans, timing of college entry, choice of college, test-taking, and application are eliminated from consideration. Given these serious limitations of NCES's pipeline

[5] The NELS:88 questions about college applications were asked during the senior year, which means that students answering affirmatively on these questions had applied to a college that required an application the year before enrollment. Many less selective institutions do not require these advance applications.

[6] Chapter 8 presents a reexamination of analyses reported by NCES (1997a) to illustrate that, because of its interpretive assumptions, NCES has systematically overlooked the role of finances in promoting equal educational opportunity in the United States. This is both sad and ironic, given that promotion of equal opportunity remains an intent of federal student financial aid, the primary form of federal investment in higher education.

model, and given that NCES's system already overlooked the role of finances in access, one of my goals in this book is to develop a more balanced approach to studying the impact of public policy on access and to considering the role of academic preparation.

An Approach to the Problem

To build an understanding of the access problem facing colleges, states, and the federal government, we need to consider both the financial and academic aspects of the access challenge. Thus, while *Refinancing the College Dream* is primarily concerned with the role of finances in improving access to higher education, it also considers the roles of academic preparation and efforts to encourage school students to pursue a postsecondary education (postsecondary encouragement). It considers how high-stakes testing accentuated the opportunity gap that has emerged since 1980, and how the new emphasis on research-based school reform and postsecondary encouragement might contribute to expanding access and narrowing the opportunity gap. However, a central concern in refinancing should be to improve coordination of public finance strategies and to improve the frequency and use of evaluation research.

We must reconsider the relationship between college finances and social justice for diverse economic interests in American society if we are to craft more workable public finance strategies. The opportunity for middle-income students to enroll and persist in college was made easier by loans in the 1980s and tax credits in the 1990s. Even if they paid more for college in part through delayed payments (i.e., loan repayment), middle-income families found it easier than did low-income families to pay the direct costs of attending. The overall participation rate for traditional college-age adults increased during the last two decades of the twentieth century (NCES 1998a), raising the possibility that loans helped the middle class finance their college choices.

However, the growth in opportunity was not evenly shared within the traditional college-age population, nor was opportunity evenly distributed among those who prepared academically. Many low-income students had more to pay, after grants and loans, than they could afford, with the limited financial support available from their families (St. John 2002). There was virtual equality in college participation rates for African Americans and Hispanics compared with Whites in 1975, but a substantial opportunity gap emerged in the last quarter of the twentieth century (NCES 1998a). The opportunity gap widened between high-income and low-income groups. For high school students from families in the low-income quartile, the college enrollment rate increased only from 57 to 60 percent between 1980–82 and 1992 (Kane 2001). During the same period, the enrollment rate for students in the highest income quartile increased from 68 to 90 percent (Kane 2001). Therefore, we need a better way of evaluating the effects of public finance strategies related to the interests of the middle-income majority, of minorities facing financial inequalities, and of taxpayers concerned about the efficient use of tax dollars.

Part I of *Refinancing the College Dream* develops a framework for evaluating the effects of finances and other policies on access and equal opportunity, then uses the framework to assess the effects of policy changes that took place in the 1970s, 1980s, and 1990s. John Rawls's highly regarded theory of justice provides a conceptual starting point for broadening the scope of the evaluation beyond the narrow confines of economic theory. The framework builds on the theory of justice, the economic theory of human capital, and other related social and policy theories. The analytic chapters examine how changes in student aid policy during the last three decades of the twentieth century corresponded with trends in key indicators (i.e., college participation rates, equity in participation, and taxpayer costs). They also review econometric studies of the impact of financial aid to determine whether these studies confirm the apparent relationships between changes in financial aid and changes in participation rates during these periods.

To address questions related to academic preparation, I also consider how changes in other educational policies (e.g., school reforms) could have influenced changes in these indicators. Evaluations of the impact of federal student aid policy and college prices on access and persistence by all students indicate that changes in policy help explain the growth in access for White and upper- and middle-income students, while studies of the impact of aid on minorities and low-income students confirm that the participation gap was created by the decline in grants. These analyses provide compelling evidence that changes in federal student aid policy were the primary cause of increased inequality of opportunity for college enrollment during the late twentieth century. However, the increased emphasis on testing and standardization in K–12 schools also may have contributed to the problem.

In part II, I propose a contingency approach to finance that can be used to rethink financial strategies in colleges, in states, and at the federal level. This approach involves coordinating financial strategies within states, as well as between states and the federal government. It also involves using research to inform policy development, with frequent evaluations to assess the effects of policies that have been implemented. Policymakers in states and institutions should routinely evaluate whether student aid is adequate to maintain financial access for low-income students, given the costs that students must pay to maintain their enrollment. A research-based approach to finance reform is needed in higher education.

In developing the contingency theory of finance, I argue that evaluations should be used to inform strategies for improving access to higher education, as well as for equalizing opportunity—crucial issues in the early twenty-first century. Part II also examines possible approaches for reforming K–12 education, providing postsecondary encouragement, and expanding the postsecondary system.

Better coordination between states and the federal government will be needed to respond to the challenge of improving access. Increased coordination of financing strategies within states can help expand financial access to higher education while constraining growth in total tax expenditures. Clearer articulation of common goals could help us expand access while equalizing access to quality higher education and reducing the total taxpayer subsidies per student.

Refinancing the College Dream takes a different position than the mainstream policy literature on higher education. Researchers working for NCES (2001d) and the American Council on Education (King 1999, 2002) have taken the position that the shift to middle-income affordability as a focus of federal policy is an acceptable policy path, and that for low-income students, the central policy issue is academic preparation (Choy 2002; King 2002; NCES 1996a, 1997a,b, 2000a). I argue that we should take a thoughtful and critical look at the claims underlying this policy position. At a minimum, it is crucial to reopen the debate on workable approaches for balancing concerns about middle-income affordability, equal opportunity for low-income families, and efficiency in the use of tax dollars.

PART I   Understanding the Access Challenge

The chapters in this part of the book assess the challenge of access to college. First, chapter 2 examines the new access challenge from a social justice perspective, focusing on access for the majority, equal opportunity for students in low-income families who prepare academically, and efficiencies in the use of tax dollars. However, to build an understanding of the ways in which changes in policy influence these three competing interests, a new framework is needed. Chapter 3 reviews theories typically used in research on college access, and chapter 4 presents the study framework and explains how it is used to assess the effects of policy changes in the last three decades of the twentieth century.

The framework provides a logical basis for assessing the influence on access of changes in educational reform and public finance. In chapters 5–7, I assess the roles of academic preparation and finances (tuition and student aid) during the 1970s, 1980s, and 1990s. These chapters systematically examine trends in access (college participation rates by high school graduates) and equal opportunity (a comparison of participation rates across diverse groups). The analyses examine the role of finances, largely overlooked in the National Center for Education Statistics' studies of access (e.g., NCES 1997a,b, 1998b), and also examine the influences of changes in K–12 policy. The analyses provide an assessment of the relative effects of changes in finances and K–12 reform on access and equal opportunity.

As a final step in building an understanding of the access challenge, chapter 8 reexamines NCES's analyses of academic preparation for students in the high school class of 1992. This chapter examines the role of finances in the transition to college by college-qualified students from low-income families compared with college-qualified students from high-income families.

Finding Justice in Public Finance

Social justice is integral to the public financing of higher and other post-secondary education. Both taxpayers and students have an interest in college finance. If the vague notion of "future economic returns" no longer provides a sufficient rationale for federal investment in need-based student aid, then as a society we need a better way to understand the consequences of the decline in public investment. Given that Congress has approved George W. Bush's plan for a decade of reductions in federal taxes (in the Economic Growth and Tax Relief Reconciliation Act of 2001), a substantial new federal investment in grants is unlikely, unless it is offset by other cost reductions. At best, perhaps states and the federal government can develop a workable collaborative reinvestment strategy. To provide background on the access challenge, this chapter first examines the eroded purchasing power of Pell grants, which provided the foundation for federal need-based aid in the 1970s and early 1980s. I use John Rawls's theory of justice (1971) to build an understanding of the three dimensions of social justice in college finance:

1. *access for the majority*, as measured by the overall opportunities to attend college;
2. *equal opportunity to enroll*, as measured by the growing gap in opportunity between minorities (African Americans and Hispanics) and Whites and between low-income and high-income students;
3. *justice for taxpayers*, as measured by tax expenditures per student enrolled in higher and other postsecondary education.

Before discussing these three sets of measures, I examine the decline in Pell grants over the past two decades. The reduction in federal grant aid after 1980 appears to be linked to a new inequality in the opportunity to attend college for minority students compared with White students and for low-income students compared with upper-income students. Since the increased gap in opportunity corresponds with the decline in Pell grants, the major federal student aid program, it makes sense to start this inquiry by examining trends in the Pell program.

The Decline in Pell Grants

The Pell grant program, created in 1972, is the one federal program with the potential for equalizing opportunity for low-income students. It is the only "portable" federal grant program. A student who is eligible for a Pell grant can take the grant to virtually any college to which he or she is admitted. Predicting demand for Pell grants was difficult, because students with low levels of need were eligible, or "entitled." The *entitlement* nature of Pell made the program difficult to evaluate. One indicator of whether aid is adequate to maintain financial access is the percentage of educational costs covered by the maximum Pell award—the amount of aid the poorest student would receive if no other grant were available. In table 2.1, the maximum Pell award is compared with the average cost of attending a public four-year college. This measure illustrates the declining purchasing power of Pell grants.

In 1975, the maximum Pell award was $4,048 (in 1997–98 dollars).[1] At that time, this maximum grant equaled 85 percent of the average cost of attending a public four-year college. However, the Pell program had a "half cost" provision: the student's award could not exceed half the cost of attending. Students attending higher-cost (private) colleges could receive the full award. This single federal program essentially created the opportunity for the poorest in society to send their children to college, if they were academically qualified.

Since 1975 the purchasing power of Pell grants has substantially declined. Between 1975 and 1995, the average cost of attending a public four-year college rose while the maximum Pell grant declined (in constant dollars). Pell grants increased slightly in 1999–2000 compared with 1995–96. The purchasing power of Pell grants decreased substantially across this period. The maximum percentage of the average cost of a public four-year college covered by a Pell grant fell from 85 percent in 1975 to 35 percent in 1995. The maximum percentage then rose slightly, to 39 percent in 1999–2000.

However, the full potential of Pell's purchasing power was never fully realized by low-income students in public colleges. Until 1986, the Pell

---

[1] All dollar amounts in this book (with the exception noted below) are adjusted to 1997–98, using the Consumer Price Index for All Urban Consumers (CPI-U) (see appendix). Some higher education analysts prefer to use the Higher Education Price Index (HEPI), which is based on changes in faculty salaries and other costs to institutions of higher education (Halstead 1995). However, since affordability is a general public concern, it seems more appropriate to adjust all monetary amounts for the CPI. Actual dollar amounts are reported in some of the evaluation studies reviewed in part I.

TABLE 2.1 Purchasing Power of Pell Grant Maximum Awards at Four-Year Public Institutions, 1975 to 2000

Year	Pell Grant Maximum Award		Average Cost of Attendance (1997–98 Constant Dollars)	Pell Maximum as Percentage of Average Cost of Attendance (1997–98 Constant Dollars)[a]	Average Cost of Attendance at Public College Minus Pell Grant Maximum (1997–98 Constant Dollars)
	Current Dollars	1997–98 Constant Dollars			
1975–76	1,400	4,048	4,769	85%	$0.5 \times 4,769 = 2,348$[b]
1980–81	1,750	3,240	4,674	69%	$0.5 \times 4,674 = 2,337$[b]
1985–86	2,100	3,095	5,419	57%	$0.5 \times 5,419 = 2,710$[b]
1990–91	2,300	2,755	5,891	47%	$5,891 - 2,755 = 3,136$[c]
1995–96	2,340	2,427	7,011	35%	$7,011 - 2,427 = 4,584$
1999–2000	3,125	2,985	7,723	39%	$7,723 - 2,985 = 4,738$

Sources: College Board 1998; 1999, 15, table 8; 2000, 13, table 7.

Note: Constant dollar figures assume 1997–98 academic year as base year. College costs and CPI estimated for 1997–98 (see appendix).

[a] Until 1986, HEA limited the Pell Grant award to no more than 50% of a student's *actual* cost of attendance. But for the lowest-income students at most four-year institutions, Pell awards did exceed 50% of *average* public four-year attendance costs. From 1986 to 1992, the 50% limit on awards was increased to 60% and likewise did not reduce the maximum award received by the lowest-income students at most four-year institutions. After 1992, the cost limitation was removed altogether.

[b] Reflects 50% cost limitation.

[c] Unaffected by 60% cost limitation.

award was limited to 50 percent of the cost of attendance. This means that rather than receiving the maximum Pell award, the average low-income student at a public college received only $2,348 in 1975–76, a little more than half of the Pell maximum. Because of the half-cost provision, in the early 1980s the federal government could reduce the maximum Pell award, maintain access to public colleges, and reduce total Pell costs (St. John and Byce 1982). Students who attended more expensive colleges received the full Pell awards, but the purchasing power of their awards eroded when Pell awards were cut. Thus, Pell grants originally promoted college choice, because low-income students received higher awards at higher-cost private colleges, but the "college choice" feature of the Pell program eroded as the maximum award declined.

Until 1985–86, then, low-income students in most public colleges could not receive full Pell awards. Thus, the highest Pell award in the average public college increased between 1975–76 and 1985–86, as did the cost of attending. In 1985–86, for example, the Pell award for the poorest student in an average-cost public four-year college was $2,710. The student was expected to pay an equal amount as his or her portion of the cost (through other grants, work, loans, and expected family contribution). Between 1975–76 and 1985–86, both the Pell award and the expected contribution increased in public colleges. After 1985–86, the poorest students' share of college costs climbed at an even faster rate than college costs for students who paid full cost, as the purchasing power of Pell grants declined even more. In 1999–2000, the maximum Pell grant was $3,125, but students from poor families would be expected to pay $4,738 after Pell, an amount higher than for any of the previous years.

The decline of Pell grants had a more substantial impact on pricing behavior (tuition and grant strategies) in private colleges than in public colleges, at least before 1985–86 (St. John 1992a). With the erosion of the maximum Pell award, low-income students in private colleges received lower Pell awards. Private colleges adapted by redirecting a portion of their tuition revenue to student grants (Hauptman 1990; St. John 1992b). However, students in public colleges began to experience a reduction in the purchasing power of Pell grants relative to the cost of attending.

Three other issues complicate any effort to understand the consequences of the decline in Pell grants. First, other federal grants declined even more substantially than Pell grants after 1975 (table A.2). Thus, the real decline in federal grant dollars for low-income students was even greater than suggested by the decline in Pell awards (table 2.1). Not only did the purchasing power of Pell grants decline, but supplemental federal grant aid was reduced even more substantially. Second, there was an expansion in federally subsidized loans, which made more resources

UNDERSTANDING THE ACCESS CHALLENGE

available to cover expected student costs. Low-income students could borrow more, but they needed to earn enough after college to pay off their debt—if they were fortunate enough to graduate.[2] And the decline in the purchasing power of Pell grants made it extremely difficult to avoid loans and afford continuous enrollment. Third, states differed greatly in the funding for state grants. In some states, sufficient aid was available to equalize opportunity, but as a general pattern, grant aid was insufficient.

Many analysts have questioned whether Pell made a difference in the first place (Hansen 1983; Kane 1995). By extension of this logic, if the implementation of Pell grants did not make a measurable difference, why would cutting Pell make a difference? Analysts therefore paid little attention to the reduction in Pell grants in the 1980s and 1990s. However, total federal grant aid declined after 1975 (table A.2). The impact of implementation of Pell was constrained by reductions in other federal grant programs. Therefore, a broader framework is needed to build an understanding of the consequences of these policy changes. The remainder of this chapter uses the theory of social justice to identify a new set of indicators for assessing the effects of change in student aid policy, including large changes in Pell funding.

Focus on Justice in Finance

Too frequently, policy debates about the financing of higher education pit arguments for equity against arguments for efficiency. Those who argue for equity rationalize that achieving equity would have high costs, but that taxpayers have a moral obligation to pay these costs—a liberal argument that laid the foundation for federal student aid programs in the 1960s and 1970s. However, since new conservatives have argued that taxpayers pay too high a share of the costs, liberals need to reexamine their old assumptions. This clash between liberal and conservative rationales was central to the decline in higher education funding during the late twentieth century. During the administrations of Ronald Reagan (1981–88) and George H. W. Bush (1989–92), federal grants were cut and loans expanded, because this strategy for providing aid had a lower cost for taxpayers. In the Clinton years (1993–2000), targeted tax relief for middle-class families with children attending college was used as a strategy for aligning middle-class voters with a tenuous new majority for

[2] A recent analysis indicates that in 2000, 30 percent of all borrowers graduated with "unmanageable student loan debt; meaning these students pay more than 8 percent of their monthly income on student loan payments" (King and Bannon 2002, 5).

the "New Democrats." This new Democratic rationale realigned student aid to support the majority of students, but it virtually ignored the original liberal arguments about equity. In fact, the gap in opportunity between low-income and middle-income students widened during the 1980s and 1990s.

Recently, a prominent group of forty liberal analysts, in an advertisement placed in the *New York Times* (republished by Mortensen 2001), argued for "just and efficient college finance." This is an important step, because it points to the need for justice for students and taxpayers. But we must take a look at the meaning of social justice as viewed from the perspective of three interest groups: opportunity for the middle-class majority (access), the special interests of low-income families (equal opportunity), and economy in the use of tax dollars (taxpayer justice). Occasionally we need to step back from the logical frameworks commonly used to examine a problem and to consider new ways of viewing the issue. Rawls's theory of social justice provides a framework that can help broaden our understanding of the affordability challenge. Rawls summarized his general conception of justice as follows: "All social primary goods—liberty and opportunity, income and wealth, and the bases of self-respect—are distributed equally unless an unequal distribution of any or all of these is to the advantage of the least favored" (1971, 303).

The opportunity for a postsecondary education is a social primary good that influences both wealth and self-respect. The distribution of the opportunity to attend college is fundamental to liberty and social justice. In the old low-tuition model, the equal distribution of opportunity was provided by state subsidies to institutions, which held down tuition; and equity for those with the greatest need was provided through need-based grant aid. In the 1970s, need-based grants helped close the opportunity gap between the massive middle class (who could afford to pay full direct costs of public colleges) and the poor (who could not afford the direct costs of public colleges). Given the need for a massive expansion in postsecondary opportunity, there is reason to take a further look at the balance among these interests.

During the 1980s and 1990s, the total federal grant dollars per student decreased while public tuition charges increased. The increase in tuition in public colleges resulted in large part from a decline in taxpayer funding per student enrolled, but there was also an increase in spending per student in public colleges. Public funding per student enrolled declined both in states and at the federal level after 1980. Thus, taxpayers' willingness to pay taxes, opportunity for the majority to attend, and equalization of opportunity are important indicators of social justice in higher education finance.

The participation rate for traditional college-age high school graduates provides one indicator of the extent to which opportunity is provided for the middle-class majority. Between 1970 and 1999, the enrollment rate for this population increased from 32.6 to 43.7 percent (table 2.2). Not only was 1972 the first year for which participation rates for diverse groups were made available, but this year also represents the status of opportunity after the development of mass systems of higher education. About one-third of college-age high school graduates were enrolled in 1975, a point when the Pell program was almost fully implemented.[3] However, for the remainder of the 1970s, the percentage of the population attending college did not change appreciably, although the size of the traditional college-age cohort increased.

Between 1975 and 1980, the average enrollment rate did not change substantially. In 1975, 32.5 percent of the traditional-age high school graduates enrolled in college. In 1980, 31.8 percent attended (table 2.2). The federal investment in grants did not expand access, as measured by the overall participation rate by high school graduates. College enrollment was actually more than 10 percent lower in 1979 than had been predicted by NCES in 1970 (table 2.3), indicating that expansion in grants during the 1970s did not expand access for the majority.

However, access for the majority did improve after 1980. Between 1980 and 1990, enrollment rates expanded substantially, from 31.8 to 39.1 percent for traditional-age students (table 2.2). Further, in both the 1980s and 1990s, college enrollments were higher than NCES had predicted. Enrollment was 20.12 percent higher in 1989 than predicted by NCES in 1980 (table 2.3), and 5.29 percent higher in 1997 than predicted in 1990. Expansion in enrollment rates by traditional-age students explained this high enrollment.

At a prima facie level, growth in loans was related to increased participation rates, but was this really a causal relationship? Or did other factors (e.g., K–12 educational reforms) explain the surge in overall participation rates after 1980? If loans enabled more middle-income students to attain a postsecondary education, given college costs, then loans may have provided a way of balancing the justice claims of conservative taxpayers and the demand for access by the majority of students. Since taxpayer costs are less for loans than for grants, this financial strategy seems to meet taxpayers' concerns about efficiency. However, if increasing

---

[3] Pell was implemented incrementally: for freshmen the first year (1973–74), for freshmen and sophomores the second year, and so forth.

TABLE 2.2 Trends in Percentage Enrollment of 18- to 24-Year-Old High School Graduates by Race/Ethnicity, Showing Opportunity Gaps, 1970 to 1999

	1970	1975	1980	1985	1990	1995	1999
White	33.2%	32.3%	32.1%	34.9%	40.4%	44.0%	45.3%
African American	26.0%	31.5%	27.6%	26.0%	32.7%	35.4%	39.2%
Gap	−7.2	−0.8	−4.5	−8.9	−7.7	−8.6	−6.1
Hispanic		35.5%	29.9%	26.8%	28.7%	35.2%	31.6%
Gap		+3.2	−2.2	−8.1	−11.7	−8.8	−13.7
Total	32.6%	32.5%	31.8%	33.7%	39.1%	42.3%	43.7%

Sources: NCES 2000a, 216, table 187.

Note: Opportunity gaps given as percentage point difference.

TABLE 2.3 Differences between Actual and Predicted Enrollment, 1970 to 1997

NCES Prediction Years	Difference between Actual and Predicted FTE Enrollment
1970 Prediction for 1979	−10.82%
1980 Prediction for 1989	+20.12%
1990 Prediction for 1997	+5.29%

Source: Calculated from NCES reports. See tables 5.1, 6.1, and 7.1 for specific sources for each time period.

loans expanded opportunity and college choice for middle-class students but not for low-income students (Advisory Committee 2001a; McPherson and Schapiro 1991; St. John 1990a), then using participation rates alone as an indicator of the effects of finance on access does not work well in efforts to assess the efficacy of student aid and other public financial strategies. At the very least, we need to consider additional ways of evaluating the influence of loans and other forms of student aid.

EQUAL OPPORTUNITY

Equal opportunity can be measured in two ways. Logically, the best way is to compare trends in enrollment rates for different income groups. Given inflation and the static nature of data-collection instruments,[4] it is not possible to compare enrollment rates across income groups over time. An alternative way to measure equal opportunity is to compare enrollment rates for historically underrepresented minorities (African Americans and Hispanics) with enrollment rates for Whites. Since the Hispanic and African American populations have larger percentages of students from low-income families than the White population, these comparisons provide an indicator of changes in equity over time.

However, using enrollment rates for diverse racial/ethnic groups should not be interpreted to mean that all Hispanics and African Americans are poor. There is substantial economic diversity within the African American population (NCES 1997a; Paulsen, St. John, and Carter 2002), as there is within each major ethnic group in American society. But a lower percentage of Whites than African Americans or Hispanics is truly economically disadvantaged. Equity is not present when students (and potential students) with the greatest financial need cannot afford to main-

[4] Current Populations Surveys has used income categories (numeric ranges) that are difficult to adjust for inflation. Therefore, most analysts have relied on participation by diverse ethnic groups as a measure of equity.

tain continuous enrollment, but equally qualified students with less financial need can. Given the substantial differences in the extent of poverty across diverse ethnic groups, we can consider participation rates across diverse groups as an indicator of equity.

In taking equal opportunity across ethnic groups as an indicator of equity, we must be open to all possible explanations for diversity in opportunity. Trends in this indicator give us a perspective on the equity aspect of the affordability problem. In 1975, participation rates were nearly equal for Whites and African Americans, while Hispanics attended college at a slightly higher rate than Whites (table 2.2). Was this relative level of equity attributable to federal grants? Recall that Pell grants covered half the cost of attending a four-year college (table 2.1). Did the growth in federal need-based grants in the late 1960s and early 1970s contribute to the emergence of these equitable conditions? Did the K–12 reforms of the late 1960s and early 1970s contribute to the condition of equity that emerged in the late 1970s? We must ask these questions precisely because it is important to build an understanding of why equity was achieved during this earlier period.

By 1996, however, a large disparity in opportunity had arisen. A substantially higher percentage of traditional college-age Whites (45 percent) than college-age African Americans participated in higher education. The college enrollment rate for African Americans was 9.3 percentage points lower than that for Whites. For Hispanics, the enrollment rate was 11.2 percentage points lower than for Whites. What explains this new inequality? Is it simply a matter of differences in academic preparation, as some school reform advocates argue? If so, did the educational reforms of the 1980s and 1990s benefit Whites more than African Americans and Hispanics? Or did the shift in emphasis of federal student aid policy, from grants to loans and tax credits, have an influence? Did the decline in the purchasing power of Pell grants influence the growth in inequality? Could loans have had a different effect on Whites than on African Americans and Hispanics?

There is certainly prima facie evidence that the erosion in Pell grants contributed to the disparity in opportunity that emerged in the 1980s and persisted through the 1990s. The decline in the purchasing power of Pell grants (table 2.1) corresponds with the growth in the opportunity gap (table 2.2) in the 1980s and 1990s. An examination of the opportunity gap across income groups provides further confirmatory evidence related to this hypothesis: 22.3 percent of college-qualified low-income students (from families earning less than $25,000) who graduated high school in 1992 had not attended college by 1994 (NCES 1997a). In contrast, only about 10.1 percent of college-qualified middle-income students did not

TABLE 2.4 Percentage of Students Who Enroll in Postsecondary Schools within 20 Months of High School Graduation, by Parental Income Quartile, 1980–82 and 1992

Parental Income Quartile	Total	Any Postseconday Schooling			
		Vocational, Technical	Two-Year College	Four-Year College	
Bottom	0.57	0.12	0.16	0.29 ⎤	
Third	0.63	0.11	0.19	0.33 ⎪	Class of
Second	0.71	0.10	0.22	0.39 ⎬	1980–82
Top	0.80	0.06	0.19	0.55 ⎪	
Total	0.68	0.10	0.19	0.39 ⎦	
Bottom	0.60	0.10	0.22	0.28 ⎤	
Third	0.70	0.07	0.25	0.38 ⎪	Class of
Second	0.79	0.06	0.25	0.48 ⎬	1992
Top	0.90	0.05	0.19	0.66 ⎪	
Total	0.75	0.07	0.23	0.45 ⎦	

Source: Kane 2001; based on figures reported in Ellwood and Kane 2000.

attend. This means that the differential in enrollment for college-qualified students between low-income students and middle-income students was 12.2 percentage points. Thus, the gap in opportunity between low-income and middle-income students is comparable to the gap between Hispanic and African American students and White students.[5]

That the new gap in postsecondary opportunity is related to family income rather than to race or ethnicity is beyond doubt. Comparisons of college enrollment rates by income quartile for students in the early 1980s (classes of 1980 and 1982) and early 1990s (class of 1992) are consistent with trends in participation rates (table 2.4). For students from the lowest income quartile, the opportunity to enroll in four-year colleges declined between 1980–82 and 1992. In contrast, students from upper-income families had substantially expanded opportunity to attend four-year colleges.

Those who believe that academic preparation is the primary explanation for inequality in opportunity must ask themselves: did changes in K–12 schools—the educational reforms of the late 1970s and 1980s—constrain opportunity for low-income students while expanding opportunity for upper-income students? After all, the conservatives who now argue

[5] To provide a better understanding of college enrollment behavior and NCES's analysis of process, the statistics reported in NCES 1997a are reexamined in chapter 8.

that school reform will solve the access problem (e.g., Finn 2001) were among the same analysts who argued that testing was essential to K–12 reform (e.g., Finn 1990). We must assess the role of federal educational reform after 1980 in widening the opportunity gap. The large gap in opportunity between college-qualified students of low income and those of middle income (NCES 1997a) indicates that academic preparation is not the problem. Clearly, we must address this question.

TAXPAYER JUSTICE

All too frequently, justice for taxpayers is left out of discussions about affordability, at least when affordability is examined using the liberal rationales put forward by most policy analysts. Indeed, the affordability measures reviewed above provide a rationale for spending more on higher education, especially spending more per student, so costs will fall. The idea that we might consider taxpayer spending per student enrolled as a "justice" indicator is probably appalling for some analysts who study higher education finance. A central assumption in this field has been that states should provide adequate state financial support (McKeown 1996), a rationale that values more funds over efficiency.

Rawls argues that taxpayers' willingness to subsidize cross-generation equity is central to the principles of justice. If we take seriously the new challenge to expand access to higher education, then we must also consider taxpayer costs per student. If only 45 percent of the high school graduate population enrolls in college and the goal is to substantially increase this percentage, then costs per taxpayer would almost double, if tax dollars per student are held constant. Thus, tax dollars spent per student (i.e., government spending on student aid and public institutions) provides a useful measure, if we also consider measures related to opportunity for the majority and equal opportunity for minorities. This approach provides insight into the taxpayer portion of the policy triangle.

In the 1980s, the Reagan administration successfully reduced income taxes in response to conservative voters concerned about the cost of federal programs. Given the need to expand higher education in the next few decades, tax dollars spent per student is an indicator that can reveal the effects of different public policies, if this indicator is considered along with other key indicators. Crafting public policy involves balancing different types of social and economic interests.

Tax expenditures per full-time student (FTE) for student aid (table 2.5), represented by federal student aid per FTE, declined in the 1980s.[6]

---

[6] This analysis assumes that subsidized loans cost fifty cents per dollar (McPherson and Schapiro 1998). No costs were attributed to unsubsidized loans.

TABLE 2.5 Trends in Tax Expenditures per FTE Student Enrolled in Higher Education, 1970 to 1999

Year	Federal Student Aid per FTE[a]	State and Local Appropriations per FTE	State Grants per FTE
1970–71	1,446	4,315	143
1975–76	2,501	4,522	169
1980–81	2,090	4,393	170
1985–86	1,655	5,078	218
1990–91	1,426	4,770	225
1995–96	1,668	4,529	304
1998–99	1,718	NA	323

Source: Calculated from trend data reported by NCES and the College Board. See appendix (especially table A.9).

[a] Federal grants from Title IV and other sources and loan subsidies (at 50 cents per dollar of subsidized loan).

However, in the Clinton years, tax expenditures per FTE for student aid rose again, but not to the 1975–76 level. Whereas in 1975–76 most aid dollars took the form of grants, by 1998–99 loans were the major taxpayer cost. Before we consider the arguments about efficiency, we also need to consider the role of tax credits. Taking into account tax credits and tax relief (about $7 billion in 1998; see chapter 7), taxpayer costs—the actual cost of student subsidies (grants, loans, and tax relief)—were actually higher in 1998 than in 1980.

Since 1998, targeted tax credits (e.g., HOPE Scholarships; see chapter 7) have been used as a means of subsidizing the direct college costs of middle-income families with students. Tax relief is also given for college savings. This method of finance essentially provides tax relief to targeted groups rather than seeking efficiency in the use of tax dollars. This development raises a serious question: are targeted tax credits more just for taxpayers than the efficient use of tax dollars? This question, framed as an issue of social justice, must be addressed as part of the debate about higher education finance. Efficient use of tax income in federal programs treats all taxpayers equally, given the extant tax rates. Targeted tax relief treats reductions in taxes as benefits to specific groups. Targeted tax credits lack a sound economic rationale, given the emphasis on optimization in economics. Should middle-income taxpayers have relief from taxes while their children are in college? In a moral sense, efficient use of tax dollars should be balanced against the broader issues related to access and equity. Targeted tax relief may stimulate the economy better than an across-the-board decrease in tax rates; both mechanisms have been used in recent years (e.g., the Tax Relief Act of 2001), and their efficacy should be evaluated. Such an assessment is beyond the scope of this study.

Thus there is now an apparent tradeoff between targeted tax relief for some taxpayers (i.e., middle-class taxpayers who are better able to afford college than low-income students who are ineligible for HOPE Scholarships) and efficient use of taxes as measured by taxpayer dollars spent per FTE student enrolled. Can concepts of justice help inform a debate about this tradeoff? Perhaps so, but when pondering this question we must also consider the issues of access and equity. One purpose of taxes is to promote cross-generation opportunity (Rawls 1971), which means we should consider the access and equity outcomes in relation to taxpayer costs (and to targeted tax subsidies).

BALANCING INTERESTS

For Rawls (1971), cross-generation equity could be attained only if citizens were willing to pay taxes. This premise has a new meaning in the twenty-first century. In the presidential campaign of 2000, strategies for returning taxes to citizens were debated more extensively than were strategies for reinvesting in higher education. Since political debates reflected the concerns and interests of citizens, higher education analysts must take taxpayers' concerns into account if they are to develop more compelling arguments for funding.

As a society, we need to balance the interests of three groups—the majority of students, who are mostly middle-class; low-income students, disproportionately represented in African American and Hispanic populations; and taxpayers—as we develop and test new financing strategies. This is not to suggest that low cost for taxpayers should be the primary concern; rather, this cost should be included in the factors analyzed when debating alternative refinancing strategies.

Refinancing higher education to accommodate a larger percentage of the population is analogous to refinancing a home to build more rooms for more children. A family could save more, earn more, borrow more, or use some combination of strategies to achieve this goal. The contingency theory of college finance (chapter 9) provides a framework that might inform such choices in states and at the federal level about how to expand opportunity for higher education in the next few decades.

Justice and College Access

An examination of changes in the purchasing power of Pell grants since 1975 in relation to these indicators of social justice reveals that

American society faces a serious college affordability problem for low-income families, just as it did before the 1970s. Affordability and social justice are related, but in complex ways. From the initial review of these indicators, we can develop three *hypotheses*:

—The decline in the purchasing power of Pell grants influenced the emergence of a gap in postsecondary enrollment rates between African American and Hispanic students and White students.
—Other forms of student subsidies—loans and tax credits—enabled more majority (middle-class) students to attend college.
—The new emphasis on loans was more efficient for taxpayers but less effective, because it has contributed to the new inequality (i.e., the opportunity gap that opened after 1980).

These hypotheses may hold true, but a more systematic analysis is needed to confirm them. Using a new analytic framework, I will take a closer look at the specific changes in student aid policy and changes in the three sets of indicators during three periods (the 1970s, 1980s, and 1990s). While there is substantial confirmatory evidence to support these hypotheses, my purpose is not merely to amass the evidence but to inform policy development. While expanding access and improving equity represent important goals, it is crucial to consider taxpayer costs when we debate the causes and consequences of the new access challenge.

The principles of social justice may be an appropriate starting point for assessing the effects on access to higher education of changes in public finance policies, but neither Rawls's theory of justice nor economic theory provides an entirely adequate foundation for assessing such effects. To assess the effects of these policies, it is important to "control" conceptually, if not statistically, for forces other than student aid that can influence enrollment in postsecondary education. To untangle further the ways in which both educational reforms and student aid affect access to and equity in higher education, an expanded set of foundations is needed.

Although my primary focus is on the role of finances in promoting access and equity, I also recognize the need to consider the role of educational reforms. Politics necessitate that we take this step. In an "opposing view" in *USA Today*, Chester E. Finn argued:

> The USA is the only land where people talk seriously about "universal" higher education, and at least some of that is due to our failure to ensure that a high school diploma represents solid proof of basic education. Indeed, our virtually open admission to college takes the heat off of the K–12 system. The Advisory Committee on Student Financial Assistance seems not to notice.
>
> Nor does it adequately meet the many non-financial obstacles in the path of low-income students. Yet these students are likely to have attended the worst of America's schools, those that prepare students least well for success in intellectual pursuits, even functional literacy. They are apt to have encountered the weakest teachers (2001).

Here Finn claims not only that improving K–12 schools is necessary to expand postsecondary access, but also that if K–12 schools were sufficiently improved, there would be less demand for postsecondary access. However, we must find better explanations for how the new inequality in opportunity came about if we are to figure out ways of reducing this disparity or increasing access. To untangle this issue further, we need to address two questions:

1. Did the new inequality (i.e., the new gap in postsecondary educational opportunity) result from the erosion in grants, as the Advisory Committee on Student Financial Assistance (2001a) argues?
2. Or was there a sudden decline in K–12 schools that caused the new inequality?

Only after considering these questions can we seriously ask: what types of remedies are likely to induce improvements in postsecondary access and equity in the future? To address the two questions above, we need a new framework. The first step toward this goal requires rethinking the assumptions commonly used to assess the impact of policy remedies on educational opportunity. It is overly simplistic to propose remedies to problems without fully considering why the problems exist in the first place. While major improvements in K–12 schools could reduce the number of people who need some postsecondary education, as Finn claims, this rationale offers little insight into why substantial inequities emerged in the 1980s and persisted through the 1990s. Or why, in the 1990s, there was an expansion in access. Did differences in the financial resources of minority families influence this disparity in gains in access after 1980? Or did K–12 reform policies favor middle- and upper-income and White students but not low-income and minority students?

To examine these questions, we need to assess the effects of changes in educational policy along with the effects of changes in funding for higher education. This chapter starts the rethinking process by reexamining the assumptions commonly—and uncommonly—used to assess the impact of policy. By reexamining the theories that have been and can be used to evaluate the impact of finance and school reforms, we can develop foundations for a new framework.

While Rawls's theory of social justice provides a basis for rethinking how educational policy and public subsidies might benefit different groups in society, we must also consider other explanations for factors that influence educational opportunity. To develop a framework for assessing the effects of student aid and other educational policies on expanding, reducing, or equalizing postsecondary opportunity, it was necessary to think through the foundational assumptions commonly used to assess public policy in higher education. In addition to Rawls's theory, I consider economic theories of human capital and price response, social theory related to educational attainment, student choice theory, and concepts in the policy sciences. The chapter concludes with a summary of some new guiding assumptions for assessing the impact of finances on educational opportunity.

The Principles of Justice

In *A Theory of Justice*, John Rawls (1971) identifies two principles that help frame the role of justice in public policy. One principle focuses on equal treatment, the other on equity of opportunity. While there have been substantial developments in theory and research since Rawls wrote this seminal work, it nonetheless provides a starting point for reconsidering the role of government in promoting postsecondary opportunity. Both of Rawls's principles merit consideration.

> "The First Principle: Each person is to have an equal right to the most extensive total system of equal basic liberties compatible with a similar system of liberty for all" (Rawls 1971, 302).

This principle argues for equal treatment of all. Expanding the opportunity for access to postsecondary education relates directly to this concept, assuming a similar system of liberty for all. Rawls suggested the "first priority rule": "The principles of justice are to be ranked in lexical order and therefore liberty can be restricted only for the sake of liberty. There are two cases: (a) a less extensive liberty must strengthen the total system of liberty shared by all; (b) a less than equal liberty must be acceptable to those with lesser liberty" (302).

Thus, while Rawls argued that the first principle is the first priority, given his lexical order, he recognized that unequal liberty presents a problem. He suggested two criteria for judging whether there is an equal basis for liberty. Both relate to the absence of impediments to equal opportunity. First, Rawls argued that the system of "natural liberty" implies that "careers were open to all, based on their talents" (72). If all college applicants had the same opportunities before they applied for college, then the equal application of a single set of admissions criteria would be consonant with this assumption and would provide a means of rationing access, or opportunity to attend higher-quality universities. However, given the history of school segregation and inequality in educational opportunity in the United States, this first case does not hold up to evidence: the system of liberty (i.e., opportunity for quality education) is not shared by all. Schools are more segregated now than before the 1954 *Brown* decision (Fossey 1998).

However, the case for inequality in higher education opportunity in the United States no longer rests on historical inequalities. There is growing evidence of declining opportunity for college-qualified students with low income (Advisory Committee 2002). While most of the analyses in part I of this book focus on the new inequality for African Americans and Hispanics compared with Whites (see table 2.2; see also chapters 5–7), there is also a growing inequality across income groups (see table 2.4). This pattern of inequity is also evident when the National Center for Education Statistics' criteria for academic preparation are controlled for: large numbers of college-qualified low-income children do not have the opportunity to attend college (chapter 8).

Rawls acknowledged that natural liberty assumes the existence of a "free market economy." He recognized that the notion of free markets assumed "that all have at least the same legal rights of access to all advantaged social positions" (72). This assumption has a different meaning for postsecondary education, which has not been accessible to all, than for K–12 schools, which are compulsory. In K–12 education, much of the current debate on educational policy centers on equal access to quality education. One strand of reform emphasizes improving the quality of troubled schools (i.e., educational standards and testing), an approach that seems to argue for equalizing the supply of opportunity. A newer and compelling strand of reform policy argues for extending school choice, to enable the K–12 market to work better. More market forces are at work in postsecondary education, but the opportunity for access is influenced by prior education, a family's ability to pay, and exposure to environmental opportunities that might influence aspirations. This means that a perfect market does not exist in either K–12 or higher education.

Thus, while Rawls's first principle of justice is important, it does not provide a sufficient basis for judging the extent of social justice in educational opportunity, which establishes the need for Rawls's second principle (examined below). In spite of these limitations, we need to consider how the first principle applies to an assessment of the impact of finance policies in higher education.

The "lexical order" assumption suggests that the first priority is equal treatment for all, based on their talents. However, exceptions must be based on equities in liberty and must be acceptable to those with less liberty. When opportunity to attend postsecondary education was allocated primarily based on academic merit, achievement in K–12 education was central, assuming there would be funds to equalize opportunity for high-achieving children from poor families. Students in the middle-ability range gained access in the 1960s, which also increased the economic diversity of students gaining academic access. Thus, as opportunity for higher education expanded during the middle twentieth century, the allocation of resources to subsidize direct costs for students from poor families (i.e., student financial aid) became more central to public finance.

If there are large numbers of college-qualified students who cannot afford to attend college, then equal treatment of all does not exist. Such an inequality would differ in both its nature and its origin from the original concept of social injustice that influenced President Johnson's Great Society programs in education. This new injustice would be a consequence of the gradual dismantling of need-based student grants over the 1980s and 1990s. In fact, a growing disparity is well established (chapter 2; Kane 2001). A goal of this analysis is to discern whether changes in finances or changes in academic preparation best explain why the new inequality came about in the first place.

> "The Second Principle: Social and economic inequalities are to be arranged so that they are both: (a) to the greatest benefit to the least advantaged, consistent with the just savings principle, and (b) attached to offices and positions of fair equality of opportunity" (Rawls 1971, 302).

Before considering application of the second principle for postsecondary education, we must examine what Rawls means by the "just savings principle." Rawls framed this concept within the notion of cross-generation responsibility. He argued that capital was and should be passed on from one generation to the next: "The just savings principle can be regarded as an understanding between generations to carry their fair share of the burden of realizing and preserving a just society" (289). This principle provides Rawls's rationale for public investment in education:

> Each generation must not only preserve the gains of culture and civilization, and maintain intact those just institutions that have been established, but it must also put aside in each period of time a suitable amount of real capital accumulation. This savings may take various forms from net investment in machinery and other means of production to investment in learning and education. Assuming for the moment that a just savings principle is available, which tells us how great investment should be, the level of social minimum is determined. Suppose for simplicity that the minimum is adjusted by transfers paid for by proportional expenditure (or income) taxes. In this case raising the minimum entails increasing the portion by which consumption (or income) is taxed (285).

Thus, Rawls's second principle of justice rests on the notion that cross-generation investment, generated through taxation, is essential for maintaining a just social system, and thus it rests on an assumption that taxpayers are willing to pay for an educational system that provides equal opportunity.

The second principle, then, introduces the concept of equal opportunity to attain an education, controlling both for students' ability/ achievement and for taxpayers' willingness to pay taxes. This is complicated, because, as illustrated in the review of new political arguments in chapter 1, an underlying claim of new conservatives has been that the system of taxation went too far and that tax rates should be reduced. However, before society moves too far backwards in its cross-generation commitment to maintaining a just system of education, we must consider how well equal opportunity to attain a postsecondary education has been maintained. The review of trends (chapters 2, 5–7) reveals a decline in equity since 1975.

Rawls's second principle of justice suggests that the moral responsibility of a just society is to equalize opportunity for education with respect to financial access. Two primary financial mechanisms used by government to promote opportunity and to equalize opportunity are (1) state subsidies to institutions, which reduce tuition charges for all students, and (2) state and federal subsidies to students (grants and loan subsidies), which reduce the costs of attending for students with financial need. Because of substantial changes in the patterns of public subsidies over the past three decades, it is important to consider how or when the system of finance equalizes opportunity to attain a postsecondary education.

Specifically, it is the taxpayers' willingness to support higher education and other social institutions that has come into question since 1980, with cuts in taxes and student grants.[1] My argument is that considering efficiency in the use of tax dollars is preferable to cutting appropriations without first engaging in this type of critical reflection. Further, the issues of opportunity for all and equal opportunity must be considered as part of the discussions about efficient use of tax dollars, but equal opportunity should take priority over reduced average cost for the majority, given the second principle of justice. This priority provides the moral basis for reexamining the logic used by NCES when it systematically overlooked the role of finances in its analyses of access (chapter 8).

The issue of taxpayers' willingness to pay not only must be balanced against any inequalities that might exist but also must consider who benefits from reinvestment strategies. Loans may have been a less costly way to expand access for the majority, but if taxpayer costs per student enrolled increase, as they did between 1990–91 and 1998–99 (see table 2.5),

[1] This is not to argue for a causal relationship between cuts in taxes and cuts in grants. Rather, it illustrates problems with the new conservative political ideology that underlies both policies.

and inequalities are not resolved, then there is reason to rethink how tax dollars are being spent.

INDICATORS OF JUSTICE

The two principles of justice, along with the just savings principle that underlies them, suggest we need to explicitly consider three sets of interests when thinking about the role of finances in rationing postsecondary opportunity. In this book, I explore whether changes in public policy have influenced changes in access, equity, and efficiency for taxpayers. While I frame these questions as being related primarily to postsecondary finance, I recognize that we need to consider other plausible explanations for changes in the indicators.

The examination of change in access uses two indicators. Enrollment rates for high school graduates provide one indicator of the extent of educational opportunity in society. Changes in participation rates have a direct influence on college enrollment. The trend review (table A.8) shows that participation rates did expand in the 1980s and 1990s. Comparisons between projected class enrollment and actual enrollment provide the second indicator of access. The NCES's enrollment projections are based on demographic trends and birth rates and do not consider the impact of either K–12 reform or affordability. If enrollment is substantially higher or lower than predicted (in the midrange projections developed by NCES), then we have evidence of expansion or contraction of opportunity for the majority compared with trend-based expectations. As the preliminary trend review shows (chapter 2), enrollment was higher than predicted in the 1980s and 1990s, indicating an expansion in access. As a next step, I consider whether student financial aid, K–12 reform, or other forces influenced expansion in access and increases in inequality after 1980. In chapters 5–7 I examine the relationship between financial and policy changes and changes in access in three distinct periods (the 1970s, 1980s, and 1990s).

Changes in access do not present the complete picture, however. Because there is not a true market or equitable opportunity for attaining a quality K–12 education, we also need to consider equity for diverse groups in society. I use a comparison of enrollment rates for Whites and for African Americans and Hispanics as the primary indicator of whether a system of "just" educational opportunity has been developed and maintained. We know a just system is possible, because there was equity in the middle 1970s. Analysts have come up with two common explanations for the new disparity in opportunity. The first is that, given the substantial differences in the average rate of poverty between African American and Hispanic families and White families (or between low-income and upper-income families), the decline in federal grants may be the cause of the new disparity. A second possibility is that forces other than finances influenced reductions in equity; specifically, the analytic chapters consider how changes in educational policy may have affected the opportunity gap.

Finally, I examine a third key indicator. The just savings principle provides a lens for reinspecting efficient use of tax dollars. I consider taxpayer costs per student enrolled in the system. Changes in taxpayer spending provide an indicator of taxpayers' willingness to pay. Rawls argues that the government's ability to finance cross-generation opportunity is based on the willingness of the general public to pay taxes. Given conservative arguments about excessive spending on higher education, it is crucial that we consider tax dollars per student, as well as opportunity to attend.

These three indicators—enrollment rates for traditional-age students, comparisons between projected college enrollment and actual enrollment, and taxpayer costs per student enrolled—provide a basis for assessing the relative costs or benefits of different approaches to student aid policy, as a balance between three sets of interests. As the percentage of traditional college-age students grows, there are pressures to reduce taxpayer costs per student. With inequity in who benefits, more efficient strategies might be more problematic, adding to systemic inequities. In contrast, strategies that promote equity are not as directly related to educational costs per student as we might first assume, given the substantial body of evidence that a high-tuition, high-grant strategy is less costly and more equitable than subsidies for all students. Thus, considering access and equal opportunity as distinct indicators, we can provide a different view of taxpayer costs than if we consider either access or equity alone in relation to taxpayer costs. Using the three indicators in combination provides a more complete basis for considering the efficacy of public finance policies than using a cost-benefit ratio that considers either opportunity for all or equity in opportunity on the benefits side of a single equation. Triangulating between the three indicators is more complex, but it is also more informative than considering costs and benefits in a single ratio.

A REFLECTION ON RACE/ETHNICITY AND SOCIAL JUSTICE

Racial/ethnic differences are central to the equity criterion used in this study. When analysts focus on the two principles of justice in relation to race/ethnicity alone, without considering the role of finances *and* academic preparation, they run the risk of assuming a racial deficit. Indeed, strict application of the second principle of justice can lead to assumptions that some groups have deficits compared with other groups. While there are still vestiges of past discrimination in higher education (Williams 1997), we must now focus on both the economic and academic aspects of the new inequality.[2] Both of these forces can play a role in remedying inequalities in educational opportunity and in expanding access. It is also important to consider forces outside education that can influence inequity in educational opportunity, including housing patterns and health care.

Economic Theory

Economic theory has had a greater influence on higher education finance policy than other theories, including the theory of justice, largely because it provides a basis for rationalizing public spending as an investment. Claims about human capital formation and economic development underlie arguments made by higher education officials when they lobby for public spending on higher education (Slaughter 1991; Trammell 1996). Most rationales for public spending also assume enrollment is responsive to prices (e.g., Leslie and Brinkman 1988; Mumper 1996), without questioning the implications of the assumption. We need to consider the ways in which students respond to pricing information in their enrollment decisions. Economic theory is important not only because it provides a rationale for public funding but also because it provides the underlying rationale for using need-based financial subsidies to equalize educational opportunity. The large body of economic theory and research in higher education finance holds up well to empirical study (Paulsen 2001a,b) and is assumed to be the foundation for the current analysis (see also chapter 1). Arguments about human capital and price response are frequently used in making policy (St. John and Paulsen 2001), but to consider other (nonfinancial) explanations for disparity in opportunity, we also must consider theories outside economics.

LIMITATIONS OF HUMAN CAPITAL THEORY

In 1964, Gary S. Becker wrote his theory of human capital, which crystallized the rationale for public "investment" in education. Becker argued that individuals and governments made their investment decisions by comparing costs and benefits. For individual students and their families, costs include both the direct costs of attending college and the for-

[2] The federal courts may ultimately decide against affirmative action in college admissions. Given the growing inequality, American society should find a new strategy for promoting equal opportunity.

gone earnings while attending, and the benefits include increased earnings and a better quality of life. For society (and government), the costs include spending on institutions and students, and the benefits include economic and social development; as the economy develops, tax revenues will increase from both corporations and individuals, assuming constant tax rates. Economic research generally confirms the basic assumptions of human capital theory, including the economic benefits to individuals and states (Leslie and Brinkman 1988; Pascarella and Terenzini 1991; Paulsen 2001a,b).

Two basic notions of price response were embedded in human capital theory. First, the basic argument that students consider costs and benefits when making educational choices could be reduced to an argument that individuals respond to a single price, or net price (tuition minus grants). Second, Becker speculated that loans also entered into students' calculations about costs and benefits. A variation on the first of these arguments (i.e., net price) was more widely tested in economic research than was the second, but both arguments merit consideration, especially with the expanded role of loans in the past two decades.

Becker, however, did not sufficiently consider the role of other forces, including family influences, on educational choices. Therefore, we also need to consider social as well as economic explanations about postsecondary opportunity. While the basic precepts of human capital theory hold up to empirical research (Paulsen 2001a), we need to be concerned about the role of other forces in expanding postsecondary opportunity. The framework developed in this book uses the claims made in human capital theory as core assumptions, but also uses a more complete understanding of the role of prices and of family background in postsecondary opportunity.

THE COMPLEXITIES OF PRICE RESPONSE

An understanding of student price response is crucial to building a framework for assessing how postsecondary policy influences access and equal opportunity. Subsidies to institutions can reduce prices and increase opportunities, while increases in need-based student aid can help equalize opportunity at a given price. Two theories of price response are germane to the study of educational opportunity.

Net-price theory has been the most widely used approach to research on the effects of public subsidies. Most researchers have considered net price to be the remainder after grant aid is subtracted from tuition (Heller 1997; Jackson and Weathersby 1975; Leslie and Brinkman 1988). Some researchers also subtract both government subsidies for loans and grant dollars from tuition in determining net price (e.g., McPherson and

Schapiro 1991, 1997). A few studies have also examined total costs (tuition plus living) minus total subsidies (grant amounts plus loan amounts) as a measure of "net cost" (e.g., St. John and Starkey 1995a). Net-price and net-cost research is important because it represents the dominant view of price effects in the community of higher education policy researchers.

An alternative approach involves analyzing the effects of different types of student aid and different types of costs on enrollment and persistence. This approach was influenced by Stephen Dresch's argument (1975) that the effects of student aid could change over time, as a consequence of changes in public finance policies. If the effects of student aid can change over time, then we need methods for assessing the effects of aid that consider the independent effects of prices and different types of subsidies.

Research comparing the two approaches—net price and differentiated price—indicates that the differentiated approach is better at measuring the enrollment effects of student aid (Paulsen 2001a; St. John 1993; St. John and Starkey 1995a). However, the alternative assumptions used in the differentiated approach to price response are not generally accepted, especially by economists, who more frequently rely on the logic of net price. I consider both explanations in this book. I review research using both methods of measuring the effects of prices and subsidies, but focus on research using differentiated price theory. Thus, both strands of price response research inform the understandings reached in succeeding chapters.

USING ECONOMIC RATIONALES

Contending with differences in the financial means of families is central to the construction of educational policy. Economic theory provides one basis for making judgments about the influence of changes in policy on changes in equal opportunity and access. However, economic theory alone is not the basis for constructing finance policy in K–12 education (Theobald 2003) or in postsecondary education (St. John 1994; St. John and Paulsen 2001). While economic rationales provide a foundation for considering the role of finances, they are not sufficient for considering how school reforms influence postsecondary opportunity. Therefore, it is crucial that we develop a broader framework.

Social Theory

An understanding of social theory is important because economic theory does not sufficiently address the role of family and other social forces in educational attainment. In constructing a framework for the study of postsecondary policy, we need to consider two distinct strands of social theory: (1) early arguments about social attainment that focused

on cross-generation uplift, and (2) more recent theory on social reproduction, which illuminates some of the impediments to equalizing
opportunity.

EDUCATIONAL AND OCCUPATIONAL ATTAINMENT

The early theories of educational and career attainment focused on
cross-generation uplift (Alexander and Eckland 1974, 1977, 1978; Blau
and Duncan 1967), consonant with Rawls's theory of justice and Becker's
theory of human capital.[3] These early theories argued that for any family,
income and parents' occupational status, along with individual achievement and aspirations, influenced both occupational and educational
attainment of succeeding generations.[4] A substantial body of social,
economic, and educational research confirms these basic assumptions
(Alexander and Eckland 1974, 1978; Geske 1996; Leslie and Brinkman
1988; Pascarella and Terenzini 1991), but the early approach used to test
this theory overlooked the role of policy in promoting opportunity for
diverse groups. Over time, researchers began to examine the influence
of family background on educational attainment for diverse groups.
Early research confirmed that the basic elements of the model were
relevant for African Americans and Whites (Wolfle 1985). More recent
research confirms that aspirations play an especially strong role in
attainment for African Americans (St. John 1991b; St. John and Noell
1989).

Given the wide acceptance of social attainment theory and the crucial role of cross-generation uplift, a consideration of the assumptions of
social attainment theory is important. In particular, this theory has
shaped arguments that improvements in K–12 schools and postsecondary
encouragement can influence (increase or reduce) the gap in opportunity between Whites and people of color. These arguments are explicitly considered in this study.

[3] While these theories leave conceptual room to explore forces that might impede
cross-generation social process, they share an optimistic view of cross-generation
uplift. One purpose of this chapter is to reconstruct understanding in a way that
better integrates the role of the diverse contexts (personal and family experiences)
in which students make choices.

[4] On parents' occupational status, the initial argument was that father's occupation
was central, but some researchers using this model have also examined mother's
education as a predictor. On students' achievement and aspirations, Alexander and
Eckland (1978) expanded educational attainment theory to include aspirations, but
the original theory did not include aspirations (e.g., Blau and Duncan 1967).

SOCIAL REPRODUCTION

Marxist theory has long been associated with an alternative view of social reproduction. Pierre Bourdieu (1977, 1990) is perhaps the leading neo-Marxist theorist to argue that social reproduction is a major inhibiting force in educational attainment. He argues that "familial manifestations of this external necessity (sexual division of labour, domestic morality, cares, strife, tastes, etc.), produce the structure of the habitus which become in turn the basis of perception and appreciation of all subsequent experience" (1977, 78). Bourdieu (1990) further argues that "cultural capital" represents a form of habitus that has a substantial influence on the educational choices families make. He argues that education is to cultural capital what money is to economic capital. The habitus of families transmits cultural capital—the values and practical choices—across generations.

Recent studies that examine how high school students make choices about postsecondary education confirm that these deeply embedded family patterns, often transmitted across generations (Hossler, Schmit, and Vesper 1999; McDonnough 1997; McDonnough, Antonio, and Trent 1997), can influence the way in which high school students develop college aspirations. Proponents of this theory argue that habitus, the situated contexts in which people make educational choices, is central to understanding class reproduction. This line of inquiry lends support to arguments that interventions designed to inform families about educational opportunities (Hossler, Schmit, and Vesper 1999) can influence who attends college. Further, researchers should give greater attention to learning environments in colleges (Hurtado and Carter 1997; Berger 2000) and the ways in which learning environments influence these culturally embedded patterns of college choice. Berger (2000) has pointed out the logical congruity between Bourdieu's concept of habitus and the "situated contexts" assumption of nexus research (e.g., St. John, Paulsen, and Starkey 1996). This logic is also integral to the framework proposed in chapter 4.

CONTENDING WITH SOCIAL FORCES

This brief review of two broad social theories—cross-generation uplift and social reproduction—reveals the two countervailing social forces that influence first-time college enrollment, especially for children from African American and Hispanic families. On the one hand, African Americans have higher aspirations, controlling for social background, which exert a substantial influence on college enrollment (Carter 1999; St. John 1991b). On the other hand, students make choices within streams of experience (i.e., habitus or situated contexts), which also exert substantial constraining or liberating influences (McDonnough 1997). If K–12 schooling is of poor quality or if parents have low aspirations for their children, then future opportunities are constrained by the situated contexts children experience. Improving K–12 schools and providing encouragement can, at least in theory, change this context in modest ways that induce college enrollment. This proposition must be examined in relation to empirical evidence.

Research on School Reform

Beginning in the 1990s, educational research was used in efforts to reform K–12 schools. Before 1980, it was widely assumed that providing equal access to quality schools would increase educational opportunity. A litany of reforms after the 1954 *Brown* decision focused on equalizing educational opportunity. Since 1980, however, school reform has focused on educational outcomes, which shifted the role of educational research. I briefly examine both developments as a way of exploring how K–12 reform might influence postsecondary access and equity in opportunity.

EQUAL ACCESS TO QUALITY SCHOOLS

After the Supreme Court's 1954 decision in *Brown v. the Board of Education*, the courts attempted to restructure school boundaries and provide bussing to equalize ratios of Whites and African Americans across schools within their districts. Two concerns guided court decisions about desegregation: to equalize access to quality schooling and to improve the quality of schools. This dual emphasis was necessary because *de jure* segregation had been based on the notion of separate but equal. However, as it became clear that not all schools were equal, the courts were forced to initiate remedies for this dual set of inequalities—in patterns of enrollment and in the quality of schools—when they desegregated public school systems.

The Elementary and Secondary Education Act (ESEA) of 1965, which through the Title I program funded supplemental compensatory education for "disadvantaged" schoolchildren (Wong 2003), was put in place to provide national support for improving the quality of schools. No particular theory of education guided these early reform efforts. Rather, additional financial resources were allocated to schools with large percentages of low-income students. Schools were required to involve parents in developing plans, but the focus of the funding was clearly on improving education for financially disadvantaged schoolchildren. Over time, the focus of the Title I program shifted to improving educational outcomes (Wong 2003), but the effects of the first few decades of funding on postsecondary access have never been systematically examined.

Unfortunately, there is now strong evidence that desegregation attempts failed to desegregate schools, especially urban schools (Fossey 1998 in press). Not only are schools more segregated now than before the *Brown* decision, but successive waves of urban school reform seem to have failed urban schools (Miron and St. John 2003), which now serve mostly minority students. Increasingly, debates about school finance focus on outcomes rather than on whether the resources of urban schools are adequate (Theobald 2003). Arguments for equalizing financial inputs and improving the quality of schools for all children have therefore given way to a new reform strategy that focuses on providing funding to promote specific outcomes.

Perhaps the new push for school choice will refocus policy on providing equal access to quality schools, but there are reasons to be cautious about making such an assumption. The advocates for school choice (Finn, Manno, and Ravitch 2001) include analysts who argue against fully funding the Pell program (e.g., Finn 2001). Given the underlying inconsistencies in the arguments of those supporting this rationale, it is possible that school choice would not be sufficiently funded to equalize access to quality schooling. Further, there is evidence that some private and suburban schools will resist admitting urban schoolchildren when these reforms are pilot tested (Ridenour and St. John 2003; St. John and Ridenour 2001). Thus, we must think critically about the empirical evidence used by reform advocates to argue for school choice and other reforms.

RESEARCH-BASED REFORM

In the 1980s, educational policy in the United States began to focus on educational outcomes (Finn 1990), and by the 1990s, federal reform strategies began to focus on translating outcomes-oriented research into educational policy. For example, research that examined the role of direct instruction in early reading (Snow, Burns, and Griffin 1998) informed the federal Reading Excellence Act of 1998, which provided competitive grants to states for interventions in early reading. Taking a different tack, the Comprehensive School Reform (CSR) demonstration provided large grants for schools to undertake schoolwide reforms that had a research base. Most of the research used to argue for both reading and CSR reforms was conducted by the advocates of the reforms, however, which raises questions about whether the widespread application of these models will have the intended effects (e.g., Madden et al. 1989, 1991). Research that examines the impact of implementing reforms indicates that no single reform model is universally successful at enabling children to achieve at grade level (St. John, Manset, Chung, Musoba, et al. 2003). Both types of reforms—research-based reading and schoolwide reforms—hold great potential, but evaluative evidence is limited (St. John and Miron in press).

Most recently, advocates of school choice schemes have used research to advocate for quasi-voucher schemes. For example, Paul Peterson (1998) has studied the effects of privately funded scholarship programs in several urban communities. There is some evidence from this research that students who received vouchers have slightly better test scores than peers who did not, and that their parents are more satisfied than the parents of students without vouchers who remained in urban schools. However, the research on school effects also shows that public school teachers faced more constraints than did teachers in private schools and that the more elite private schools did not open their doors to voucher students (Ridenour and St. John 2003).

These newer reforms raise a number of questions. For example, will they increase the percentage of children who achieve at grade level and go on to attend college? Of course, it will take another decade to determine whether these reforms affect college participation rates, but we can assess how they affect student progress. There is some evidence that the latest round of research-based reforms can produce improvement in equity-related outcomes (i.e., reductions in failure rates and special education referral rates) and can improve test pass rates (St. John and Miron 2003). But it is crucial to continue to scrutinize the research produced by these reform advocates.

UNTANGLING THE EFFECTS OF SCHOOL REFORMS

Because school reform is routinely offered as an alternative strategy for improving college access, we must consider the effects of previous school reform efforts on postsecondary opportunity. While the issue is a secondary focus of this book, it was crucial to develop a framework that considered this alternative explanation for access to college and equity in participation.

Research on College Students

Research on college students provides an additional foundation for building an understanding of the role of government in fostering just approaches to educational opportunity. Early research on college students used developmental theories to study traditional-age college students (e.g., Chickering 1969, 1976; Perry 1970), but these models had few direct policy applications because the research did not consider the influence of policy variables. Over time, a new set of theories evolved that enabled researchers to examine the influence of finance and other types of policies on students' educational choices. Early studies of the impact of student aid on specific outcomes, as well as recent attempts to link student outcomes, have informed the development of the framework for this study.

EARLY RESEARCH ON STUDENT CHOICE

Change theories that examined the influence of the college environment on student outcomes, including research by Alexander Astin (1975, 1993), enabled researchers to focus on how policies influence student outcomes. In particular, Astin (1975) considered how different types of student aid were associated with long-term persistence between the freshman and junior years. Astin's research helped other scholars conceptualize the ways in which educational policy influenced students' educational choices. In the late 1970s, new models for research on enrollment and persistence decisions were developed that borrowed from both research on college students and economic research on price response.

Some scholars used the National Longitudinal Study of the High School Class of 1972 to study the impact of student aid on enrollment, controlling for student background and student characteristics. Jackson (1978) developed a theory of student choice that was widely accepted as a basis for theory on college choice (Hossler and Gallagher 1987). In addition, Manski and Wise (1983) developed economic models that had better statistical controls for student background than did earlier studies; they confirmed that Pell grants influenced college choice, but their study was ignored and Hansen's (1983) more simplistic comparison of averages for 1972 and 1980 surveys received attention.

The longitudinal databases (NLS:72, HSB:80, HSB:82, NELS:88)[5] were also used in studies of college persistence. Terkla (1985) developed a path model that examined the influence of the receipt of student aid on persistence to graduation (using NLS:72). Others adapted Tinto's

[5] The National Longitudinal Study of the High School Class of 1972 (NLS:72), High School and Beyond Senior Cohort (HSB:80) and Sophomore Cohort (HSB:82), and National Education Longitudinal Study of 1988 (NELS:88) are major data collections administered by NCES. While each of these studies had multiple follow-ups (and different years could be used to designate specific surveys), I consistently use the base survey year to refer to each longitudinal study. For example, "NELS:88" refers to the base survey and follow-up surveys for NELS.

year-to-year persistence models[6] (and used HSB:80) to examine the effects of student aid on persistence (Cabrera, Stampen, and Hansen 1990; St. John, Kirshstein, and Noell 1991). These newer models provided the foundation for a rethinking of the role of finances in persistence (St. John, Cabrera, et al. 2000).

Recent research considers students' ability to pay and continuity of perceptions about finances across a sequence of educational choices (St. John, Cabrera, et al. 2000). These more recent models examine how students' perceptions of their financial ability to pay for college influence their subsequent decisions about persistence (Cabrera, Nora, and Castaneda 1992, 1993; St. John, Paulsen, and Starkey 1996).

SITUATED CONTEXTS AND PATTERNS OF STUDENT CHOICE

The concept of habitus (Berger 2000; Bourdieu 1977) informs two assumptions in student choice theory: (1) students make choices in situated contexts and (2) the patterns of educational choices vary for diverse student groups in diverse contexts. Students and potential students make choices based on their circumstances. These newer theories examine continuity across a sequence of student choices (Berger 2000; St. John and Hossler 1998; St. John, Kline, and Asker 2001; St. John, Paulsen, and Starkey 1996; Stage and Hossler 2000). They offer a foundation for thinking more critically about the role of government policy aimed at expanding access and equalizing postsecondary opportunity. However, in order to take into account the full set of arguments about access, we need to further reconceptualize the role of policy by considering the role of K–12 educational reform, along with postsecondary encouragement and improvements in K–12 schools that improve academic preparation for potential college students.

Policy Perspectives

There has long been a tension between two perspectives on policy: (1) rational arguments about policy and the exceptions these arguments create and (2) political processes that undermine the continuity anticipated from rational models, especially as a consequence of the politics of implementation. Both perspectives inform the framework used in this study.

---

[6] Tinto's persistence model (1975), initially tested by Pascarella and Terenzini (1979, 1980), rapidly became the dominant model (Braxton 2000). In addition, Bean (1990) developed a year-to-year model that was widely replicated (Cabrera, Nora, and Castaneda 1992).

Rational policy models (e.g., Schultz 1968; Weathersby and Balderston 1972) used structural assumptions about linkages between educational policies and educational outcomes. Economics in particular is influential in rational conceptions of policy, both because of the "rational person" notion of decision making and because economic theory is used as a rationale for public policy in education. These early rational models have had an especially substantial influence on higher education policy.[7]

Policy analyses using a rationale based on economic theory had a large influence on the evolution of student aid programs. The Higher Education Act of 1965 was introduced as part of the Great Society programs, which were created using planning, programming, and budgeting models (Schultz 1968). This legislation treated federal loans and grants as strategies for expanding opportunity. Then, with passage of the Education Amendments of 1972, the federal student aid programs were reorganized with a greater emphasis on equalizing opportunity (Gladieux and Wolanin 1976). These policies were heavily influenced by economic research on price response.

There is also growing evidence, however, that policy development in higher education finance is essentially a political process (Hearn 2001b; Mumper 1996). In particular, Hearn (1993, 2001b) points out that rational models and analyses had little influence on the evolution of student aid policy. It is also apparent that state finance policies shifted as new conservative ideological arguments emerged in the 1980s (Heller and Rasmussen 2001; St. John 1999).

Thus, when assessing the causes and consequences of policy shifts, we must consider how federal student aid programs have changed, as well as how new political rationales influence shifts in policy. Chapters 5–7 consider how the federal student aid programs changed as a consequence of these arguments.

Guiding Assumptions

This review informs a set of guiding assumptions for a new framework for assessing the impact of finances on educational opportunity. To achieve this intent, it was necessary to control logically for the role of K–12 reform in promoting postsecondary access. While the principles of social justice and applications of economic theory provide a basis for assessing the direct effects of tuition and aid subsidies, a broader frame-

[7] The new conservatives revised the rational model to focus on the link between academic preparation and educational outcomes, but ignored the role of finances altogether (e.g., Finn 1990; NCES 1997a).

UNDERSTANDING THE ACCESS CHALLENGE

work is needed here. The assumptions that guide this inquiry are summarized below.

Assumption 1: The concept of social justice provides a way to think about crucial indicators for assessing the efficacy of financial aid: access to postsecondary education, equity of participation across diverse groups, and efficient use of tax dollars.

These justice-related indicators provide a basis for assessing whether access and equity are being provided at a reasonable cost to taxpayers. Each of these indicators represents the interests of a major social group. Equity is a concern to low-income families, which are overrepresented in African American and Hispanic populations. It can be measured by comparing participation rates for traditional-age college students, informed by an analysis of whether enrollments are higher or lower than predicted by demographic projection models. Finally, efficiency in the use of tax dollars, as measured by tax expenditures per student enrolled, provides an indicator of interest to wealthy and conservative taxpayers who have advocated cuts in public funding of higher education. At a surface level, these indicators provide visibility into whose interests were represented in the student aid system at different points in time.

Assumption 2: In addition to providing the conceptual basis for need-based student financial aid, economics has provided a rationale for appeals for funding of higher education and student aid (human capital) and a framework for evaluating the effects of student aid.

This assumption acknowledges the central role of economic theory. On the one hand, economic theory provides a basis for assessing need and allocating resources to need-based financial aid. On the other hand, economic theory is frequently used as a rationale for increasing funding for student aid and institutional subsidies in higher education. The irony is that appeals for funding often ignore the value placed on optimization in economic theory. The reasoning for focusing on need is lost in appeals for funding and in efforts to build political coalitions. This tension in the political aspects of the use of economic theory is seldom acknowledged by economists. The analyses in subsequent chapters therefore consider how the rationales for student aid have evolved. In addition, chapters 5–7 summarize studies that examine the direct effects of student aid.[8] These studies illuminate whether student aid was adequate to maintain afford-

---

[8] The studies reviewed in these chapters used statistical models that controlled for students' background, college experiences, and achievement, as appropriate and necessary, to assess the impact of student aid.

ability for students who received the aid. In particular, I consider whether the studies help explain patterns of change in the indicators of access and equity. To the extent that studies of the impact of aid help explain trends in key indicators, the studies provide a form of verification that student aid policy influenced these outcomes.

> Assumption 3: The tension between social reproduction and cross-generation uplift can inhibit efforts to improve postsecondary access through school reform, postsecondary encouragement, and financial aid.

Social theory provides part of a broader framework for untangling the effects of different types of educational policies on access and equity. If access improves overall, but the opportunity gap increases, then it is crucial to untangle what forces are responsible for the differential effects of policy. For example, is it possible that a particular school reform might favor some groups in society (i.e., White or middle-income families) more than others? Certainly the federal educational policies of the 1960s and 1970s were aimed at equalizing opportunity by providing more resources to those who had historical disadvantages. Did these policies help equalize the opportunity for college enrollment? We also need to ask whether the educational reforms of the 1980s and 1990s widened the opportunity gap. These questions are seldom asked but merit attention. To ponder these questions, however, we need to consider how K–12 education and other policies might influence the aspirations, achievement, and educational progress of diverse groups. While these questions were not my primary concern, they need to be considered.

> Assumption 4: The shifts in focus of educational reform—from equal access to quality education and improvement in outcomes—complicate efforts to assess the role of academic preparation in promoting postsecondary access.

While conservatives consistently use arguments about postsecondary preparation to counter arguments about the adequacy of student aid, they seldom ask whether the reforms they advocate have actually helped improve academic preparation and college access. The new conservative reforms include increased emphasis on testing and curricular alignment rather than on addressing the learning needs of diverse populations. Has the new focus on outcomes helped maintain equity in postsecondary opportunity? Do we have as much equity now, after about twenty years of the excellence movement, as in 1980, before these reforms? Given the time that has passed since the focus of policy shifted from equalizing access to improving the quality of schools, it is possible to build an understanding of how empirical evidence relates to these questions. Thus, while my inquiry focuses primarily on student aid, it also addresses the academic preparation argument. It is important to consider whether the new conservative educational policies have influenced improvement in academic access.

Assumption 5: Postsecondary choices are made in situated contexts—prior family experiences and educational choices—that both constrain and enable educational attainment processes.

When assessing the effects of student financial aid, it is important to consider whether this aid is adequate to enable students to maintain continuous enrollment in public four-year colleges. This standard broadens the definition of access to include the opportunity to persist. We must investigate whether students who have the academic preparation to attend public four-year colleges also can afford continuous enrollment. Further, this measure takes into account the patterns of student choice: concern about the ability to pay for college can constrain college choice as well as negatively affect persistence.

Assumption 6: Policy formulation is a political process that can be informed by rational arguments and research evidence.

In the history of student aid policy, there have been times when research evidence has been used to inform policy, but most decisions about federal student aid and state financing of colleges and students remain essentially political. The tendency of politicians and practitioners to filter through research evidence to find studies that support their positions militates the use of rational decision models. In spite of this limitation, we should make the effort to generate objective research evidence that can inform policy choices. In fact, in recognition of the political nature of policy decisions, I suggest in part II a contingency approach to finance as a means of amassing evaluative evidence and using this evidence to inform policy development.

Assessing the Effects of Policy

With the new guiding assumptions presented in chapter 3, we can develop a more complete framework for assessing the ways in which public
policies influence educational opportunity (fig. 4.1). For K–12 education,
families have a substantial direct influence on educational attainment, but
the percentage of the population completing high school and student's
level of achievement in public school also can be influenced by school reform (*educational policy*) and the social context (*social and economic forces*)
to which children are exposed (e.g., parents' work settings). For the postsecondary transition, access for qualified students is influenced by students' aspirations (career and education) and by policy interventions (tuition and student aid, postsecondary information, and admissions
policies). The percentage of the population completing a postsecondary
education can be affected by changes in educational environments, labor
markets, and public funding of colleges and students. Educational
attainment results in personal growth, which influences *earnings* and *congruence*. Taxation on increased earnings provides a rationale for public investment and leads to economic development from research. Congruence between education and personal development provides the basis for
personal satisfaction with education and a willingness to support higher
education (as parents or taxpayers).

Educational policies also influence achievement and attainment outcomes. If school reform affects access, it must happen as a result of
changes in K–12 outcomes. College-age adults who complete a high
school education (or, according to stricter definition, complete a college
preparatory curriculum) are prepared to attend college. School reform
influences the size of the pool of college-eligible students, *not* the college
participation rate of the college-eligible population.[1] Providing encouragement for postsecondary education can expand the college-eligible
population by increasing the percentage of high school students who pre-

[1] While most of this discussion uses high school graduation as an indicator of college preparedness, chapter 8 uses the stricter definition of college preparation used
by NCES (1997a).

pare for college and by increasing access. However, logically, encouragement cannot increase enrollment by academically qualified low-income students who cannot afford to attend, unless there is adequate student financial aid. College prices and student aid influence whether low-income students can afford sustained enrollment, after student grants, loans, and work income. Academic policies in college also can influence persistence (completion of college), as well as students' college choices.

The new logical framework for assessing the effects of policy changes on access and equal opportunity in postsecondary education helps distinguish between different types of claims about the linkages between policy changes and enrollment outcomes. In this chapter, I first reconsider the definitions of *access* and *equal opportunity*. Then, using the assumptions developed in chapter 3, I present the framework used to assess the impact of financial aid and other interventions on access and equal opportunity (fig. 4.1). Finally, I describe how I have used the framework to make informed judgments about the impact of student aid and other policies on changes in access and equity.

Rethinking Academic and Equity Outcomes

REDEFINING ACCESS

Given the claims that K–12 reforms, postsecondary encouragement, and higher education finances influence access and equity, it is appropriate to define these outcomes in ways that can be used to assess the relative effects of each type of policy intervention. We need to distinguish between two forms of access: financial access and academic access.

Financial access is the ability to afford continuous enrollment in low-cost two-year *and* four-year programs available to applicants based on their ability and prior performance. This definition of the financial access goal incorporates the idea that the financial opportunity to attend college cannot be realized if students do not have the opportunity to *persist* in the program to which they have academic access. Limiting this goal to low-cost programs constrains the boundaries more narrowly than the broader notion of equal educational opportunity, which also includes the freedom to choose a private college.[2] And by focusing on access to both two-year and four-year programs, this definition assumes that students

[2] In the current system of student aid, we need to recognize that private colleges are more affordable for their students than public colleges (Paulsen and St. John 1997; St. John, Oescher, and Andrieu 1992), because they invest more of their money in grant aid. If the average Pell award increased, private colleges would recoup some of this investment, because public colleges are no longer affordable for low-income students.

FIG. 4.1 Framework for assessing policy influences on educational opportunity, linking educational policy to educational outcomes. PSE, postsecondary education.

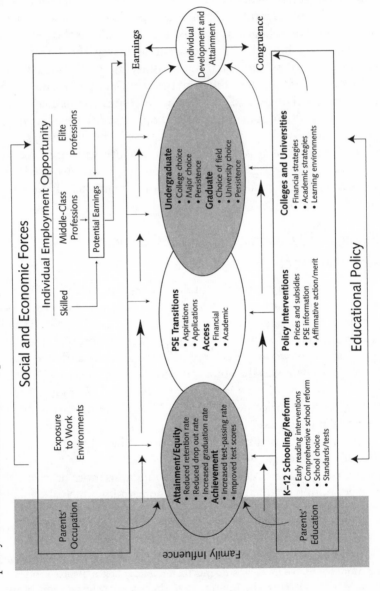

should have the opportunity to attend any level of program to which they can gain academic access.

Constraining access by students' *ability* and *prior performance* leaves higher education in control of setting parameters for *academic access*: students being academically prepared for initial and continued enrollment. The academic qualifications required for admission vary by college. Elite colleges have high admissions standards. At the other extreme, the minimum standard for postsecondary access is the ability to read and comprehend at a tenth-grade level; this standard is consistent with the requirements of the GED examination and a growing number of high-stakes graduation tests. In its 1997 study, the National Center for Education Statistics (1997a) used a college qualification index that considered the types of high school courses taken by students and standardized test scores. This standard can help distinguish qualifications for a moderately selective four-year college.

This definition of academic access implies that the rationalization of academic access to two-year and four-year programs depends on institutional practices (and possibly state policies) governing admissions and academic progress. By acknowledging that colleges have an obligation to make decisions about admissions and judgments about academic progress in college, this definition clarifies how to assess the roles of academic preparation and postsecondary encouragement. If we assume that K–12 education should prepare students for college, then we can assess how well K–12 schools promote academic access. Further, postsecondary encouragement can influence students' decisions about high school courses, which relates to academic preparation. However, postsecondary encouragement that focuses on finances can raise false expectations about financial access if it is not truthful about the inadequacy of aid.

These definitions of financial and academic access are more precise than are the empirical indicators of access used in this book to make prima facie judgments about access. Each of the analytic chapters (5–7) summarizes studies of persistence by students enrolled during the specified time period. The evaluation studies reviewed in these chapters controlled for family income, parents' education, child's prior education, and so forth. This approach provides an appropriate method of analyzing whether financial aid was adequate to promote financial access. I use the new logical framework to make informed judgments about the relative influence of school reform and financial aid. The impact of changes in financial aid on financial access will become apparent if we also consider the possible effects of K–12 reform on high school graduation rates and college participation rates by high school graduates (the approach used in chapters 5–7). We can also consider differences in enrollment by college-qualified students from high-income and low-income families (the approach used in chapter 8). The combination of the two methods provides a good indication of whether student aid was adequate to promote financial access and provides insight into whether school reforms affected academic preparation.

Equal educational opportunity is appropriately defined as equal opportunity to enroll, given the correct academic qualifications, regardless of financial means. This definition provides a way to think about equal educational opportunity in relation to efforts to improve financial affordability and academic preparation. First, with respect to the role of finances, I argue that the role of government in student aid is to equalize opportunity to enroll, controlling for ability and prior performance. Further, based on the definition of financial access given above, I argue that one role of government is to equalize financial access to public four-year and two-year programs. If this standard were reached, it would improve affordability and equal opportunity above current practices in most states. However, this definition stops short of the old goal of enabling college choice without regard to costs.

OUTCOME MEASURES

Based on these definitions and the new assumptions presented in chapter 3, I suggest four types of outcomes related to both the academic preparation perspective and equity perspective on access (fig. 4.1):

1. *K–12 outcomes*: Educational reforms should be evaluated with respect to their influence on both student achievement (average scores and pass rates) and equity outcomes (percentages of students who achieve at grade level and graduate). Improving both types of outcomes would be a balanced reform approach. Improving achievement outcomes while reducing graduation rates could be viewed as a deceptive reform strategy with false gains in outcomes. Improving equity while reducing achievement could be viewed as a dilution in quality of education.
2. *College transitions*: Academic access can be measured by participation rates for high school graduates, an indicator of whether there are gains in academic access. Financial access can be measured by comparisons of college enrollment rates for academically prepared students (students who graduated high school or have completed a college preparatory curriculum).[3] These outcomes are the focal point of the current study.

[3] Chapters 5–7 consider participation rates for high school graduates. Chapter 8 uses NCES's definition of college qualification as a basis for reexamining the causes of the new inequality.

3. *Postsecondary attainment*: Improved rates of degree attainment provide an indicator of improvement in the academic aspect of attainment, while narrowing the gap in rates of degree attainment across diverse groups indicates improvement in equity in attainment.
4. *Economic and social outcomes*: The consequence of gains in academic and equity outcomes include *congruence* between education and employment (a social and educational outcome) and increased *earnings* (an economic outcome for the individual and society).

My primary focus is on the transition to college, but I also consider research related to the role of school reform in promoting K–12 outcomes as a means of discerning the effects of policy on the academic and financial aspects of access. The long-term outcomes—postsecondary attainment and economic and social outcomes—are beyond the parameters of this study. However, research focusing on the employability of college graduates, as measured by congruence between degrees (and fields of degrees) and employment opportunity, as well as earnings, does have policy relevance, and these additional outcomes merit further study using this type of analytic framework.

Assessing the Impact of Policy on Access

Using the definitions presented above, I have constructed a logical framework for assessing the effects of governmental policies, programs, and funding on opportunity and equity in postsecondary attendance, as measures of social justice in postsecondary finance. In the logical framework for assessing the effects of governmental policy on academic attainment and equal opportunity in postsecondary education (fig. 4.1), the effects should be viewed in three distinct, yet interrelated ways:

1. as consequences of changes in the situated contexts in which students and their families make educational choices;
2. as educational choices made by students and prospective students, within a continuous stream of educational and career choices;
3. as individual decisions that are influenced by educational policy, controlling for students' situated contexts and their prior educational choices and experience.

SITUATED CONTEXTS FOR EDUCATIONAL CHOICES

Students and their families make educational choices within situated contexts. While many researchers have historically examined educational attainment and postsecondary choices through the lens of social class, it is now evident that much analysis of the role of class has oversimplified the role of social contexts. When a simple, continuous measure of socioeconomic status (SES) is used in analyses of discrete decisions (e.g., the decision to enroll or to attend a private college),[4] it is difficult to control for the ways in which educational choices have been influenced by situated family contexts, because these measures do not consider differential effects of parents' education and occupation.

Research that takes into account the differential effects of family income and parents' education reveals differences in the situated contexts in which students make their educational choices (St. John, Kirshstein, and Noell 1991; St. John, Paulsen, and Starkey 1996). The recent "nexus" studies also provide insight into the diversity of situated contexts facing different types of students. With some colleagues, I have developed a method of assessing how financial perceptions, formed during the college-choice process, have a confounding influence on college experiences and on the ways in which students react to tuition and student aid (St. John, Paulsen, and Starkey 1996). Below, I summarize nexus studies of the roles of social class (Paulsen and St. John 2002) and racial differences (Paulsen, St. John, and Carter 2002). The studies illustrate the underlying influence of social class and race on the ways in which students make their postsecondary choices.[5] I then reconsider the role of situated contexts.

The Influence of Social Class

Three distinct patterns of college choice emerged from the nexus study of social class (Paulsen and St. John 2002). First, when the low-income students were examined as a distinct group, we found that students who lived in poverty had a distinct pattern of choice. Most chose colleges because of high financial aid, low tuition, or both. And a large percentage also chose their colleges so they could work while in college. Further, low-income students who chose colleges because of low tuition were less likely to persist. Low-income students who chose colleges because of aid had a slight competitive advantage compared with students who did not consider aid important, even though aid was adequate in the late 1980s. As the analysis of the decline in purchasing power of Pell grants indicates (chapter 2), this was a period of low affordability.

---

[4] Typically in educational research, social class influences are "controlled" for with a measure of SES, which is imputed from a combination of parents' education and occupation (Blau and Duncan 1967).

[5] The nexus studies used the National Postsecondary Student Aid Survey of 1987 (NPSAS:87). (The late 1980s were similar to the 1990s with respect to availability of need-based grant aid.) The original studies used national samples of all students enrolled in four-year colleges (St. John, Paulsen, and Starkey 1996; Paulsen and St. John 1997); the class and race studies used samples of all students in two-year and four-year colleges (Paulsen and St. John 2002; Paulsen, St. John, and Carter 2002).

Second, the analyses of lower-middle-income students revealed a working-class pattern of student choice. Most of these "working-class" students considered work and living costs very important in their college choices. Financial aid and low tuition were also important. However, this group was even more responsive to tuition than the students from poor families. Some lower-middle-income families appeared to be unaware of student aid, or to be aware of the inadequacy of aid. They were more likely to choose their colleges because of low tuition than were poor students, and their choices were more directly affected by tuition. While they were also somewhat less likely to consider aid, grants and loans were adequate for these students once living costs were controlled for.

Third, the analyses of middle-income and upper-income students revealed a middle-income pattern of student choice. These privileged students were less likely than other groups to choose colleges because they were close to work. They were also less likely to choose colleges because of financial aid, but choosing a college for this reason had a positive influence on persistence.

Thus, finances are central in educational choice processes for poor and working-class college students. Both groups considered tuition and aid in their college choice more than did wealthier students. However, while student aid was more important in college choice for low-income students, grant aid was inadequate for them, inhibiting their persistence in college. In contrast, students from working-class families were more likely to choose colleges because of low tuition, and their persistence decisions were more substantially influenced by tuition. Aid was still minimally adequate for working-class students. For wealthier students, from middle-class and upper-class families, choosing colleges because of high aid was positively associated with persistence. Thus, by the late 1980s, financial aid policies accentuated class privileges. There were far fewer economic constraints on choices by middle-class students, and aid was adequate for these students.

The Role of Race/Ethnicity

There are also distinct patterns of college choice across racial/ethnic groups, but these group differences also accentuate class differences in American society (Paulsen, St. John, and Carter 2002). I summarize here the distinct patterns evident among African Americans, Hispanics, Asian Americans, and Whites.

African Americans were highly sensitive to finances in their college choices and in their persistence decisions. Tuition and student aid played a substantial role in the college-choice process for African Americans, and grants and tuition had a substantial and direct influence on persistence.

Further, choosing a college because of student aid was positively associated with persistence, even when the direct effects of student aid were controlled for. This majority pattern among African Americans was similar to the pattern of college choice by students from low-income families observed in the analysis summarized above (Paulsen and St. John 2002).

A substantial percentage of African Americans in the survey were from high-earning families with high levels of education. Higher levels of parents' education were associated with persistence for African Americans, indicating that those with cultural capital aspired to reproduce this capital in their families. Thus there is clearly a pattern of economic diversity within the African American population that accentuates the role of finance in college choice and college persistence.

The dominant pattern among Hispanic Americans is appropriately characterized as working class (Rendon, Jalomo, and Nora 2000). In 1987, nearly 45 percent of Hispanic college students chose their colleges because they were close to work (Paulsen, St. John, and Carter 2002). Further, choosing a college for this reason was positively associated with persistence, before living costs were controlled for, a pattern similar to that for working-class families across ethnic groups (Paulsen and St. John 2002). In addition, loans had a negative influence on persistence by Hispanic students, even after living costs were considered. Thus, working to pay their way through college held a higher value for the majority of the Hispanic community than did borrowing to pay living costs while in college.

Asian Americans placed a greater value on higher education relative to income than did the other racial/ethnic groups (Paulsen, St. John, and Carter 2002). They attended more expensive colleges, had mothers with higher levels of educational attainment, and persisted better than other groups. But their average income was lower than the average for Whites. Yet, Asian Americans were less responsive than other groups to student aid. This suggests a pattern of family savings and/or a pattern of extended family support.

Finally, Whites were more economically advantaged than students from the other racial/ethnic groups. There was economic diversity among the White populations, however, which helps explain why they were responsive to tuition and student grants. But while loans were negatively associated with persistence, they ceased to be significant when living costs were controlled for. This indicates that loans were sufficient to enable Whites to persist in college but were not sufficient for other groups.

Situated Contexts

Race/ethnicity and social class have a pervasive influence on educational choice processes. The research reviewed above illustrates that the decline in Pell grants had a more substantial impact on poor and working-class students than on middle-class students, and on minorities than on Whites. Clearly, different groups in society reacted to changes in policy (financial or academic) in different ways. These different patterns of choice provide a compelling reason for examining how policy changes (i.e., K–12 reforms and reduction in grants) have influenced the new disparity in postsecondary opportunity that emerged in the 1980s and increased in the 1990s.

PATTERNS OF EDUCATIONAL CHOICE

For a fuller understanding of the role of government in expanding access to higher education, it is important to consider three spheres of influence: K–12 education, the formation of aspirations (for career and education), and postsecondary choices. When attempting to build an understanding of how changes in educational policy have influenced postsecondary opportunity, we need to consider how policy links to educational outcomes. Here, I briefly examine both traditional and nontraditional patterns of choice.

Traditional Patterns

Given the diversity in experience of families and children, it is startling how much research on *traditional* patterns of educational attainment and choice informs governmental policies and institutional strategies for improving opportunity. Most of the research on college students focuses on traditional-age students (Pascarella and Terenzini 1991). And while the national longitudinal databases (e.g., NLS:72, HSB:80, HSB:82) enabled researchers to explore the complexity of the college-choice process, including the impact of financial aid (Jackson 1978, 1988; Manski and Wise 1983; St. John and Noell 1989), these databases contained only traditional-age college students and generally did not even include students who had dropped out of high school.[6] Thus, most of the research on college students, including research on the impact of financial aid, can be generalized only to traditional-age students.

Research that focused on the school experiences of traditional students has been widely used to inform strategies for promoting postsecondary opportunity. In the late 1980s, the Reagan administration commissioned a set of studies that examined the explanations for the

---

[6] For HSB:82, the sample included high school sophomores and thus included some students who would drop out of school. However, NLS:72 and HSB:80 were national samples of high school seniors and thus would include fewer students who dropped out before graduating.

downturn in minority participation rates in the middle 1980s. The initial study (Chaikind 1987) used the national databases to examine the influence of family background and academic preparation, without considering student aid. The more noted follow-up study by Pelavin and Kane (1988, 1990) extended this approach. They found a correlation between high school courses (e.g., algebra) and college attendance, a finding that has since led to such courses being widely advocated (e.g., NCES 1997a). Thus, the study findings for a restricted group of students, those who followed traditional patterns, have been used as the basis for the rationale that "educational improvement" can expand postsecondary opportunity. However, although high school course-taking behavior may influence academic preparation and academic access, a substantial percentage of low-income students who are academically qualified do not apply to or attend college (NCES 1997a). These students lack financial access, which has become a serious policy problem in the United States.

Nontraditional Patterns

With the current effort to expand postsecondary opportunity to a point of nearly universal access, we must begin to consider the scant research on students who have followed nontraditional patterns. Many people do not follow the traditional lockstep process through education. Many who drop out before completing high school can eventually benefit from college. Some of these individuals eventually complete GED exams and go to college. Others attempt to enter technical postsecondary programs without completing high school.

Graduation rates for 17-year-olds have declined slightly since the 1970s (table A.7). Thus, two decades of "educational improvement" by the Reagan, Bush, and Clinton administrations did not improve the primary outcomes of K–12 schools. Students who do not graduate from high school, along with some who do graduate, lack the academic preparation (and functional literacy) necessary for college study. Thus, colleges will need to provide academic support for underprepared students.

The population that has not been well served by traditional approaches—those who did not complete high school, did not attend college, or dropped out of college—is more diverse in racial/ethnic origins than is the traditional population that has been better served by K–12 schools and traditional colleges and universities. This means that research on diverse groups may be more informative to the construction of policies to increase postsecondary participation than studies focusing on those who have successfully negotiated the educational system.

There is a legitimate reason for concern about the quality of education (Finn 2001), especially in urban communities (Fossey 2003). The most recent wave of school reform has not served urban schools well. Whereas Title I once provided financial support—with only modest restrictions—to schools with high percentages of low-income students (Wong 2003), over time the funds for Title I have been targeted and restricted to practices thought to be linked to improvement in educational outcomes. At the same time, states have implemented new high-stakes tests (Manset and Washburn 2003) and other accountability measures. This creates a number of contradictory mandates in schools (Manset and Washburn 2003) that seem to promote academic failure in urban schools (Franklin 2003). Indeed, it appears that the most recent round of school reforms could be failing in urban schools, adding to the number of students needing remedial support as they make the transition to college.

THE ROLE OF POLICY IN PROMOTING OPPORTUNITY

During the first few decades of the twenty-first century, educational policymakers in states and at the federal level will be increasingly concerned with finding better ways for improving—both expanding and equalizing—the opportunity for postsecondary education. While finances play a role in expanding and equalizing opportunity, they are not the only strategies government can use. To build a foundation for future efforts to expand opportunity, it is crucial that educational researchers assess the effects of efforts to date.

The influence of family backgrounds—and the situated contexts in which students make educational choices—should not be overlooked when considering how governmental policy affects students. Parents' educational experiences influence the ways in which students enter educational systems, including the schools they enter, as do parents' expectations about their children's success in school. While the federal government and states historically enabled about one-third of the population to attain at least some postsecondary education, they are now attempting to extend opportunities to children whose parents have had little success in school. As policymakers attempt to construct policies that further increase postsecondary opportunity, they will need to refocus on strategies that help equalize all levels of educational opportunity.

It is frequently argued that improvements in K–12 schools are the best way to improve access (e.g., Pelavin and Kane 1990; NCES 1997a). When filtering through these claims, we need to distinguish between claims based on research that focused on traditional students and those based on studies that included nontraditional students. When we make this distinction, it becomes apparent that researchers have (1) documented correlations evident among majority and minority students and (2) assumed that K–12 reforms could expand opportunity for nontraditional students. But when these new rational models examined the link-ages between educational policies and student outcomes, they over-looked the role of finances (e.g., Finn 1990; NCES 1997a).[7] A correlation does not mean causation. The logic of the logical models used to ana-lyze academic access, if they ignored the role of finances as an explana-tion of inequality when finances were a cause of inequality, was mis-specified. In that case, policies aimed at improving educational outcome could increase inequalities, if these policies lead to changes in financing that contribute to the inequalities. For example, focusing policy on rais-ing educational standards while reducing funding for grants would be consistent with the new conservative rationale, but it could create new disparities while improving some outcomes. Therefore we must use the timeline of history to untangle how policies have changed in relation to changes in educational outcomes. Chapters 5–7 focus on the possible effects of the major educational (K–12) policy developments in the last half of the twentieth century.

By the 1970s, it became possible to see whether the reforms of the 1950s and early 1960s had produced results. New approaches to math and other "research-based" reforms were introduced as a result of the Na-tional Defense Education Act. The Elementary and Secondary Educa-tion Act of 1965 introduced a focus on educational improvement for the "historically disadvantaged" through the Title I program, which gave ad-ditional funding to schools with high percentages of low-income stu-dents. And a pattern of pulling special needs students out of classrooms was established. The high school graduation rates and college enrollment rates for high school graduates in the 1970s (1970, 1975, and 1980) pro-vide insight into the impact of these early educational reforms.

The 1980s were a period of transition in educational policy. During the 1970s, programs for special needs students were expanded as the portfolio of programs authorized through ESEA increased. Then, in the early 1980s, an emphasis was placed on consolidation of federal pro-grams. While the Title I program was maintained,[8] an emphasis shifted to "schoolwide" programs in schools with high needs. There was also a greater focus on statewide testing, largely as a result of national report-ing on comparative test scores. Transitions in the key indicators during the early 1980s (1980–85) correspond with the reforms in the late 1970s,

[7] This issue is central to the current study. As chapter 8 illustrates, NCES systemati-cally overlooked the role of finances; in that chapter, NCES's assumptions are reex-amined using evidence from its own reports.

[8] For a time the program was designated Chapter 1, due to changes in enabling legislation.

while changes in these indicators during the late 1980s (1985–90) correspond with the early effects of the shift toward educational excellence.

Trends in the two indicators in the 1990s corresponded with the ongoing effects of the new policy environment. The climb in college participation rates by high school graduates and the decline in high school
graduation rates—trends reviewed briefly in chapter 2—correspond
chronologically with these policies. In the 1990s "research-based reforms" were emphasized, a pattern now evident in states' efforts to promote reading reform, comprehensive school reform, and postsecondary
encouragement. However, it is too early to look for any substantial effects
of the latest round of policy changes.

Did K–12 reforms improve academic access to postsecondary education? While I do not assess how these reforms influenced academic
preparation and access, this study is informed by such assessments.[9] Logically, educational reforms should influence both achievement outcomes
(improved test scores and pass rates) and equity in K–12 attainment outcomes (higher percentage of students who perform at grade level). Improvement in both types of outcomes can improve access to college. If
students achieve better on standardized tests, they probably are better
prepared for college. And if more students complete high school, the percentage of the traditional-age population going to college should also increase. I focus here on attainment/equity outcomes, since they relate directly to the goal of increasing postsecondary opportunity.

POLICY INTERVENTIONS THAT PROMOTE ACCESS

Financial Access

Financial access only recently resurfaced as a major policy issue,
when the Advisory Committee on Student Financial Assistance (2001a)
called the attention of the press to problems with college affordability
(USA Today 2001). The coordination of financial strategies at the state
and federal levels is necessary to promote financial access. In this study
I use multiple indicators of financial access, including general measures

[9] As a researcher interested in educational policy, I have collaborated on a comprehensive review of urban school reform (Miron and St. John 2003) and on critical
studies of reading reform (St. John, Manset, Chung, Simmons, et al. 2003), comprehensive reform (St. John, Manset, Chung, Musoba, et al. 2003), and school
choice (Ridenour and St. John 2003; St. John and Ridenour 2001). These and
other research efforts inform the statement about specific reforms. However, my
purpose here is not to focus on K–12 reform but rather to encourage readers to
put these reforms in perspective as they think about strategies for reforming K–12
policy.

of enrollment and participation, to discern whether there is a problem. I also examine studies of the effects of financial aid on first-time enrollment and persistence (chapters 5–7). In combination, these types of evidence provide a systematic and cohesive analysis of the effects of changes in student aid policy.

Postsecondary Encouragement

The notion that encouragement to pursue postsecondary education might improve enrollment and somehow equalize opportunity has only recently emerged, at least as a federal policy initiative. The federal government has long had the "TRIO" programs (Talent Search, Upward Bound, Special Services) that provided encouragement as an integral part of postsecondary educational policy. Indiana was one of the first states to undertake a statewide effort to provide information on postsecondary opportunities, as a means of promoting opportunity in postsecondary education (Hossler and Schmit 1995; Hossler, Schmit, and Vesper 1999). More recently, the federal government has initiated an effort to promote states' expansion of postsecondary encouragement through a new federal program, Gaining Early Awareness and Readiness for Undergraduate Programs (GEAR UP).

These incremental efforts suggest that encouragement can make a difference, even if the research on these programs is still modest (St. John and Hossler 1998). Encouragement can function in three ways:

1. *Improving information on postsecondary programs for all students*: Getting better information to middle-school and high-school students about postsecondary opportunities provides a potential means of expanding opportunity by enabling more high school students to learn how high school course work is related to postsecondary options (Hossler, Schmit, and Vesper 1999; Perna 2000). These strategies expand both financial and academic access.
2. *Providing information about student financial aid*: Providing information on college costs and financial aid can help families plan for college (Hossler and Schmit 1995; Hossler, Schmit, and Vesper 1999). Such information can improve financial access only if there is adequate financial aid to ensure access; otherwise it increases the level of false hope among low-income families.
3. *Affirmative and merit-aware approaches to admissions*: Refining admissions strategies to consider the strengths of diverse groups can expand opportunity for these groups to attend elite institutions (St. John et al. 2001), and information linked to this can help equalize opportunity to attend elite colleges.

Since the national data on postsecondary encouragement are modest, I explore how encouragement converges with other policies to promote academic access (i.e., to encourage high school students to prepare for college) and informs students about financial access.

Postsecondary Strategies

Colleges and universities also have a substantial and direct influence on educational attainment. Both financial and academic strategies can influence students' educational choices and educational attainment. Ultimately, however, the ways in which students experience their learning environments have a substantial and direct influence on students' choice and attainment, especially if there are sufficient financial resources.

FINANCIAL STRATEGIES. The strategies colleges use to finance their enterprises—their decisions about spending, tuition, student aid, and other revenue acquisition—directly influence affordability. In public colleges, state subsidies function as part of the educational revenues, along with tuition. In the current financial context, public colleges, as well as private colleges, are faced with the challenge of generating sufficient supplemental revenues for student aid. A principal concern of the analyses in this book is how well colleges maintain financial access, as measured by the ability of students to continue their enrollment.

ACADEMIC STRATEGIES. Changes in academic strategies can have a substantial influence on the distribution of enrollment. In the 1980s there were large-scale changes in the academic and financial strategies used by private colleges, which enabled these colleges to compete more successfully for students (St. John 1992a,b, 1994). In particular, more thought needs to be given to meeting the educational needs of new clientele as colleges further expand opportunity. In this study, I consider these changes and reflect on whether this topic merits further exploration.

LEARNING ENVIRONMENTS. Research on college students increasingly shows that students' engagement in their learning environments in college has a direct and substantial effect on their persistence (Kuh and Love 2000; Tinto 2000). However, for low-income families, students must have adequate resources to engage in the academic and social opportunities provided by colleges. While I am concerned primarily with the role of finances in keeping college accessible, I recognize that students' engagement in the college environment is more crucial to academic success once financial access is maintained. In the future, researchers should extend the framework employed here by examining college outcomes, including employability of graduates and congruence of majors and employment.

Assessing the Impact of Finance Policy

The framework developed above guides the analysis of the effects of financial aid policy and academic preparation in the next three chapters. First, I use the framework to examine three periods: the 1960s and 1970s (chapter 5), the 1980s (chapter 6), and the 1990s (chapter 7). This provides an understanding of the relationship between changes in policy and changes in student outcome. The final chapter in part I reexamines NCES's analysis (1997a) of the college enrollment process by students in the high school class of 1992, using NELS:88. This reanalysis further illustrates how the analytic framework used by NCES has systematically overlooked the role of finances in promoting access and equal opportunity.

ANALYSIS OF THE CONSEQUENCES OF POLICY CHANGES

The next three chapters examine the impact of changes in federal policy during different periods:

—during the emergence of student aid programs, when equal educational opportunity was a policy goal (the late 1960s and 1970s; chapter 5);
—during the refinancing of higher education, a period when the efficient use of tax dollars became a political priority in educational policy (1981–92; chapter 6);
—during the expansion of loans and emergence of tax credits, when the interests of middle-class taxpayers were paramount to maintaining a political coalition (1993–2000; chapter 7).

Four questions guided the analyses of each period. I used a systematic and logical process to build an empirical understanding of the role and impact of policy changes. The questions that guided the analyses are discussed in relation to the analytic framework.

Step 1: Identify Changes in Policy

How did federal financial aid and state finance policies change during the period?

The framework (fig. 4.1) proposes that changes in prices and subsidies, including changes in federal student aid policy, have a direct impact on financial access. As a first step in assessing how changes in policy have influenced changes in financial access, I examine the changes in federal student aid policy during the three distinct periods. The roles of theory and ideology are also examined, along with trends in funds provided by the major student aid programs. The literature on student aid has assumed that student aid funding influences enrollment, an assumption also evident in the framework outlined in this chapter. Unlike many other analyses of student aid (e.g., Hansen 1983; Kane 1995), my review considers trends in funding for both generally available aid programs (now funded through Title IV of the Higher Education Act) and specially directed funds (for veterans, health professions, and so forth).

The analysis considers changes in policy for both types of federal student aid, because both can influence enrollment behavior, consistent with the intent of the two types of programs. While veterans' benefits and other forms of aid are limited to the military and provided as a reward for service, they enable enrollment in much the same way as generally available need-based aid. Indeed, these specially directed programs often induce people of limited financial means to make life choices: some high school students will choose the military as a means of financing a college education. Ignoring these other federal programs is a serious oversight. To contend with the tendency of other analysts to focus exclusively on Title IV aid, when assessing the impact of aid I consider both generally available aid and total aid (generally available plus specially directed).

Further, changes in state finance policies are also examined in the three analytic chapters. I examine the literature on state financing strategies, along with trends in state subsidies to institutions, tuition, and state grants. Changes in state finances are considered because federal student aid and changes in state financing of higher education have simultaneous and interrelated effects on students' enrollment decisions.

Step 2: Assess Changes in Key Indicators

> How did the key indicators—access, equal opportunity, and efficient use of tax dollars—change during the period?

As a second step in the analysis, I examine whether there is a relationship between changes in finance policy (federal student aid and state funding) and the indicators of financial access and equity, as well as whether these changes have higher or lower costs for taxpayers. This step establishes a prima facie case for making informed judgments about the impact of policy changes on student outcomes. The three indicators provide a logical basis for linking considerations about social justice, from diverse perspectives, to the impact of student aid. Specifically, I consider how three types of indicators changed over time. (The trend tables used in these analyses are in the appendix.)

ACCESS. I examined two access indicators: trends in the overall enrollment rate for three periods (table A.8) and actual FTE enrollment in relation to the midrange predictions developed by NCES a decade earlier. Projections and actual enrollment (see tables 5.1, 6.1, and 7.1) are examined by institutional control (public or private institutions) and level (two-year or four-year), when available (see the appendix for a description of the methods used in these analyses). This provides an assessment of whether enrollments ran higher or lower than predicted by a demographic prediction model. Both of these measures relate to issues of financial and academic access.

EQUAL OPPORTUNITY. The primary indicator of equity used for this study was the comparison of trends in college enrollment rates for African Americans and Hispanics with those Whites (see tables 2.2 and A.8). If better data were available on participation across income groups, I would have used this measure as well. However, the availability of consistent data on participation by racial/ethnic group made it possible to ponder a set of related questions about academic preparation and academic access.

TAXPAYER COSTS. I focus primarily on tax dollars spent per FTE student enrolled (table A.9). I assume that the cost to taxpayers is one dollar for every dollar of government aid for grants and fifty cents for every dollar of loans.[10] In addition, I ponder the role of tax credits and examine the costs of these subsidies in chapter 7.

Step 3: Summarize Evaluation Studies

> Did evaluation studies of students enrolled during the period help explain the apparent relationship between changes in policy and changes in access, equal opportunity, and the efficient use of tax dollars?

As a third step I consider whether statistical analyses that control for the effects of student background (family income, ethnicity, student achievement, and so forth) further explain how student aid policies during specific periods influenced student educational choices. I summarize evaluation studies by examining evidence of the effects of student aid on financial access.

This step is necessary to provide confirmatory evidence of a relationship between the changes in policy and corresponding trends in key indicators. Establishing that indicators changed during a period when policy changed does not provide statistical proof of causality. Rather, sound

[10] This assumption is frequently made in the literature (e.g., McPherson and Schapiro 1997). However, with the lower default rates and interest rates in the 1990s, the costs may actually be lower.

logical and statistical models are needed to assess how prices and subsidies influenced student outcomes. I review studies that examine the effects of student aid on students enrollment and persistence in educational programs (either high school students making the transition to college or college students making the choice to continue their enrollment) during the three distinct periods. These studies illuminate how policy influenced students' educational choices during these historical periods.

However, we should be cautious in generalizing from the reported statistics. The evaluation studies reviewed in chapters 5–7 analyzed large student databases using logical models that controlled for student background and achievement. The analyses all used delta-p statistics to measure the direct effects of student aid. Readers should use caution when comparing the size of the delta-p statistics reported in summary tables (Peng et al. 2002). These statistics apply only to otherwise average students in the samples analyzed and should not be compared or generalized across studies.

Step 4: Examine Other Explanations

> Did changes in K–12 schools or in postsecondary encouragement influence observed changes in access and equity?

While the evaluation studies I have reviewed provide statistical controls for student achievement, other educational policies that could have influenced students' educational choices in these evaluation studies were beyond the statistical analyses summarized below. Therefore, I take a step back and consider whether other educational policies—including prior K–12 reforms and prior efforts to provide postsecondary encouragement—might also have affected the patterns observed.

In this final step I use the entire framework (fig. 4.1) as a logical basis for building an understanding of how changes in educational policy have influenced these students' enrollment decisions. Admittedly these are indirect and speculative interpretations, but they are precisely the types of retrospective analyses that are needed to untangle questions about the relative effects of financial strategies, postsecondary encouragement, and academic preparation.

A REEXAMINATION OF NCES ACCESS STUDIES

The historical analyses in chapters 5–7 provide one view of how changes in school reform and finance influenced changes in student outcomes. Given the overwhelming conclusions from these analyses—that changes in student aid policy affected the new inequality in postsecondary opportunity—there is reason to question the logical models

NCES has used to analyze national databases. Chapter 8 proposes a model that considers the role of academic preparation, as measured by NCES, and finances in the transition to college by students in the high school class of 1992. This analysis documents how the frameworks used by NCES precluded a full consideration of the role of finances and the influence of financial aid in its analysis of access and persistence using national databases.

5   The 1970s: Equalizing Educational Opportunity

The federal role in student aid expanded in the late 1960s and early 1970s, as did the state role in funding public higher education. States expanded public systems in response to growth in the size of the traditional college-age populations (i.e., the baby boom generation), founding new campuses in large state systems (Lee and Bowen 1971, 1975). The earliest federal student aid created before the 1960s, such as the GI Bill, was made available to special groups in society. The Higher Education Act, passed in 1965, formalized the federal role in student aid by making aid generally available. After 1965, the federal government awarded need-based grants as a means of providing financial access for low-income students. In 1972, the notion that student aid should equalize the opportunity to attend a private college was firmly established by a reauthorization of HEA. However, in 1978 student aid programs were broadened to include middle-income students as well as low-income students. The price tag for the new programs was considered too high, given the emerging concerns about the cost of social programs. Analysts soon began to examine alternative ways of constraining the costs of federal student aid (Hansen 1983; St. John and Byce 1982). Thus, federal aid programs were adequately funded for only a brief period in American history, a period of *equalizing educational opportunity*.

Step 1: Changes in Policy

The federal role in student financial aid emerged after World War II, with the GI Bill of Rights. Many of the earlier student aid programs were workforce related, and some began before World War II (Finn 1978). The early federal grant programs, including the GI Bill, were specially directed, aimed at addressing workforce needs in specific areas (e.g., health care, the military). The National Defense Student Loans program (NDSL),[1]

[1] NDSL, created by the National Defense Education Act, was renamed National Direct Educational Loans and reauthorized in the HEA of 1965. It continued to be referred to as NDSL.

the first generally available federal program, was created in 1958. The *generally available* programs provided aid to students based on their financial need.

In 1964, the federal government created the Social Security Survivors Benefits program as the major specially directed program. It provided generous grants to children of a deceased parent who had contributed to Social Security. It was the largest federal grant program in the 1960s. The program played an important role because of its size and focus on poor families. Social Security Survivors Benefits provided a safety net that enabled many children in at-risk situations to attend college who might not have been able to attend without this aid. However, since benefits were not awarded based on a generally accepted need-analysis formula, they were often overlooked in analyses of the effects of student aid. Such *specially directed* aid supports students in specific circumstances and can influence students' choices in much the same ways as need-based aid.

Federal programs that provided generally available loans and work-study were created before the passage of HEA in 1965, one of President Johnson's Great Society initiatives (Gladieux and Wolanin 1976; Finn 1978). HEA consolidated generally available programs, NDSL and College Work-Study (CWS); created a major new grant program, the Educational Opportunity Grant (EOG) program;[2] and created a major new loan program, Guaranteed Student Loans (GSL, renamed the Federal Family Education Loan Program [FFELP] in 1992; I refer to this program as GSL throughout the book). Students could apply directly to a state guarantee agency or the federal government for a GSL loan. It was the first generally available and *portable* federal aid program. Under GSL, students made a choice of where to go to college. The loan functioned as a *quasi-entitlement*, something like a voucher. The other programs included in HEA were distributed to campuses based on applications made by colleges and universities. And while the federal government required that the *campus-based* programs be awarded aid according to financial need,[3] these programs were not portable. Students could not take their grants with them from one campus to another.

Thus, the foundation for federal student aid was established in 1965, with substantial programs that were both need-based and specially directed. The new programs focused on equalizing opportunity (i.e., the

[2] EOG was renamed Supplemental Educational Opportunity Grant (SEOG) in 1972, after the Basic Educational Opportunity Grant program (now Pell program) was created in 1972.

[3] The SEOG, CWS, and NDSL programs were named "campus-based" programs in 1972, as described later in the text.

HEA Title IV programs), while the older programs focused on expanding demand by special populations (i.e., specially directed programs). Logically, changes in federal programs during the 1970s could have affected total enrollment, equal opportunity, and other types of educational choices (i.e., type of program, level of aspiration). Therefore, I examine how the rationales used to argue for student aid and funding levels changed during the decade. I also consider the role of state finance policy during this period.

THE RATIONALE FOR EXPANDING STUDENT AID

The Higher Education Act, one of President Johnson's Great Society programs, was initially rationalized based on emerging beliefs about social justice. The early Title IV grant programs distributed funds to universities based on grant applications. The institutions were awarded grants according to financial need. At the time, however, equal opportunity was viewed largely as a social goal. Desegregation of schools was still a major policy issue, and college desegregation was still being litigated. The emphasis on equal opportunity in the 1965 legislation was influenced by these changes in the policy environment. Two arguments were made in the 1960s that influenced the emergence of the generally accepted notions about market forces in higher education. These early market arguments also had a substantial influence on the 1972 reauthorization of HEA.

First, Milton Friedman's argument (1962) that funding students was a more appropriate means of financing higher and vocational education than direct institutional subsidies gave conservatives another point of view to consider. In the 1960s and 1970s, most conservative politicians and economists supported the dominant progressive notion that tax dollars should directly fund schools and colleges as a means of meeting demand. The primary question dividing conservatives and liberals during this still progressive period was not "should taxes be used to support institutions?" but "how expansive should this support be?" Friedman's argument stimulated some conservative politicians and analysts to question their assumptions. These arguments made it easier for the Nixon administration to consider portable grants as an alternative to institutional aid in the debates about HEA in the early 1970s.

Second, the emergence of human capital theory in the 1960s also stimulated thinking about student subsidies as an alternative to institutional subsidies. In his foundational work on human capital theory, Gary S. Becker (1964) argued that when faced with investment decisions, both government and individuals explicitly considered costs and benefits in deciding how much to invest in higher education. Becker speculated that the types of federal loans generally available through the National Defense Education Act (i.e., NDSL) could serve as a subsidy to individuals in their cost-benefit calculations. This framework provided a logical basis for the first wave of econometric studies of the effects of prices, which soon followed. These economic arguments persuaded liberals in the U.S. Senate to consider an alternative federal strategy in the 1972 reauthorization of HEA (Gladieux and Wolanin 1976).

During the 1970s, a temporary consensus emerged that the goal of federal higher education programs was to promote equal educational opportunity (Gladieux and Wolanin 1976). The 1972 reauthorization of HEA restructured the federal student aid programs: NDSL, CWS, and SEOG were combined into the campus-based programs, and two new grant programs were created. The State Student Incentive Grant program (SSIG) provided a financial incentive to states to create need-based grant programs. The major new federal grant program, Basic Educational Opportunity Grants (BEOG; now Pell grants),[4] was need-based and portable and thus functioned like need-based vouchers. Pell grants were phased in over a four-year period, with freshmen being eligible the first year, freshmen and sophomores the second year, and so forth.

The introduction of the Pell program enabled institutions to exercise more discretion over the use of SEOG grants. At the same time, the new Pell program created an opportunity for "innovation" by new institutions. Some of the early advocates had hoped this program would stimulate innovation in traditional higher education (e.g., Newman 1971), but the major new development was stimulated by the proprietary schools sector. The Pell program had been created by the Nixon administration in response to demands to expand the federal role in higher education.[5]

The Pell program became the preoccupation of many analysts who advocated the rational market model (e.g., Hansen 1983; Kane 1995; Manski and Wise 1983). Introduction of the Pell program also substantially complicated federal budget processes. Since Pell grants functioned as a quasi-entitlement for need-eligible students, the federal government could not simply set program funding in the budget each year. Rather,

[4] For readability of the text, I refer to BEOG as Pell from this point forward. The reader is reminded, however, that the change in name did not occur until the 1980 reauthorization of HEA; at the same time, NDSL was renamed Perkins Loans and GSL was renamed Stafford Loans—symbolic changes that more closely identified the programs with their legislative sponsors (chapter 6).

[5] Rather than support the major new institutional aid program introduced in the House version of the Education Amendments of 1972, the Nixon administration introduced the idea of portable grants, which had been advocated by Newman (1971) and other study groups (e.g., Carnegie Commission 1973).

it became necessary to predict program costs for the federal budget and to reconcile the annual program costs in subsequent budgets (St. John and Byce 1982). Setting award schedules in the federal budget (i.e., limiting maximum awards) became an indirect method of controlling Pell program costs.

In the 1970s there were also changes in the GSL program, as the federal government tried to manage this complex quasi-entitlement program (Hearn 1993). The GSL program was difficult to manage because of the large number of actors—state guarantee agencies, private lenders, federal processors, secondary markets, and colleges and universities—that played a substantial role in the administration of the program. Further, in part because of the entitlement nature of the program,[6] it was difficult to predict program costs.

While political support for promoting equal opportunity goals held together during the decade, there were challenges by advocates of tax credits. At the time, many analysts considered tax credits an ultraconservative idea. Jimmy Carter was confronted by these proposals during his presidency. His response was to extend need-based aid to the middle class. The Middle Income Student Assistance Act (MISAA) extended eligibility for Pell grants to middle-income students and expanded eligibility for GSL. These program changes further increased the capacity of colleges with campus-based programs to offer SEOG grants to students from middle-income families (St. John and Byce 1982).

TRENDS IN AID AWARDS

Trends in the amount of aid awarded illustrate this expansion in federal student aid during the decade (table A.2, part A). Pell grants totaled $2.7 billion in 1975–76 and rose to nearly $4.46 billion in 1980–81, after MISAA. In contrast, awards through SEOG changed very little. GSL decreased slightly in the early 1970s, due to a period of regulatory tightening, but tripled in size in the late 1970s after MISAA. The $12.9 billion in federal generally available loan awards in 1980 was substantially greater than total federal spending on generally available grants ($5.3 billion).[7]

---

[6] If students qualified for GSL, they were "entitled" to a loan. The amount of demand for loans depended on the number of students who exercised this entitlement.

[7] Note that table A.2 indicates aid awarded, not federal spending on aid programs. This makes little difference for grant programs but is important when considering loans and work-study. GSL dollars are provided by private lenders, but the federal government subsidizes in-school interest, processing costs, and insurance against loan default. In CWS, the federal government required matching funds from institutions. Perkins Loans created a "revolving" fund in institutions that enabled them to lend money collected from prior loans.

Awards through CWS also increased, but remained a relatively small part of generally available federal student aid.

The federal budgets for the older campus-based programs were easier to predict and manage than the newer quasi-entitlement programs (e.g., GSL and Pell). The federal budget could set funding for NDSL, CWS, and SEOG, then the Department of Health, Education and Welfare would allocate funding to institutions. There was little difficulty in reconciling budgets at the end of each fiscal year. The quasi-entitlements—Pell and GSL—were much more complex to administer. Under GSL, the program eligibility criteria and subsidy levels (for state agencies, lenders, and students) influenced costs, and decisions on each of these factors could influence students' educational choices. For the Pell program, the award criteria had a major influence on award levels, but in the early years it was difficult to predict where students would enroll. Also, the impact of the new grant dollars was mitigated by the awarding of Pell grants to many students who would have entered college without the new grant program and by reductions in other federal grant programs.

There were also changes in the specially directed student aid programs during the decade (table A.2, part B). Spending on Social Security Survivors Benefits increased throughout the decade, from $2.0 billion to $3.5 billion. Veterans' benefits nearly tripled in the early 1970s, reaching $12.2 billion in 1975 as the program subsidized Vietnam veterans, then dropped substantially in the late 1970s (to $3.2 billion). Specially directed federal loans declined slightly during the 1970s. These other programs are important because they influenced enrollment along with the generally available programs.

When the funds for both generally available and specially directed federal programs are combined, a more complete picture emerges of the changes in federal student aid during the 1970s (table A.2, part C). Somewhat surprising when trends in total awards are examined is that veterans' benefits comprised more than half of total grants in 1975, then declined in the second half of the decade. Indeed, total federal grants actually declined in the late 1970s, from $19.3 billion in 1975 to $12.6 billion in 1980. Thus, the magnitude of changes in specially directed programs overwhelmed the growth in Title IV grants (Pell). Analysts who focused exclusively on Pell grants overlooked the major federal role during the period (e.g., Hansen 1983). It is also interesting to note that grants actually declined as a percentage of total federal aid awarded during the decade, from 55 to 47 percent. This is a different picture than that created by analysts who focused exclusively on need-based aid. Analysts who concluded that the increased investment in Pell had little effect on enrollment (e.g., Hansen 1983; Kane 1995) overlooked the effects of specially directed student aid. They focused on increases in Pell grants but ignored the decline in total federal grants (Pell plus other federal grants).

UNDERSTANDING THE FEDERAL ROLE

In the 1960s and early 1970s, a substantial portion of federal student aid was *specially directed* to target populations (i.e., veterans' benefits, Social Security Survivors Benefits). These programs induced enrollment and had a financial cost to the federal government, but they were not need-based and were generally overlooked by economists who studied the impact of federal student aid. There was a shift in the focus of federal student aid, from specially directed to *generally available* aid focused on equalizing opportunity. When some economists have pondered why the increased investment in generally available aid (i.e., Pell grants) did not increase enrollment, they have ignored the impact of decreases in specially directed student aid, an approach that led to false conclusions about the impact of student aid.

Consider Hansen's argument about measuring the effectiveness of the Pell grant program:

> The effectiveness of student financial aid programs in widening access to college can be assessed in two ways, both of which involve comparing enrollment rates to ascertain the extent that the number of college-age youths attending or planning to attend college increased as a consequence of the greater availability of federally provided student aid. The first compares enrollment rates for college-age youths from families with different income levels, on the assumption that need-based financial aid should raise the enrollment rates of lower-income youths relative to higher-income youths. The second standard compares planned and realized enrollment rates for high school seniors by socioeconomic status and ability levels (1983, 91).

Hansen specified the outcome related to spending on need-based student aid. He assumed that changes in enrollment by low-income youths of college age compared with their high-income peers were the best indicators of change in opportunity. This simple approach ignored the millions of dollars spent on specially directed aid, along with the reduction in total federal grants. Both specially directed and generally available aid can induce enrollment and enable persistence in college, especially if low-income students are eligible for funds. Hansen also ignored the fact that loans can influence college choice by middle-income students, as well as help low-income students pay their basic costs of attending college. A final problem was that his analysis overlooked changes in participation by women. Generally available aid expanded opportunity for women as well as men.

Hansen (1983) compared participation rates for traditional college-age men below the median-income level to those above the median-income level and concluded that need-based aid, which had expanded substantially during that period (between 1972 and 1980), had not influenced access. Participation rates for low-income African American students and low-income women did improve, but participation rates for low-income men declined sufficiently to create a slight net loss in participation rates between 1972 and 1980.[8] Hansen concluded that aid had functioned as an income transfer rather than as a mechanism for supporting access. Despite a number of logical and methodological problems with this approach,[9] it remains a method many economists use to assess the efficacy of generally available federal aid programs (e.g., Kane 1995).

Hansen's research was taken seriously by the Reagan administration (St. John 1994). It is ironic that Hansen concluded there was expansion in aid that had no effect. Clearly, he focused on only one form of aid: need-based, generally available Pell grants. Had he considered other forms of aid, he might have reached a different conclusion about the impact of federal student aid. In addition, with a more comprehensive set of measures, it is possible to build a better understanding of the effects of aid during this period.

THE STATE ROLE IN FINANCING HIGHER EDUCATION

Given the substantial changes in the federal role in financing higher education, states made only modest adaptations of their financial strategies in the 1970s. Master planning, the process of setting a general direction for a state system and providing funding to move toward the goals, was central to the literature (e.g., Halstead 1974). State strategies for funding institutions changed very little in the 1970s, but state grant programs adapted to the federal government's SSIG program.

The 1973 report of the National Commission on the Financing of Postsecondary Education (NCFPE) (see also Carlson, Farmer, and Weathersby 1974) received attention in some states, along with related planning models (e.g., Balderston 1974; Weathersby and Balderston 1972). However, there was a stable approach in state finance (Glenny et

[8] For example, other market forces in the 1970s, including the perception of over-education (Freeman 1976), could have caused some prospective students (who might otherwise have had access) to seek employment.

[9] There have been many critical examinations of Hansen's study (e.g., Leslie and Brinkman 1988; McPherson and Schapiro 1991).

UNDERSTANDING THE ACCESS CHALLENGE

al. 1974) in spite of changing conditions within and across states (Glenny 1974–75). Many groups argued for more substantial changes in state policy (e.g., NCFPE 1973; Carnegie Commission 1973; Committee on Economic Development 1973), but changes in state finance strategy were modest. Between 1975–76 and 1980–81, the average state appropriation per student in the public system and state tuition and fee charges remained nearly constant, changing by less than one percentage point over the period (table A.3). State appropriations covered about 21 percent of educational and related expenses in the public sector in 1975–76 and 1980–81 (table A.3).

In the early 1970s, state grants grew substantially after the introduction of SSIG, increasing from $0.96 billion in 1970–71 to $1.5 billion in 1980–81 (table A.4). State grants increased only modestly in the last half of the decade. As a general pattern, most states implemented grants in response to change in federal student aid strategies but did not substantially alter their financing strategies.

These adaptations added to the total amount of grant aid available to students in the 1970s. However, while state grants increased modestly in the late 1970s, by 4.7 percent (table A.4), federal and institutional grants declined in the last half of the decade, by 34.7 percent at the federal level and 11 percent at the institutional level. Thus, while states made incremental increases in grants during the last half of the decade, the total amount of grants available to students actually declined slightly.

ASSESSING THE EFFECTS OF CHANGES IN FINANCE POLICY

While the period 1965–80 was a time of growth in federal student aid focused on equal opportunity, there were major changes in the philosophy, structure, and funding of student aid programs throughout the period. The original specially directed programs—veterans' benefits under the GI Bill and Social Security Survivors Benefits—eventually gave way to generally available, need-based programs. There were also changes in the philosophy of generally available aid programs. The original Title IV programs focused on equalizing opportunity (e.g., EOG). However, the focus was expanded to include providing opportunities for middle-income students to attend private colleges. The full provisions for massive middle-income grant programs were never funded. This expansion lacked a sufficient rationale. The political ethos of valuing equal opportunity had a foundation in economic theory. But coupling the interests of the middle class and the economically disadvantaged into a single set of aid programs did not work well. By 1980, total federal grant dollars had already started to decline, even though a larger percentage of students were eligible. What impact did the decline in grants have on access and equal opportunity? What impact did the expansion and contraction of aid have on taxpayer costs?

Step 2: Changes in Key Indicators

Most sound economic research demonstrates that student aid has an impact on enrollment decisions (Heller 1997; Leslie and Brinkman 1988; McPherson and Schapiro 1998; Manski and Wise 1983), but when some economists compared trends in need-based aid (i.e., Pell) and enrollment, they concluded that aid did not influence enrollment (Hansen 1983; Kane 1995). Trend and cross-sectional studies on the impact of net price on enrollment consistently found that student grants influence the probability that students will enroll or persist in college (Heller 1997; Kane 1999; Manski and Wise 1983). However, given the lingering doubts about the efficacy of Pell grants, it is important to reexamine this issue. Here I examine three indicators of the impact of federal student aid.

ACCESS

It is important to situate the federal programs in their historical context. The movement to mass higher education in the 1950s and 1960s expanded access to children of the growing middle class. State efforts to build low-tuition systems of public higher education created accessible college opportunity for children of this expanding middle class. The student aid policies of the 1960s and 1970s essentially set a new standard: they were intended to expand access to a college education to academically qualified children of poor families. These policies were consonant with a growing awareness of the need to equalize opportunity for higher education in the post-*Brown* period. Providing the opportunity for low-income students was clearly the intent of the early Title IV grant programs. When analysts assumed that enrollment should correspond with Title IV funding, they ignored the fact that each increase in aid would increase funding for students who would have enrolled under earlier conditions. Thus there have long been logical reasons to question the net-price assumption that expansion in need-based grant aid would directly correspond with increases in enrollment.

First, although there may not have been a direct correspondence in increases, enrollment rose across all sectors. Enrollment in public four-year colleges increased from 3.053 million FTE students in 1970 to 3.524 million FTE students in 1980 (table A.6). Enrollment in private four-year colleges increased from 1.407 million FTE in 1970 to 1.585 million FTE in 1980. Enrollment in public two-year colleges increased from 1.413 million FTE to 2.484 million FTE, and in private two-year colleges increased

TABLE 5.1 Total FTE Enrollments Compared with NCES Projections, Fall 1970 and Fall 1979

Type of Institution	FTE Enrollment (Thousands)		
	Public	Private	Total
1970 Actual	4,953	1,785	6,738
1970 Projection for 1979	7,491	2,026	9,517
Predicted percentage difference	51.24%	13.50%	41.24%
1979 Actual	6,393	2,095	8,487
Difference (actual minus projected)	−1,048	69	−1,030
Percentage difference between predicted and actual	−14.66%	3.41%	−10.82%

Sources: Actual enrollment for 1970 and 1979 from NCES 1980; projected enrollments from: NCES 1970, table 12.

Note: Breakdowns for two-year and four-year institutions were not available. These numbers include both undergraduate and graduate students.

from 105,000 FTE to 173,000 FTE. However, most of this increase was attributable to growth in the size of the traditional college-age cohort rather than to change in the participation rate for this cohort. The social transition to mass higher education—the increase in participation by traditional-age students—had occurred by 1970. The 1970s saw the end of the baby boom college cohort, so enrollment continued to expand even though participation rates changed very little.

Second, enrollment did not increase as much as had been predicted by NCES before Pell was created. In 1970, two years before the Pell program started, NCES predicted an FTE enrollment of 9.5 million in 1979 (table 5.1). However, actual FTE enrollment in 1979 was only about 8.5 million, 10.82 percent lower than predicted. The biggest difference was in the public sector, with enrollment 14.66 percent below the prediction. Private college FTE enrollment was 3.41 percent higher than predicted.

Third, access, as measured by the percentage of the traditional-age population attending college, did not change in the 1970s. The enrollment rate for traditional college-age high school graduates changed very little: 33.7 percent in 1967, 32.6 percent in 1970, 31.9 percent in 1972, 32.5 percent in 1975, and 31.8 percent in 1980 (table A.8). High school graduation rates declined from 75.9 percent in 1970–71 to 71.7 percent in 1980–81 (table A.7). These trends suggest there were sound reasons for the concerns about academic preparation in the early 1980s. Thus, the enrollment growth in the 1970s was attributable to the change in the size of the college-age cohort (i.e., the baby boom generation) rather than to changes in overall access. There were no visible gains in academic preparation. Indeed, the decline in high school graduation rates suggests the reverse.

To understand these trends we need to consider what happened to federal student aid. In spite of an increase in Pell funding (table A.2, part A) in the late 1970s (from $2.7 billion in 1975–76 to $4.46 billion in 1980–81), total federal grants actually declined by 35 percent during the late 1970s (from $19.3 billion in 1975–76 to $12.6 billion in 1980–81). This decline in total grants was due to a reduction of veterans' benefits. However, since enrollment was influenced by veterans, especially veterans returning from the Vietnam War, it is shortsighted to ignore the effect of these other grant programs on enrollment. The postsecondary participation rate in 1975 (32.5 percent) was higher than that in 1980 (31.8 percent), when total federal grant aid was lower.

Thus, postsecondary access eroded after the decline in total federal grants in the late 1970s. The mystery of the impact of the Pell program is really an artifact of mistakenly focusing exclusively on Title IV aid (or generally available aid). When total grant aid is examined in relation to enrollment, it is simply not reasonable to have expected a more substantial impact from Pell. However, the other part of the problem in interpreting the effects of Pell pertains to the comparative impact on diverse groups.

EQUAL OPPORTUNITY

The quest for equal opportunity is appropriately situated in the context of efforts to end racial discrimination in K–12 and higher education (St. John and Hossler 1998; Williams 1997). Historically, equal educational opportunity was denied to a generation of African American students as an artifact of segregation. In higher education, however, litigation over segregation was delayed and limited to the South. By the time of the *Adams* decisions, which set in motion a process of desegregation of public higher education in the South (in the late 1970s), a framework of federal student aid was firmly established. In this historical perspective, the potential equalizing effect of student aid was vitally important. President Johnson did not appeal to the issue of racial justice when he argued for the Great Society programs in K–12 education (ESEA) and higher education (HEA). However, the historical context of racial injustice is the reason for considering racial equity, an issue that transcends economic arguments about access. Therefore it is crucial that we consider trends in postsecondary opportunity across racial/ethnic groups in American society.

When we examine trends in participation rates for high school graduates by racial/ethnic group (table A.8) in relation to trends in federal student aid, a complex story unfolds. To understand the relationship between student aid and equal opportunity, we need to examine each half of the decade. Between 1972 and 1975, participation rates for all traditional college-age high school graduates increased slightly, from 31.9 to 32.5 percent. The opportunity gap between traditional-age Whites and African Americans narrowed slightly, from a differential of 5.4 percentage points to a differential of 0.8 percentage points. For Hispanics, the disparity in opportunity disappeared. Traditional college-age Hispanics actually had a higher participation rate (35.5 percent) than Whites (32.3 percent) in 1975. Pell grants were almost fully implemented in 1975, and veterans' benefits were near their peak. Thus, the growth in federal grant dollars could explain the apparent equalization process.

In the late 1970s there was a slight regression in this pattern. In 1980, 32.1 percent of traditional college-age White high school graduates were enrolled in higher education, compared with 27.6 percent for African Americans and 29.9 percent for Hispanics. Improvement—an equalization in rates—occurred over the decade, but not in the last half of the decade. The decline in veterans' benefits and the shift of total grant dollars from low-income to middle-income students (St. John and Byce 1982) could explain the reduction in equity across racial/ethnic groups.

This evidence indicates a direct linkage between participation rates for diverse groups and federal spending on grants. Minorities appear to be responsive to changes in the total amount of grants, including Pell grants. It is a mistake to assume that federal student aid was not effectual. Focusing exclusively on generally available aid (i.e., Pell) led to misunderstandings about the impact of changes in student aid policy in the 1970s, misunderstandings that have continued among the community of scholars who study higher education finance.

TAXPAYER COSTS

Federal spending on grants per FTE student changed across the decade (table A.9); it was substantially higher in 1975 ($2,276) than in 1970 ($1,127) or in 1980 ($1,428), and only slightly higher in 1980 than in 1970. This pattern parallels my earlier observations about racial/ethnic equality of participation rates (e.g., table A.8). The taxpayer costs associated with loans are more difficult to estimate. Subsidized loans are generally thought to cost about fifty cents per dollar loaned (McPherson and Schapiro 1998). However, changes in default rates and increased uses of unsubsidized loans decreased these costs. Thus, while loans increased substantially in the second half of the decade, the cost of these increases to taxpayers is unclear. Total federal loans were $319 per FTE in 1970–71, dropped to $225 per FTE in 1975–76, then rose to $662 per FTE in 1980–81 (table A.9).

Thus, total taxpayer costs per FTE increased in the decade but declined after 1975. The total federal taxpayer expense per FTE was $1,446 in 1970–71, $2,501 in 1975–76, and $2,090 in 1980–81 (table A.9). Tax spending on grants declined substantially in the last half of the decade, a period during which minority participation began to decline. As noted above, federal grant awards per FTE fell from $2,276 in 1975–76 to $1,428 in 1980–81. There was a relationship between total aid and total enrollment as well as between grants and minority participation rates.

Other components of taxpayer costs increased modestly during the decade. State and local subsidies to institutions were lower in 1970 ($4,315 per FTE nationally) than in 1975 ($4,522) or in 1980 ($4,393) (table A.9). State grants rose slightly, from $143 to $170 per FTE during the decade, but changed very little in the late 1970s. Total state and local spending per FTE was also lower in 1980 than in 1975.

The total state and federal tax expenditure per student was $5,904 in 1970–71, $7,192 in 1975, and $6,653 in 1980. Thus, the mystery of Pell should be debunked once and for all. Less was spent per student in 1980 than in 1975. The increased emphasis on need-based grants probably improved taxpayer efficiency, a fact completely overlooked in previous analyses. Too much attention was cast on analyses that considered the implementation of Pell in relation to enrollment trends without considering the total federal investment in student grants.[10]

RELATING KEY INDICATORS TO CHANGES IN POLICY

A look across all three indicators illuminates the relationship between public spending and student outcomes. There was a relationship between total spending and maintaining total enrollment. The disparity in participation rates between African American and Hispanic students and White students was closely linked to total federal spending on grant aid. The reasons for this disparity are related to the level of unmet need for diverse groups rather than to ethnicity per se (Advisory Committee 2001a, 2002).

By the early 1980s it was apparent that equal opportunity was related to the levels of student grant aid available to students with financial need. However, the relationship between total grant and loan aid and overall

[10] To some readers this may seem a redundant point—or perhaps even a point that should not be made—but since this study focuses on the role of policy analysis as much as (or more than) on the results of econometric studies, it is important to point out how analysis of one aspect of a policy problem can misinform policy. In this study, I am concerned as much about the limited theoretical frames used by economists as about the limited theoretical frames used by new conservative educational analysts.

enrollment could obscure the effects of the decline in grants, given the growth in loans in the late 1970s. Further, because total aid awarded from Title IV programs had increased during the decade, the decline in total grants in the last half of the decade went largely unnoticed. By the early 1980s, the attention of policymakers shifted away from student aid altogether.

These developments raise questions about the federal commitment to equal opportunity. Federal efforts to desegregate colleges began in earnest only in the late 1970s (Williams 1997), and it is a cruel irony that the total federal commitment to student grants peaked at about the same time. If we simply follow the funds available for students—grants and loans—and examine these patterns in relation to total participation rates and participation by race/ethnicity, the effects of the policy changes seem readily apparent. However, this simultaneous occurrence of trends—the rise and fall of grants and the rise and fall of equal opportunity—does not confirm a causal relationship.

Step 3: Evaluation Studies

To make a judgment about whether changes in student aid were causally linked to changes in financial access, as measured by first-time enrollment or persistence, we need to use well-designed statistical studies that control for the influence of critical variables related to student background (e.g., income, race/ethnicity) and achievement (in high school and/or college). Analyses of national databases on college students provide insight into the effects of student aid at particular points in time. While trend review (i.e., the indicators discussed above) reveals a relationship between student aid and equal opportunity, only studies with appropriate controls can establish a causal linkage between student aid and equal opportunity. The longitudinal studies—the National Longitudinal Study of the High School Class of 1972 and High School and Beyond survey—followed cohorts of students from high school through college. NLS:72 followed students in the high school class of 1972, and HSB followed the classes of 1980 (HSB:80) and 1982 (HSB:82). Evaluation studies using these data provide a basis for examining the effects of student aid during this early period. Using these databases, I tested some more refined approaches to assessing the effects of (1) aid packages and (2) amounts of student charges and price subsidies. These studies used sound logical models with appropriate statistical controls. A summary review of the results adds to our understanding of how student aid influenced student outcomes during this earlier period.

STUDENT PRICE RESPONSE

Many financial analysts focused on response to net prices, commonly communicated as a change in probability of enrollment per hundred dollars differential in aid or tuition[11] (e.g., Jackson and Weathersby 1975; Leslie and Brinkman 1998). In contrast, Stephen Dresch (1975) argued that students could respond differently to different types of prices and subsidies and that these responses could change over time, as a result of changes in aid policy and the labor market. To test Dresch's idea, I conducted a series of studies on the effects of amount of tuition charged and different types of aid awarded.

In the initial study using the new price-response approach, I used HSB:80 to assess the effects of prices and price subsidies on first-time enrollment by students in the high school class of 1980 who applied for college (St. John 1990a). I examined first-time enrollment by all students and by students in different income groups (table 5.2). The key findings from the study were as follows:

—Students were responsive to the amount of tuition charged, as well as to the amounts of grants, loans, and work-study awarded (all-college-applicants model). Further, students were slightly more responsive to grants and work-study than to loans, but were more responsive to all types of aid than to tuition charges.
—Low-income students were substantially more responsive to grants than to tuition, but were not responsive to other forms of student aid.
—Lower-middle-income and upper-middle-income students were more responsive to loans than to grants or tuition.
—Upper-income students were not responsive to student aid and were only modestly responsive to tuition charges.

This study supported Dresch's hypotheses (1975): comparing first-time enrollment and persistence, there were differences in the ways students responded to prices and subsidies and differences in price response. Subsequent analyses (St. John and Noell 1989; St. John, Kirshstein, and Noell 1991) also informed the alternative perspective on aid (St. John and Starkey 1995a): they confirmed the assumption that loans influence enrollment decisions (e.g., Becker 1964; Dresch 1975), along with other forms of aid.

These studies substantiate the conclusions reached above about the

---

[11] The analyses of the effects of tuition charges and aid presented in table 5.2 provide a delta-p per $1,000. To convert to a standardized price response coefficient (SPRC), one could divide these figures by 10. However, the notion of a standardized measure is problematic, so this conversion is not recommended.

TABLE 5.2 Effects of Prices and Price Subsidies on First-Time Enrollment, 1982

| | Changes in Probability, Delta-p (Dollars per $1,000) | | | |
1982 Cohort	Tuition	Grant	Loan	Work-Study
All	-0.028	0.043	0.038	0.046
Low-income	-0.034	0.088	NS	NS
Lower-middle-income	-0.039	0.035	0.053	NS
Upper-middle-income	-0.033	0.031	0.063	NA
Upper-income	-0.014	NS	NS	NA

Source: St. John 1990a.

Note: The delta-p statistics are based on 1982–83 dollars. Delta-p statistics are given when the beta coefficients are significant at the .01 or .05 level.

impact of changes in grant aid on equal opportunity. The results indicate that reduction in grant aid would probably have a more substantial influence on participation by low-income students than on that by middle-income students. The trends in participation rates in the late 1970s for minorities compared with Whites were consonant with this finding. Results also indicate that loans would help keep colleges affordable for the majority, a pattern that was also apparent in the review trends described above.

THE EFFECTS OF AID PACKAGES

By the middle 1980s, a few educational researchers had examined the effects of the receipt of aid (any type) on first-time enrollment (Jackson 1978) and persistence (Terkla 1985). However, the debates about the efficacy of loans raised questions about the impact of different types of aid. After a review of the research used in the earlier studies, I refined the receipt-of-aid approach. It involved coding the types of aid packages students received into four types: (1) grants only, (2) loans only, (3) loans and grants, and (4) other packages. When the types of packages received were included in a logistic regression model, along with other variables that influence persistence, the models estimated the change in probability of persisting that was attributable to receiving an aid package of a particular type. Essentially, these analyses compared the average recipient of each type of aid package with the otherwise-average student who did not receive aid. Two of the studies are reviewed below.

First, in a study of the effects of student aid on persistence, Jay Noell and I examined the impact of aid packages on first-time enrollment by all students in the high school classes of 1972, 1980, and 1982 (using

NLS:72, HSB:80, and HSB:82). In addition, we conducted separate analyses of persistence for Whites, African Americans, and Hispanics (St. John and Noell 1989). The results (table 5.3) led to the following conclusions:

—All types of aid packages increased the probability of persistence in the 1970s and 1980s for all students. This indicated that student aid remained effective in promoting first-time enrollment, at least at the aggregate level.
—Hispanics in the high school class of 1980 responded positively to packages with grants, including packages with loans and grants, but did not respond positively to loans as the only form of aid or to other packages (usually loans and work-study).
—African Americans in the high school classes of 1980 and 1982 responded positively to packages with loans only, but were more responsive to packages with grants only than to packages with loans.
—Whites in the high school classes of 1980 and 1982 responded positively to packages with grants and loans, but were more responsive to loans only than to grants only.

In retrospect, this study also provided an explanation for the initial decline in participation rates for minorities in the last half of the 1970s. Larger percentages of students received packages with loans as well as grants in the early 1980s than in the early 1970s. Further, in the fall of 1972, receiving other packages (mostly grants and loans) was positively associated with enrollment for Whites, African Americans, and Hispanics. In the fall of 1980, however, these other packages were no longer significant for African Americans and Hispanics, but were for Whites. In 1982, other packages (grants and loans) were significant and positively associated with enrollment by Whites and African Americans, but not by Hispanics.

Second, analyses of the impact of aid packages on year-to-year persistence, following the three high school classes through the college years (St. John 1989), provided a comprehensive assessment of the effects of different types of aid on persistence in the 1970s and 1980s. The key findings (table 5.4) were as follows:

—In the 1970s, packages with grants were positively associated with year-to-year persistence by students enrolled in four-year colleges.
—In the 1970s, packages with loans were negatively associated with persistence between the first and second years of college, but were not significantly associated with persistence by upper-division students.
—In the early and middle 1980s, packages with both grants and loans

TABLE 5.3 Effects of Aid Packages on First-Time Enrollment, 1972, 1980, and 1982, with Special Consideration of Minority Enrollment in 1980 and 1982

	Changes in Probability, Delta-p			
	Grant Only	Loan Only	Work-Study Only	Other Package
Freshmen Cohorts				
Freshmen in 1972	0.062	0.108	0.149	0.147
Freshmen in 1980	0.101	0.095	0.110	0.082
Freshmen in 1982	0.062	0.078	0.097	0.095
Ethnic Groups for the 1980 Cohort				
Whites	0.089	0.088	NA	0.071
African Americans	0.177	0.145	NS	NS
Hispanics	0.141	NS	NA	NS
Ethnic Groups for the 1982 Cohort				
Whites	0.042	0.072	NS	0.081
African Americans	0.150	0.112	NA	0.186
Hispanics	0.038	0.131	NS	NS

Source: St. John and Noell 1989.

Note: Delta-p statistics compare students receiving packages with students not receiving aid. Delta-p statistics are given when the beta coefficients are significant at the .01 or .05 level. Not significant (NS) indicates equal probability of enrollment. NA indicates not a sufficient number of cases for analysis.

were positively associated with persistence across the first three years of college.

—In the 1980s, loans were negatively associated with persistence (continued enrollment or graduation) by seniors.

These detailed analyses of persistence did not fully support the earlier conclusion that loans as well as grants promoted equal opportunity (e.g., St. John and Noell 1987). There was still a need to be cautious about loans. Packages with loans were not consistently positive in either the 1970s or the 1980s.

A REFLECTION

Looking back at these findings from the perspective of the early twenty-first century, we can see that student aid was indeed effective in the 1970s, but federal aid began to erode in the last few years of the

TABLE 5.4 Impact of Aid Packages on Year-to-Year Persistence by Students in the 1972, 1980, and 1982 Cohorts

	Changes in Probability, Delta-p				
	Grant Only	Loan Only	Grant/ Loan	Grant/ Work-Study	All
Freshman to Sophomore					
1972 cohort	NS	−0.072	0.025	0.099	NS
1980 cohort	NS	0.048	0.056	NS	0.065
1982 cohort	0.039	NS	0.073	NS	0.115
Sophomore to Junior					
1972 cohort	0.039	NS	0.089	0.099	0.105
1980 cohort	0.047	NS	0.105	NS	0.100
1982 cohort	0.056	NS	NS	NS	NS
Junior to Senior					
1972 cohort	0.049	NS	0.053	−0.038	0.118
1980 cohort	NS	0.054	NS	0.062	NS
1982 cohort	0.049	0.053	0.080	NS	0.095
Senior to Graduate (or Fifth Year)					
1972 cohort	NS	NS	NS	NS	NS
1980 cohort	NS	−0.069	NS	NS	NS

Source: St. John 1989.

Note: Delta-p statistics compare students receiving packages with students not receiving aid. Delta-p statistics are given when the beta coefficients are significant at the .01 or .05 level. Not significant (NS) indicates equal probability of persisting.

decade. The 1970s were a period when adequate aid was available and the types of aid packages offered generally had a positive association with student outcomes. However, in retrospect, it appears that the efficacy of federal student aid in promoting access also eroded somewhat in the early 1980s compared with the early 1970s. More students were offered packages with loans in the 1980s than in the 1970s, and these packages were not positively associated with first-time enrollment by minorities (St. John and Noell 1989). Further, packages with loans were not as consistently positive in their effect on persistence as packages with grants. This could have been a warning sign about overemphasizing loans, especially if grants were inadequate. The linkage to the adequacy of grants is clearer only when we also consider that low-income students were responsive to the amount of grants offered but not to the amount of loans (St. John 1990a). It also is possible that debt burden had become a problem for students who were overreliant on loans in the early 1980s.

THE IMPACT OF STUDENT AID

The evaluation studies reviewed above provide confirmatory evidence for an initial interpretation of the relationship between changes in policy and changes in related student outcomes (from step 2). Specifically these studies confirm that student aid was sufficient to be positively associated with enrollment and persistence in the 1970s and early 1980s. However, the studies also suggest that there would be a downturn in enrollment by low-income and minority students if grants were reduced, a condition that eventuated in the late 1970s and persisted into the early 1980s.

Step 4: Possible Explanations

Equal educational opportunity improved in the 1970s, a decade of expansion in student aid programs and other federal reforms. However, the overall participation rate by traditional-age high school graduates changed very little, which means that the growth in enrollment was an artifact of the growing number of college-age youths rather than a result of student aid policy per se. However, there was equity in opportunity in the middle 1970s. Federal student aid was not the only type of educational reform that could have had a positive influence on the gains in equal opportunity evident in this decade.

STUDENT FINANCIAL AID

As the analyses above indicate, student financial aid played a central role in equalizing opportunity in the middle 1970s. The Pell grant program, implemented alongside the older campus-based and specially directed programs, created a new confluence of aid programs that equalized opportunity. However, since the total amount of grant aid did not grow, aid did not influence a further expansion in opportunity (i.e., there was a relatively modest change in overall participation rates). The evaluation studies provide confirmation of the equalizing effect of aid, and they demonstrate that the probability of persistence for students who received aid was equal to or greater than that for students who did not receive aid. However, total grant aid was cut and equal opportunity eroded after 1978. Thus, when aid is adequate and targeted to low-income students, it can help equalize educational opportunity. But are there other possible explanations for the changes in participation rates?

STATE FINANCE POLICY

To assess the effects of federal student aid, we need to control, logically and empirically, for the influence of state subsidies to institutions on tuition and student aid. In the 1970s, state finance policies were relatively static. States funded the same percentage of expenditures through the decade; tuition charges also remained stable. State grants grew in response to federal policy in the late 1970s. Thus, other than changes in state grant programs, state finance policies changed very little during the decade and had little impact on the indicators noted above.

SCHOOL REFORM

The Great Society educational reforms could also have affected the relative equality in educational opportunity. The Elementary and Secondary Education Act, also passed in 1965, created a major new federal program under Title I that provided supplemental education to students with economic disadvantages that could inhibit educational opportunity. During the early years of ESEA Title I, funds went mostly to elementary schools with relatively large percentages of students receiving free or reduced lunches. The program required parental involvement in school decisions about the use of these funds. Most schools implemented interventions that used teachers' aides, many of whom were parents. There were many early experiments in reading and math. Students who had the opportunity to participate in these programs in the late 1960s and early 1970s may have been among those who enrolled in college in the late 1970s. Perhaps college students benefited from the early years of the Title I program, a period when supplemental aid was provided to schools with high percentages of low-income students (Wong 2003).

During the early period of the ESEA Title I program, schools had more freedom to develop their own unique approaches than they did in the late 1970s, when the program was more tightly regulated. For example, there is evidence that schools and university researchers worked collaboratively on experiments aimed at discovering better ways to teach early reading (e.g., Ellison et al. 1965; Ellison, Harris, and Barber 1968). That early period of innovation may have had positive effects on students who participated in these programs, thus helping to equalize postsecondary opportunities in the middle 1970s.

While the educational reforms may have helped equalize opportunity, high school graduation rates did not increase in the 1970s (table A.7); in fact, the graduation rate declined. This indicates that an erosion in total opportunity in K–12 schools was occurring at the same time as federal K–12 reforms (e.g., ESEA Title I), and student aid helped to equalize the college participation rates.

POSTSECONDARY ENCOURAGEMENT

There is also reason to expect that early efforts to encourage postsecondary education for first-generation college students had an influence on equalizing opportunity for high school graduates in the 1970s. Title IV of HEA included the TRIO programs—Upward Bound, Talent Search, and Special Services—which provided postsecondary encouragement to students who were historically disadvantaged. Most universities with campus-based aid offered summer programs for disadvantaged high school students (e.g., Torbert 1976) and provided other outreach services and support services once students were enrolled. Further, institutions had the opportunity to develop these services in comprehensive ways, given that most federal aid funded under Title IV of HEA was campus-based before 1972. And while the Education Amendments of 1972 included funding of the portable Pell program, this new program was administered in the same offices as the campus-based programs. Thus, during the early period of student aid, the focus of administrators was on extending opportunity as well as on providing aid. Indeed, the student aid profession often had a missionary quality to it during this period, with close linkages to counseling and student affairs.

The intent of the student aid administration changed after 1978. After MISAA, the federal government emphasized quality control in financial aid offices (St. John and Sepanic 1982). By the early 1980s, the early justice orientation of student aid had given way to a more managerial approach, in response to the expanding focus of aid programs and the increased regulation of the administration of student aid.

A CONVERGENCE OF REFORMS

A convergence of policies in the late 1970s—adequate and targeted student aid, an emphasis on postsecondary encouragement for the historically disadvantaged, and a residual effect of early school reforms—combined to have a substantial influence on equalizing educational opportunity. With this historical perspective, it is relatively easy to see that all three sets of policies contributed to the gains in educational outcomes.

From this evidence alone, it is difficult to assign greater value to any one of these areas of reform. However, the analyses make clear that when financial aid was adequate and targeted to meeting financial need for students from poor families, this aid helped to equalize postsecondary opportunity. In fact, in the 1970s, an adequate threshold of aid ensured that finances did not inhibit opportunity. But unfortunately, this period of adequate aid did not last. Indeed, the efficacy of aid actually eroded during the last few years of the 1970s.

Conclusion

This review provides strong evidence that student financial aid played a substantial and direct role in equalizing educational opportunity in the middle 1970s. To summarize the review, I revisit the four guiding questions.

How did federal financial aid and state finance policies change during the period?

Federal student aid programs were founded on the rationale that need-based grants would help equalize educational opportunity. The early rationale was based primarily on the arguments about justice (i.e., the Great Society) but was influenced by research by economists as well. These programs were developed during a period in which K–12 schools were being desegregated and there were other moral reasons for focusing policy on equal opportunity. However, desegregation of higher education did not begin in earnest until after 1977. Soon thereafter the focus on need-based programs shifted from equalizing opportunity for the poor to promoting choice for middle-income students. And while generally available grants through HEA Title IV did grow consistently through 1980, the federal investment in specially directed grants declined substantially in the late 1970s. Total grant aid also declined during the late 1970s, and loans grew substantially.

State finance policies changed very little during the decade. Consequently, federal policies had a more substantial influence on student outcomes.

How did the key indicators—access, equal opportunity, and efficient use of tax dollars—change during the period?

The analysis of trends in key indicators for the 1970s suggests that loans influenced total enrollment but that grants were linked to equal opportunity. While participation rates remained high after the peak in total federal investment in grant aid, the equality in enrollment rates began to erode. These trends provide reason to ponder whether grant aid is more crucial to maintaining financial access for low-income students, while the combination of grants and loans could maintain general access. It appears from the trends that low-income (and racial/ethnic minority) and middle-income (and White) students were influenced in different ways by different types of aid. Further, taxpayer costs per student generally rose during the decade. While there was a shift from grants to loans during the 1970s, only a modest gain in efficiency (tax dollars spent per FTE student) was realized.

Did evaluation studies of students enrolled during the period help explain the apparent relationship between changes in policy and changes in access, equal opportunity, and the efficient use of tax dollars?

The evaluation studies provided confirmatory evidence of a link between changes in financial aid and changes in access and equal opportunity. Low-income students and African Americans were more responsive to grants than to loans, which may help explain why participation rates by minority students declined when federal spending on grants dropped in the last few years of the decade. Further, middle-income students' responsiveness to loans may help explain why the modest shift in emphasis from grants to loans in the late 1970s did not negatively affect access.

Did changes in K–12 schools or in postsecondary encouragement influence observed changes in access and equity?

The Great Society educational programs invested in educational opportunity by providing additional funding for schools with high percentages of minority students (Title I of ESEA) and providing postsecondary encouragement (the TRIO programs). These programs apparently strengthened the foundations for realizing equality in participation rates for minorities and Whites by 1976. This is a remarkable development, given that the federal government did not actively promote desegregation of state systems of higher education until after 1977. However, the sound base provided by these federal interventions was not adequate to maintain participation after 1976, when total federal grants began to erode.

6

The 1980s: Middle-Class Assistance

Finding an efficient way to fund college choice by middle-class students loomed as a major challenge at the start of the 1980s. The Middle Income Student Assistance Act and the 1980 reauthorization of the Higher Education Act had liberalized federal grant programs so that, had this legislation been fully funded, they would have subsidized college choice for the middle class. However, since the provisions of MISAA had not been fully funded by the time President Carter left office, there was little chance that the new conservative administration of President Reagan would support the full funding necessary to expand Pell to the authorized level (St. John and Byce 1982). The Reagan administration did not even try to find funds for the full funding of federal grant programs, but it did find a way to promote college choice by middle-class students. Thus, finding a more economical way to provide *middle-class assistance* represents a theme for the decade.

The Reagan administration came into office facing another challenge in education. Reagan had campaigned against the Department of Education, created in the Carter years, and against excessive federal spending on education and other social programs. However, his constituents were interested in educational improvement. The Education Consolidation and Improvement Act of 1980, planned by the Carter administration and passed before Reagan took office, set in motion a process of consolidating and simplifying federal K–12 programs. Terrell Bell, secretary of education in Reagan's first term, responded to the new context by promoting the idea that the federal government could provide leadership by fostering educational improvement. In K–12 education, Secretary Bell started the educational improvement movement, which promoted reforms aimed at improving test scores for all students. He created the National Commission on Excellence in Education, which published *A Nation at Risk* in 1983. This sparked a new wave of federal educational reform. In higher education, Bell promoted the idea of "self-help," which argued that loans and work-study should be the first tier of student aid (Hearn 1993). If students were required to work or borrow before getting a grant, then the costs of funding college choice for middle-class families would be substantially lower than if a grant-first approach were taken. While this argument did not gain support in the higher education community, it did have an influence on the evolution of educational policy, especially the emphasis placed on loans.

In the second Reagan term, Secretary William Bennett (1986) began an attack on higher education institutions for being inefficient and for raising prices to increase the amount of federal aid their students received. Bennett's leadership team argued that colleges were greedy and raised tuition unnecessarily (Finn 1988a,b). These arguments influenced the popular press and public attitudes about higher education finance. They also provided a form of "spin control," obfuscating the erosion in federal grants and the new emphasis on loans. Meanwhile, the lobbying community tried to find ways to defend grant programs (Parsons 1997). These new conservative arguments affected the entire financing system.

Thus, the decade of the 1980s was a period of *refinancing*. Debt became the mechanism used by middle-class students to expand their postsecondary options, while the shift in emphasis from grants to loans reduced taxpayer costs. This refinancing process also changed the foundations of the federal system of student aid that had been established in the late 1960s and 1970s. The new policies changed the balance in the emphasis placed on the interests of taxpayers, middle-class students, and students from poor families.

Step 1: Changes in Policy

To call the changes in funding in the 1980s *refinancing* focuses attention on the changes in underlying assumptions about student aid, as well as on the emphasis placed on loans. In this section I examine first how student aid policy changed in the 1980s, then two issues that provided the foundations for the new direction in policy: the college cost controversy and the role of loans in promoting educational opportunity.

POLICY DRIFT, IDEOLOGICAL SHIFT

The 1980s were also a period of *policy drift*, as major budget battles each year determined the course of aid policy (Hearn 1993). The intent of the enabling legislation ceased being a central concern. Each year the Reagan administration would propose major reductions in funding for Pell and elimination of other federal grant programs. It was successful in eliminating Social Security Survivors Benefits, once the largest federal grant program for undergraduates. Further, while Congress rebuffed proposals to eliminate Supplemental Educational Opportunity Grants and State Student Incentive Grants, funding declined for these programs. In contrast, the administration tried to shift the emphasis to loans, based on new rationales about the efficacy of loans.

The changes proposed by the Reagan administration were resisted by the higher education lobbying community and by Congress (Parsons 1997). Indeed, the Democratic majority in Congress renamed the major federal student aid programs during the decade as a means of demonstrating their support. The Basic Educational Opportunity Grants were renamed after Senator Pell, Guaranteed Student Loans after Senator Stafford, and National Defense Student Loans after Senator Perkins. Congressional defense of the Pell program was an important annual budget issue. The combative environment added to the lack of consensus and the sense of policy drift.

The 1980s were also a period of *ideological shift*. The federal student aid program had been created based on social progressive beliefs (St. John 1994). Throughout the 1970s, most Republicans and Democrats in Congress supported growth in student aid as a means of promoting equal educational opportunity and economic development (Slaughter 1991). Richard Nixon, a conservative politician for the 1970s, was the force behind the development of the Pell program. However, the Reagan administration ushered in a fundamentally new ideology. The new conservative Republicans argued that social programs, including student aid, were excessive and wasteful. A new wave of "quality control" studies (e.g., Advanced Technology and Westat 1983) documented high levels of error in the administration of these programs and attempted to redesign their delivery systems (e.g., St. John and Robinson 1985). Thus, while members of Congress successfully resisted major cuts in "their" need-based student grant programs, they did not stem the tide of ideological shift in beliefs about student aid. Rather than being viewed as important to both social equity and economic development, student aid came to be viewed as troubled programs that were "out of control." Colleges and universities were increasingly characterized as wasteful and unproductive (e.g., Finn 1988a,b).

On examining trends in the amount of federal student aid awarded for the 1980s, it might appear that Congress successfully "protected" the Pell program, at least compared with other grant programs. Pell increased by nearly 20 percent in the early 1980s and by more than 10 percent in the late 1980s (table A.2, part A). Other Title IV grants declined, however, reducing the impact of the Pell increases. Generally available loans increased more substantially. Viewed from this vantage point, one might conclude that Congress held its ground. However, as noted earlier (see table 2.1), the purchasing power of Pell fell in the 1980s because the maximum award eroded. To understand more fully the shift in student aid that started in the 1980s, we must also consider specially directed federal aid. The decline in the purchasing power of Pell grants is only part of the story.

Too little was written about the decline in specially directed student aid, given that the most substantial change in federal student aid occurred in these programs. Total grants awarded from these specially directed programs dropped from $7.3 billion in 1980–81 to $1.4 billion in 1990–91 (table A.2, part B). Not only was the Social Security Survivors Benefits program eliminated, but awards through veterans' grants dropped substantially as well. Loans from other federal programs increased substantially in the early 1980s.

Putting aside the debates about the adequacy of student aid, one could argue that this shift in funding from *specially directed* grants to *generally available* grants and loans helped streamline and rationalize student aid. For example, there would have been little need for Social Security Survivors Benefits if Pell had been adequately funded. Indeed, even President Carter had proposed eliminating this program. Thus, while I agree with observations about organizational problems with Title IV programs (Hearn 1993), I conclude that federal programs were streamlined (i.e., elimination of Social Security Survivors Benefits) in ways that enhanced their underlying rationale in the 1980s. Unfortunately, there was also a reduction in funding for federal programs. The reduced funding of grant programs was far more problematic than any of the organizational problems in the administration of student aid.

When we examine trends in the composition of aid, the real decline in funding for federal grants becomes a bit more evident. Federal grant awards dropped from $12.6 billion in 1980–81 to $8.0 billion in 1985 and 1990. In 1980–81, grants comprised about 47 percent of total federal aid awarded, but they were only 31 percent of total aid in 1990–91, when loans comprised 65 percent (table A.2, part C). Given the increases in tuition and other educational costs during this period, the shift clearly illustrates a movement toward high tuition and high loans. This development, then, is one of the more serious affordability problems that emerged from the gradual refinancing that took place in the 1990s.

THE COLLEGE COST CONTROVERSY

The cost of attending college had become a major policy issue by the late 1980s. The cost grew substantially (table A.1), and this escalation was controversial during most of this period, with a wave of criticism in the press each year when tuition charges were announced. At times the causes of the college cost increases were the subject of politically motivated inquiries, and disagreements over the causes of price escalation were the subject of special studies mandated by Congress. I briefly review trends in college costs, summarize research on the causes of the tuition increases, and consider how public and private colleges adapted their academic and financial strategies after 1980.

Trends in College Costs

As a review of trends in college costs reveals, a new pattern of escalation in college pricing emerged in the 1980s (table A.1). In the late 1970s, tuition charges were stable in public colleges and universities, consistent with the pattern during the prior few decades. The idea that grants should be generally available and awarded based on financial need is consistent with the rationales used to argue for student aid programs (Committee on Economic Development 1973). In 1980, tuition charges began a steady climb, increasing substantially more than inflation in each subsequent half decade. Indeed, both the total costs of attendance (tuition and fees plus room and board) and tuition and fee charges increased substantially faster than inflation between the fall of 1980 and fall of 1996.

The average tuition charged by both public and private four-year colleges increased markedly between 1980–81 and 1990–91, from $1,502 to $2,281 in public four-year colleges and from $6,757 to $10,972 in private four-year colleges (table A.1). Yet, even though tuition charges increased in both sectors, the tuition gap between public and private colleges also grew substantially.

Research on College Costs

In the early 1980s, the sudden upturn in tuition charges caught Congress's attention. At a time when the federal government, under President Reagan's leadership, was attempting to cut taxpayer costs for social programs, colleges greatly increased their charges. This was a crucial issue for colleges as well as for Congress. The reports commissioned by the higher education community focused on the effects of increasing faculty salaries, declining federal student aid, rising technology costs, and declining state support (e.g., Davis 1997; Eiser 1988). In contrast, the Department of Education focused on excessive spending, attempts to maximize student financial aid, and greed (Bennett 1986, 1987; Finn 1988a,b; Kirshstein, Sherman, et al. 1990). There were also a number of studies from the academic community that focused on discerning explanations for the sudden increase (Breneman 1994; Hauptman 1990; Leslie and Rhodes 1995; St. John 1991a, 1992a). These studies revealed a number of contributing factors:

UNDERSTANDING THE ACCESS CHALLENGE

—Spending on instruction and student services increased, contributing to expenses. Some argued that private colleges used tuition revenue to improve academically and thus became different institutions (Breneman 1994). These trends were evident through the 1980s (table A.5).

—Spending on institutional student aid increased, which resulted in an increase in the ratio of aid to tuition (Hauptman 1990; St. John 1992a). Some concluded that institutions substituted for the loss in federal student aid by increasing tuition revenue (Eiser 1988). These trends continued in private colleges from 1980 through the middle 1990s (table A.5). A similar pattern was evident in public colleges, especially in the late 1980s.

—State support per FTE student declined over time (Kane 1999; St. John 1991a, 1994). Many argued that the decline in state support had a direct influence on tuition increases (Atwell and Hauptman 1986; Hauptman 1990). A review of financial trends (table A.5) confirms these claims. The percentage of educational expenditures paid for by families increased in the 1980s, while the percentage paid for by taxpayers declined.

—The percentage of expenditures going to administration increased. Many concluded that growth in administration was an explanation for rising tuition (Leslie and Rhodes 1995). Again, the trends in expenditures (table A.5) further confirm that administrative expenses grew faster than expenditures on instruction.

—Technology costs increased at a rate substantially higher than inflation. Many analysts considered these costs to be a contributing factor to rising tuition (Davis 1997). The emphasis on new technologies is still increasing in higher education, but technology costs are not separately reported as part of federal data collections.

Each of these trends continued through the next two decades, indicating that a new pattern of postsecondary finance was set in motion in about 1980. In retrospect, this pattern was evidence of the emergence of the new higher education market, with its increased emphasis on quality and its new array of factors that might influence perceptions of quality held by students, prospective students and their parents, and taxpayers. The costs to students for attaining a higher education increased substantially after 1980, especially the costs of a four-year degree.

LOANS AND EDUCATIONAL OPPORTUNITY

During the 1980s, as grants lost some political support, a number of questions surfaced about loans. The Reagan administration pushed loans, but it was encountering disbelief about the efficacy of loans (e.g., Newman 1985). Loans had long been viewed as a necessary evil within the student aid community. Clearly, most financial aid administrators and many policy analysts believed in the efficacy of grants; they thought grants were a more just form of aid than loans. However, the potential value of loans was overshadowed by doubts among policymakers and researchers about the role of debt. Thus, the Reagan administration confronted considerable opposition when it began to promote loans.

If we simply review the trends in the amount of loans awarded (table A.2) and in enrollments in the 1990s, we find that enrollment did not plummet (see the analysis of enrollment predictions later in this chapter) as had been predicted (Carnegie Commission 1973). Did loans increase opportunity for the majority of students? Traditional rationales for funding public systems and students (i.e., net price) did not consider the effects of loans. But the problem was even deeper than this logical oversight might suggest. Even when researchers found a positive association between loans and enrollment, they viewed the findings with disbelief (e.g., Astin 1975). Below, I examine the evolving logic used to interpret research on loans.

During the 1960s and early 1970s there was little research on the effects of loans. Most analysts wrote about loans based on opinion rather than research evidence. The one exception was Alexander Astin (1975), who used data collected through the Cooperative Institutional Research Program (CIRP) to examine the effects of different types of student aid on four-year persistence. This research combined a CIRP freshman survey and a follow-up survey of seniors. Astin found a significant and negative association between loans and freshman-to-sophomore persistence. He also found a statistically significant and positive association between loans and long-term persistence (freshman-to-senior years). Because more students had loans as seniors than as freshmen, he concluded that this positive association between loans and aid in four-year persistence was an artifact, attributable to the greater use of loans by students who persisted. He did not view this finding as evidence that loans could have, or actually did have, a positive effect on persistence.

At the time, Astin's interpretation seemed reasonable. The CIRP data included three points of time—the freshman, sophomore, and senior years—and his models lacked sufficient controls to make more refined judgments. However, when NCES's longitudinal databases became available, it was possible to test Astin's interpretations. Initial studies using these databases lacked the specificity needed to untangle how loans influenced persistence (e.g., Peng and Fetters 1978; Terkla 1985). After Pascarella and Terenzini (1979, 1980) demonstrated the logic of analyzing persistence on a year-to-year basis, a systematic assessment of the effects of loans became possible.

Michael Tierney (1980) was one of the first scholars to consider separately the effects of loans on college choice. His research, conducted under contract with the U.S. Department of Education, concluded that loans were a workable and lower-cost approach to promoting choice, especially the choice to attend private colleges. However, the doubts about loans lingered, and Astin's findings continued to be used to support arguments against expanding loans (e.g., Newman 1985).

In an analysis conducted for the Department of Education, some colleagues and I examined how different types of aid packages influenced year-to-year persistence, using the High School and Beyond survey.[1] Our analyses revealed that packages with loans were positively associated with persistence, and they cast doubt on Astin's artifact conclusion. We concluded that "loans as well as grants and work are effective in promoting persistence. When the increased likelihood that persisters will take out loans is controlled for, loans appear to have a positive impact on persistence" (St. John, Kirshstein, and Noell 1991, 399).[2]

Given these initial findings, we began to explore further the diverse sets of claims that had emerged about loans. A claim made by some observers was that the increased emphasis on debt could be affecting the new vocationalism; that is, the increased debt could be influencing more college students to choose applied majors (Kramer and VanDusen 1986). In one paper, Jay Noell and I put these findings on debt together with the analyses of first-time enrollment and persistence to examine whether debt influences educational opportunity. In a paper presented at a 1987 conference, we tried to address doubts about the efficacy of loans. Our conclusions from this study were as follows:

> There has long been a belief in the higher education community that loans are not effective in enhancing opportunities in higher education. Thus the increased emphasis on loans in the 1980s had led some in the student aid community to express concern that opportunities in higher education were declining because of changes in student aid policy. This paper examined the belief that loans are not an effective form of aid in enhancing student opportunities. Our analysis suggests that:

[1] The empirical results from these studies were summarized in chapter 5. This section focuses on the politics of the research process.

[2] This paper was originally presented at the 1987 American Educational Research Association meeting. It was moderately controversial when presented, which is why I took some time to revise it before it was published. The quotation here is from the published version but is identical to the passage in the original paper.

- Grants/scholarships, loans, and work are effective in promoting access to higher education.
- Loans as well as grants/scholarships and work-study are effective forms of aid in promoting student persistence in college.
- Cumulative debt does not have an effect on student decisions to select majors with higher expected earnings.

Our primary conclusions are that loans are an effective form of aid and that the mixture of loans and grants available for student aid through the mid-1980s was effective in enhancing higher education opportunities. This does not necessarily suggest that an increased emphasis on loans would be more effective than the mix that was evident in the early 1980s. Since aid is theoretically packaged to promote access and choice, observations on the actual mix do not indicate what would happen if this mix changed. And although our analysis cannot show that higher levels of student debt will not result in negative consequences, we can conclude that the level of debt that was present in the early 1980s did not influence students to choose majors with higher potential earnings. It would seem prudent, of course, to continue to monitor student debt and to assess whether its positive effects continue to outweigh possible negative effects. (St. John and Noell 1987, 19–20)

Subsequent, more detailed analyses have revealed that the first half of this statement is not entirely accurate (St. John 1989). The second half of the statement attempted to address the policy implications of the issue. In fact, this statement took a step further into the policy domain than I was comfortable with at the time.[3] The studies examined the effects of aid on enrollment and persistence by students who had entered college when different policies were in place. They provided evidence that the new policies worked reasonably well in the early 1980s: specifically, most types of aid packages were adequate to promote enrollment (St. John and Noell 1989) and persistence (St. John, Kirshstein, and Noell 1991). However, this research made it easier for Department of Education officials to push loans. There was at least some acceptance of the viability of loans in the student aid research community.[4]

---

[3] This research was conducted under federal contract and had to go through extensive review before being released; to get it released, we had to speculate about current policies. After this experience, I ceased trying to have papers released. Instead I focused on providing balanced analyses, even if they were not released.

[4] Most of this research (examined further below) took a balanced approach to assessing the effects of aid policy.

During this period, the leadership in the Department of Education was pushing loans as an integral part of its student aid strategy through the federal budget process. Its arguments about the problems with federal student aid programs essentially made similar claims about grants and loans. For example, Bruce Carnes made the following argument about the availability of loans forcing up prices: "Student aid does not itself push up college prices but it does facilitate their rise. As Michael O'Keef put it in *Change*, 'the increased availability of loans in recent years . . . feeds the cost spiral. Sizable tuitions become less formidable when translated into relatively modest payments per month. The magic of "buy now, pay later" has come to higher education, making it almost painless to raise costs.' When the majority of those costs are passed on to taxpayers . . . raising prices becomes easier" (1987, 70–71). This argument implies that loans, as well as grants, mitigate the effects of price increases. It implies that loans and grants have similar effects, but it stops short of explicitly arguing that loans promote opportunity. Rather, it carries forward the criticism of aid that was a crucial part of the Reagan administration's arguments against increasing spending on student aid. This bundling together of grants and loans, however, also facilitated a shift in emphasis from grants to loans. Using this logic, there was an implied argument that loans as well as grants made payment of the costs of college easier, which allowed the rationalization that expanding loans rather than grants was a less expensive way for taxpayers to subsidize educational opportunity, at least for the majority of students.

CHANGING PATTERNS OF STATE FINANCE

In contrast to the prior decade, state financing strategies changed markedly during the 1980s. While the rhetoric of federal officials (e.g., Bennett 1987; Carnes 1987; Finn 1988a,b) may have influenced some conservative state legislators to look critically on state funding of institutions, there were serious fiscal constraints on many states (Hearn and Anderson 1989; Hearn and Longanecker 1985; St. John 1991a). A high-tuition, high-aid policy evolved in Minnesota as a consequence of purposeful planning (Hearn and Anderson 1989), but financing strategies changed in other states as a response to declining state tax dollars (St. John 1991a).

Regardless of the cause, a substantial shift in state financing strategies occurred during the 1980s. State funding per student enrolled in public higher education increased by 17 percent during the first half of the decade, from an average of $5,761 in 1980–81 to an average of $6,740 in 1985–86 (table A.3), but it declined during the second half of the decade, to $6,243 in 1990–91. Public sector tuition revenue per student rose substantially during the decade, from an average of $1,567 in 1980–81 to $2,105 in 1985–86 and $2,439 in 1990–91. Tuition revenue covered about 20.6 percent of education and related expenditures in public institutions in 1980–81, compared with 23.4 percent of this total in 1985–86 and 26.58 percent in 1990–91. Clearly, the burden of paying for public college shifted from taxpayers to students and their families during the decade.

Expenditures changed substantially during the first half of the decade, rising from $7,614 in 1980–81 to $8,996 in 1985–86. These increases were the subject of intense speculation, included federally funded studies that considered the role of revenue theory and other greed-related theories (e.g., Kirshstein, Sherman, et al. 1990; Kirshstein, Tikoff, et al. 1990). However, as the dust settled on these divisive debates, it became apparent that institutions did not gain federal student aid dollars from increasing tuition, but did increase their own spending on student aid as tuition rose, even in the public sector (NCES 2001d). Also, there clearly was a relationship between increases in spending during the first half of the decade and increased tuition (St. John 1994), but given only a modest increase in spending in the late 1980s, this pattern did not continue (table A.3). Rather, the more predominant pattern over the decade was the shift in the locus of funding from taxpayers to students and their families.

State grants per student grew at about the same rate as tuition revenue in public colleges over the decade. State grants increased by 30.21 percent in the first half of the 1980s, then by an additional 15.30 percent in the second half of the decade, increasing from an average of $1.5 billion in 1980–81 to $2.2 billion in 1990–91 (table A.4). Further, since state grant dollars go to students in public and private colleges, it is clear that states were moving toward a more market-oriented approach during the decade (Zumeta 2001).

However, the growth in state spending on grant programs did not fill the void created by the massive decline in federal grants. Total federal spending on grants was $12.6 billion in 1980–81, but only $8.0 billion in 1990–91 (table A.4). Thus, in spite of a $1.7 billion increase in state grant funding from 1980–81 to 1990–91, total government student grants actually declined, while total enrollment increased slightly.

Thus, although it may appear that states were moving incrementally toward a market-oriented model of public finance in the 1980s, the potential of this shift was not realized. Instead, public sector tuition charges rose substantially faster than grants. States tried to adjust their grant programs to provide more support for students in public and private colleges, but these increases were overwhelmed by reductions in federal grants. In spite of an apparently constructive pattern of change to a market approach across the states, a high-loan, high-tuition environment evolved, a hybrid market model that undermined the historical commitment to equal opportunity, as the following analysis of the impact of these changes reveals.

Step 2: Changes in Key Indicators

Examination of the changes in higher education policy during the 1980s reveals that the shift in policy from grants to loans had different effects for different groups in American society. In this section I explore the outcomes of these developments from the perspectives of the majority of students, students from ethnic groups with greater concentrations of poverty, and taxpayers.

ACCESS

Starting in the early 1970s, most analysts predicted that college enrollment would decline substantially in the 1980s, due to a decline in the traditional college-age cohort. Throughout the 1970s, forecasters predicted enrollment declines for the 1980s (Carnegie Commission 1973; Cartter 1976; Freeman 1976; NCES 1970). The only disagreement was on how much the decrease would be. Those who considered labor market forces (e.g., Freeman 1976) predicted larger decreases than did those who considered only demographic trends (e.g., NCES 1980). Therefore it is reasonable to conclude that other social forces, including aspirations for cross-generation uplift, have a stronger influence than the labor market.

In 1980, most analysts thought enrollment would drop substantially during the next decade. However, college enrollments were higher than predicted (table 6.1). This merits attention because of the changes in student aid. In 1980, NCES predicted that overall enrollment would decline 10.84 percent by 1988 and that enrollment would decline even more substantially in public four-year colleges (by 15.44 percent) and private four-year colleges (by 16.15 percent). The increase in enrollment during a period of declining grants defied the dominant assumptions about college affordability.

Total FTE enrollment was 7.77 million in 1980 and 8.76 million in 1990 (table A.6). Each sector of the higher education system—public and private two-year and four-year colleges—increased its total enrollment during the decade. There were some half-decade declines in the 1980s, but not the declines that were expected in private four-year colleges (Breneman, Finn, and Nelson 1978). Instead, enrollment in public two-year colleges declined slightly in the first half of the decade and enrollment in the private two-year sector declined slightly during the second half.

TABLE 6.1 Actual FTE Undergraduate Enrollments Compared with NCES Projections, Fall 1980 to Fall 1988

| | FTE Enrollment (Thousands) | | | | |
| | Public | | Private | | |
Type of Institution	Four-Year	Two-Year	Four-Year	Two-Year	Total
1980 Actual	3,524	2,484	1,585	174	7,767
1980 Projection for 1988	2,980	2,473	1,329	135	6,925
Predicted percentage difference	−15.44%	−.44%	−16.15%	−22.41%	−10.84%
1988 Actual	3,828	2,591	1,690	209	8,318
Difference (actual minus projected)	848	118	361	74	1,393
Percentage difference between actual and predicted	28.46%	4.78%	27.17%	54.82%	20.12%

Sources: Actual enrollment for 1980 and 1988 from NCES 1995b, 47, table 24; 48, table 25. Enrollment projections from: NCES 1980, 44, table 12A; 45, table 12B. Middle alternative projections were used. (Three ranges of projections were reported: high, medium, and low.)

There was a substantial increase in the college enrollment rate for traditional college-age high-school graduates, which explains why enrollment was higher than predicted. Specifically, 31.8 percent of traditional college-age high school graduates attended in 1980, compared with 39.1 percent in 1990 (table A.8). Indeed, this was a notable expansion in the opportunity to attend for traditional college-age students, especially given the instability in student aid. This increase is even more dramatic when we consider that participation rates for traditional-age students had remained stable in the 1970s, a period of substantial growth in enrollment (chapter 5).

The most widely accepted explanation for the higher than expected enrollment is that the labor market improved. Economists, in particular, have made this argument (Kane 1995, 1999; McPherson and Schapiro 1997). This is certainly a reasonable argument. At the very least, the labor market induced more people to attend college. However, had the labor market been the overwhelming force compelling people into the system, we would expect more adults to return to higher education, which did

UNDERSTANDING THE ACCESS CHALLENGE

not happen. Thus, the labor market provides only a partial explanation. Improvements in academic preparation (i.e., raising standards) provide another possible explanation, one overlooked by most economists.

The prospect that loans could enable more students to enroll also merits serious consideration by economic analysts. Indeed, growth in loans during the 1980s corresponds with growth in participation by the traditional college-age population. Indeed, it is possible that the availability of capital enabled more families to send their children to college. Loans appear to have helped a larger percentage of the middle-class adult population to pay for their children to attend and to attend more expensive colleges. Thus it would be shortsighted to overlook the role of loans when attempting to explain the growth in participation rates during the 1980s. The role of loans is further examined below.

EQUAL OPPORTUNITY

A different picture emerges when opportunities for diverse ethnic groups are considered. The percentage of traditional college-age Whites attending college rose from 32.1 percent in 1980 to 40.4 percent in 1990, a dramatic increase in opportunity (table A.8). However, the college participation rate for African Americans increased to only 32.7 percent in 1990, from a low of 27.6 percent in 1980. The participation rate for Hispanics actually declined during the decade, from 29.9 percent in 1980 to 28.7 percent in 1990. Thus, the disparity in opportunity was substantially greater in 1990 than in 1980. Did school reform fail minorities? Or did the decline in grant aid have an effect?

The total amount of federal grant dollars declined during the decade, from $12.6 billion in 1980 to $8.0 billion in 1990 (table A.2, part C), but the number of FTE students increased by almost one million (table A.6). Thus there was a marked reduction in expenditures on federal grants per FTE student. The amount of federal grants declined substantially during the decade. State grants increased (from $1.5 billion to $2.25 billion), as did institutional aid (from $3.0 billion to $7.0 billion) (table A.4). The total amount of all grants (state, federal, and other) did not change substantially, with institutional and state grants offsetting the loss in federal grants. But since enrollment increased, grant aid per student declined. Further, with the substantial increase in tuition during the decade, net prices rose considerably.

Thus, the increase in net price apparently did make a difference for the African American and Hispanic populations. These groups have much larger percentages of students from poor households. There are good reasons to expect that the changes in grants and tuition helped to reduce opportunity for low-income students (Kane 1999; McPherson and

Schapiro 1997; St. John and Starkey 1995a). In spite of the increase in net price, there was a slight gain in participation by African Americans and only a slight decline by Hispanics. Thus, loans could have had a mitigating influence and the labor market could also have had an impact (Kane 1999).

The opportunity gap increased, but total enrollment was higher than most of us who study finance would have predicted in 1980, had we known there would be a substantial increase in net price. Thus, we have good reason to ponder why disparities were not greater. Some redistribution of low-income students to lower-cost colleges occurred during the decade (St. John 1994), but this was modest overall, given that two-year colleges did not grow as substantially as four-year colleges (Kane 2001).

TAXPAYER COSTS

From the perspective of conservative taxpayers, the trends reviewed above confirm the claim that it was possible to expand opportunity at a low cost for taxpayers. Had the first Reagan administration, or a second Carter administration, chosen to seek full funding for Pell and campus-based grant programs, the spending on grants would have been substantially higher—but would participation have been as high? There is no reason to expect that higher grant aid would have decreased enrollment. But it is surprising that high loans worked as well as they did, at least from the traditional viewpoint on college affordability.

The federal grant subsidy per FTE student decreased substantially during the decade, from $1,428 in 1980–81 to $801 in 1990–91 (table A.9). Federal loans increased, but total federal spending (grants and loans) was lower in 1990 ($1,426) than in 1980 ($2,090) (table A.9). Loans cost substantially less than grants, so there was a substantial savings in tax dollars in 1980 compared with 1990, along with gains in opportunity for the majority, as indicated by the two access indicators.

However, state funding per FTE student enrolled in higher education also increased during the decade, from $4,563 in 1980–81 to $4,995 in 1990–91 (table A.9). Thus, the burden of paying for college shifted from the federal government to the states. Tuition also rose, however, because educational expenditures in public colleges grew faster than did state subsidies.

The mixture of policies—more loans plus higher tuition—worked relatively well, at least for the middle-class majority. Fewer tax dollars were spent on student aid, but the dollars that were spent enabled more students to enroll. There was a serious problem, however. This pattern of finance apparently contributed to the disparity in opportunity, a conclusion that is confirmed by the evaluation studies for this period.

Step 3: Evaluation Studies

The 1980s were a period of reductions in federal grants and increases in tuition and loans. Private institutions adapted their pricing strategies to optimize enrollment, but state and public institutions were slow to make these adjustments. As the analysis of participation rates above revealed, the opportunity for minorities to enroll and persist in college declined, as evidenced by the increased gap in participation rates. However, these trends alone do not confirm that changes in federal aid policy actually influenced the disparity in opportunity. To establish this linkage empirically, analysts needed to conduct studies with appropriate statistical controls.

In 1986–87, the federal government conducted the first National Postsecondary Student Aid Survey (NPSAS 87). This database provided the first random national sample of the records of all students enrolled in the fall term of an academic year, including their student aid records and aid awards, as well as a follow-up survey of all students. NPSAS:87 provided a nearly ideal sample for examining the effects of student aid on within-year persistence.[5] In the early 1990s, I worked with graduate students at the University of New Orleans to conduct a comprehensive set of studies on the impact of aid on within-year persistence, or whether students who enrolled in the fall term could afford to stay enrolled. I review here both price-response and aid-package studies.

PRICE RESPONSE IN PERSISTENCE

The NPSAS:87 survey was the first study of all students enrolled in the public system, and the study sample was of sufficient size to allow for a range of group comparisons. Table 6.2 summarizes studies that examined different populations.[6] By 1986–87, a very different pattern of price response from that of the late 1970s or early 1980s had emerged (chapter 5). Key findings about differences in response to tuition charges were as follows:

— There was substantial variation in price response to tuition by traditional college-age students. Among traditional-age undergraduates,

[5] Subsequent NPSAS surveys had a revolving sample of all students enrolled throughout the year. This approach complicated efforts to examine within-year persistence. However, a few analysts are starting to replicate the studies cited here (e.g., Cofer 1998).

[6] The studies reported in table 6.2 had a coding problem with respect to college grades: students for whom no grade was reported were included with the B grades (Paulsen and St. John 2002). A reanalysis reveals that this coding error did not change the effects of aid reported in table 6.1.

TABLE 6.2 Effects of Prices and Subsidies on Persistence: Summary of Delta-p Statistics for Tuition and Aid Amounts

	Tuition		Grants/Scholarship		Loans		Work-Study/Asst.	
	Delta-p	Sig.	Delta-p	Sig.	Delta-p	Sig.	Delta-p	Sig.
I. *Graduate Students* (Andrieu and St. John 1993)								
All	−0.0192	***	NS		NS		−0.0055	***
Public	−0.0234	***	NS		NS		−0.0067	*
II. *Undergraduates* (Wells 1996)								
A. All								
All	−0.0506	***	NS		NS		−0.0479	***
Health programs	−0.0581	***	NS		−0.0231	***	NS	
B. Traditional-age undergraduates in all postsecondary institutions (Kaltenbaugh, St. John, and Starkey 1999)								
African American	−0.0425	***	−0.0124	**	NS		−0.0492	**
White (European American)	−0.0273	***	NS		−0.0039	**	−0.0166	***
C. Traditional-age undergraduates in four-year institutions								
All (St. John and Starkey 1995a)	−0.0262	***	NS		−0.0036	**	−0.0191	***
Private (St. John, Oescher, and Andrieu 1992)	−0.0210	***	0.0022	*	NS		−0.0195	***
Public (St. John, Oescher, and Andrieu 1992)	−0.0494	***	−0.0152	***	−0.0060	*	NS	
Low-income (St. John and Starkey 1995a)	−0.0345	***	−0.0100	***	NS		NS	
Lower-middle-income (St. John and Starkey 1995a)	−0.0335	***	NS		−0.0352	***	NS	

Upper-middle-income (St. John and Starkey 1995a)	−0.0227 ***	NS	NS	NS
D. Adult undergraduates (St. John and Starkey 1995b)				
Private	−0.0640 ***	NS	NS	−0.0560 **
Public	−0.0130 ***	−0.0220 ***	−0.0160 **	NS
E. Part-time undergraduates (Starkey 1994)	−0.1105 ***	−0.0257 **	NS	NS
F. Traditional-age undergraduates in two-year institutions (St. John and Starkey 1994)				
All	−0.1399 ***	−0.0569 ***	NS	NS
G. Adult undergraduates in two-year institutions (Hippensteel, St. John, and Starkey 1996)				
All	−0.1755 ***	−0.0412 ***	NS	NS
H. Students in proprietary schools (St. John et al. 1995)				
All	−0.0573 ***	NS	NS	NS

Sources: Analyses used data from the NPSAS:87 survey. Sources for the individual analyses are given in the table.

Note: Analyses examined actual dollars; amounts are dollars per $1,000. The delta-p statistics were not adjusted for inflation.

* Significant at .1 level; ** significant at .05 level; *** significant at .01 level. Not significant (NS) indicates aid adequacy.

African Americans were more responsive to tuition than Whites, and students in public colleges were more responsive to tuition than students in private colleges.

—Adult students and part-time students were more responsive to tuition charges than traditional-age students.

—Students in community colleges were more responsive to tuition charges than students in four-year colleges.

—Graduate students were less responsive to tuition charges than were undergraduates.

In addition, there was substantial variation in the ways that diverse groups of students responded to student aid. Overall, student aid ceased being positively associated with persistence. For all traditional-age undergraduate students (St. John and Starkey 1995a) and all undergraduates (Wells 1996), grant amounts were not significant (and presumably not adequate), while loan amounts were negatively associated with persistence. The following are the other key findings:

—Grants were positively associated with persistence in private colleges and negatively associated with persistence in public colleges (St. John, Oescher, and Andrieu 1992), indicating that adaptations by private colleges had helped keep aid viable.

—Grants were not significant in proprietary schools (St. John et al. 1995), indicating that a minimum level of aid was adequate.

—Grant aid was insufficient (and negatively associated with persistence) for African Americans, but was adequate for Whites (Kaltenbaugh, St. John, and Starkey 1999).

—Grants were not adequate for low-income and lower-middle-income students, but were adequate for upper-middle-income students (St. John and Starkey 1995a).

—Grants were insufficient for adults at public institutions (St. John and Starkey 1995b), part-time undergraduates (Starkey 1994), and students in community colleges (Hippensteel, St. John, and Starkey 1996).

—Loans, when they were significant, were negatively associated with persistence (St. John, Oescher, and Andrieu 1992; St. John and Starkey 1995b; Wells 1996), indicating that excessive debt burden was becoming a problem.

—The amount of work-study, when significant, was also negatively associated with persistence, indicating that either the low wages or the time required for on-campus work had become problematic.

Thus, a general pattern of aid inadequacy had emerged by the late 1980s. The institutions that had made the fewest adaptations—public colleges, and especially community colleges—had the most substantial affordability problems. Unfortunately, the most vulnerable in society—minorities and low-income students—faced greater affordability problems than students from middle-income families, Whites, and students in private colleges. In fact, the disparity in participation rates continues, which further confirms the linkage between aid adequacy and minority participation. The inadequacy of government aid was clearly contributing to the growing gap in opportunity in the late 1980s.

THE EFFECTS OF AID PACKAGES

In another study we compared five different ways of measuring the effects of student aid on within-year persistence by traditional-age undergraduates in four-year colleges (St. John et al. 1994). These included (table 6.3): tuition charges and aid amounts (version 1); unmet need, tuition charges, and aid amounts (version 2); aid packages (version 3); aid packages with unmet need (version 4); and aid packages with tuition and unmet need (version 5). The comparisons provided insight into the interactions among tuition charges, aid amounts, and aid packages,[7] including the following findings:

—The amounts of loans and work-study awarded were negatively associated with persistence, and the delta-p of these aid amounts did not change substantially when unmet need was considered (compare versions 1 and 2).

—Aid packages with grants only, loans only, and grants and loans were negatively associated with persistence, indicating inadequacy of these packages (version 3).

—Aid packages with all three types of aid were significantly and positively associated with persistence, indicating that total aid was adequate only when all forms of aid were combined (versions 3, 4, and 5).

—Controlling for unmet need did not substantially change the direct effects of the aid packages (compare versions 3 and 4). This means that adequacy (or inadequacy) of aid affects student decisions, but "unmet need" may not capture this effect.

—Controlling for the effect of tuition and unmet need did change the significance of loans. The negative effect of receiving loans was related to tuition charges (compare versions 4 and 5).

—The effects of aid packages changed after the direct effects of tuition and unmet need were controlled for (compare versions 3, 4, and 5). When tuition was considered (version 5), the amount of loan

[7] The analysis by St. John, Andrieu, et al. (1994) miscoded college grades (Paulsen and St. John 2002), but this coding did not influence the analyses reported in table 6.3.

awarded was no longer negatively associated with persistence. This finding further confirms that the negative association between aid and continued enrollment is related to aid adequacy.

These analyses show a pattern of relationship between tuition and aid packages. They suggest a very tight link between the effects of loans and the effects of tuition (compare versions 4 and 5). Specifically, loans as the only form of aid were significantly and negatively associated with persistence when tuition was not considered, but these packages were not significantly associated with persistence when tuition was considered. Further, packages with grants and loans had a stronger effect before tuition was controlled for than after. These findings suggest students might borrow more to pay for tuition increases.

UNDERSTANDING AID INADEQUACY

For a decade, some well-intentioned policy analysts have been aware that student aid was inadequate for low-income students in the 1980s (Mumper 1996; Orfield 1992). The set of studies described above provides confirmatory empirical evidence of this hypothesis: *in the late 1980s student aid was inadequate for students from low-income families due to inadequate federal grants.*

By the late 1980s, institutions had to invest their own funds in student aid to maintain aid adequacy—both public and private colleges (Paulsen and St. John 1997; St. John, Oescher, and Andrieu 1992). Further, students with the greatest financial need were most negatively affected by these new conditions. It is also evident that different approaches to assessing the effects of aid had different meanings. Based on the results of multivariate studies reviewed above, however, the aid-packages approach provides an appropriate way of assessing the adequacy of aid.

In the 1980s, tuition revenues grew substantially faster than revenues from state and local sources. In the early 1980s, both sources of revenue grew, but tuition revenues increased at twice the rate of state revenues (a 34 percent increase in tuition revenues compared with a 17 percent increase in state revenues). Then in the late 1980s, state funding per FTE declined (by 7 percent), while tuition revenues continued to increase (by 16 percent). The ratio of tuition revenues to educational and related expenditures rose to almost 27 percent in 1990–91, while the percentage from states dropped to 68 percent. These developments took place during the period of ideological shift and policy drift at the federal level.

TABLE 6.3. Comparison of Five Approaches to Assessing the Impact of Student Financial Aid: Summary of Delta-p Statistics for Aid Amounts and Aid Packages

	Delta-p[a]				
	1	2	3	4	5
Unmet need dollars		−0.002		−0.003	−0.002
Grant dollars	NS	NS			
Loan dollars	−0.004	−0.005			
Loan dollars	−0.019	−0.020			
Tuition dollars	−0.026	−0.026			−0.026
Grant only			−0.019	−0.021	−0.018
Loan only			−0.011	−0.015	NS
Work-study only			NS	NS	NS
Grant and loan			−0.023	−0.026	−0.013
Work-study and loan			NS	NS	NS
Grant and work-study			−0.029	−0.032	−0.470
All three			0.042	0.044	0.047

Source: St. John, Andrieu, et al. 1994. The analysis used data from the NPSAS:87 survey.

Note: These analyses used actual dollars. The delta-p statistics are not adjusted for inflation. Not significant (NS) indicates adequate aid. Blank indicates the analysis did not consider that variable. Delta-p statistics are given when the beta coefficients are significant at the .05 or .01 level. Logistic regression analyses controlled for student background, aspirations, college characteristics, and college experience.

[a] For versions 1 through 5, delta-p statistics for amounts are in dollars per $1,000; delta-p statistics for packages compare students with and without aid.

Step 4: Possible Explanations

The 1980s were a period of substantial change in higher education finance policy. For those with a new conservative perspective, these changes may symbolize "improvements," including an increased emphasis on outcomes and reduced costs for federal student aid programs. However, all of American society should be concerned about the disparity in postsecondary opportunity that emerged during the decade. From a liberal perspective, these developments are especially troubling, particularly given the gains in equality in prior decades. Here I explore some of the reasons this disparity developed, focusing on school reform, postsecondary encouragement, and student aid as plausible explanations.

SCHOOL REFORM

The notion that postsecondary participation was closely linked to the reform of K–12 schools emerged in the 1980s. When the disparity in participation began to surface, African American leaders requested that the Reagan administration study the issue. The first funded study used regression analysis to examine the role of academic achievement, arguing that disparity in test scores and grades helped explain the disparity in opportunity (Chaikind 1987). I also conducted a study, using sequential logistic regressions to examine the relative effects on college enrollment of academic preparation and high school courses, aspirations (which can be influenced by postsecondary encouragement), and student aid. While all three variables were significant, it was clear that student aid had the most substantial direct influence on minority enrollment (St. John 1991b).[8] The most widely referenced study in this area focused on academic preparation and virtually ignored the role of student aid, especially research on the effects of student aid (Pelavin and Kane 1988, 1990). One of the major conclusions from Pelavin and Kane's study (1990) was that taking an algebra course in high school was highly correlated with college attendance. These findings fueled speculation that K–12 reform could help equalize opportunity.

However, when we examine the changes in K–12 policy in relation to college participation rates, a different and more complex set of questions emerges. The 1980s were a period of educational reform, most of which focused on national standards and testing. Is it possible that reforms implemented in high schools during the 1980s increased the disparity in opportunity to attend institutions of higher education? Since minority enrollment rates were lower in the 1990s than in the late 1980s, there is reason to question whether the K–12 reforms of the 1980s had the opposite of their intended effect. If advocates of K–12 reform argue that increasing standards and tests can increase postsecondary opportunity, couldn't the reverse be true? There was an improvement in overall participation rates in the 1980s, which supports part of the new conservative rationale. But there was increased inequality, as illustrated by trends in participation rates for diverse ethnic and income groups. Was this new inequity caused by the educational reforms of the period? Probably not. The decline in grant aid provides a better explanation.

The reasons for the disparity are not easy to untangle from published statistics. The high school graduation rate for 17-year-olds increased from

---

[8] This study (summarized in chapter 5), conducted with federal funding, was completed several years before it was published. The research was conducted during the same period as the Pelavin and Kane (1988, 1990) study.

UNDERSTANDING THE ACCESS CHALLENGE

71.7 percent in 1980 to 73.2 percent in 1990 (table A.7). However, the graduation rate was lower in 1990 than in 1970 (75.9 percent) and 1975 (73.7 percent). Thus, the educational reforms of the 1980s did not restore education to its status prior to the "conservative revolution," but it did have an apparent influence on educational outcomes. Further, college participation rates increased for high school graduates (total population) in the 1990s (table A.8). But since college participation rates did not increase for African Americans, should we question whether K–12 educational opportunities eroded for African Americans? The more reasonable explanation is that the reduction in grants caused the new disparity.

The gain in overall participation rates, and especially the expansion in middle-class opportunity that occurred in the 1980s, was probably influenced by school reform. Indeed, increasing the emphasis on testing could have increased opportunity for the majority. However, given the increased disparity in opportunity, these trends should raise new concerns. Why would standards and related reforms benefit Whites more than minorities? What types of school reforms would improve opportunities for African Americans and Hispanics? If we examine K–12 reforms in relation to overall participation rates, we see that early standards-driven reform and testing enabled more White students to attend college. If we make this leap, however, we must also ask why the disparity developed. If K–12 reforms were not the reason, we must explore other explanations.

POSTSECONDARY ENCOURAGEMENT

The campus-based programs included under Title IV of HEA did not fare well during this period, and the TRIO programs suffered from a lack of attention and funding. The idea that postsecondary encouragement could make a difference did not receive much attention. Indeed, there were proposals to reduce funding for these programs during the decade. The lack of emphasis on student grants was probably discouraging enough, but the lack of emphasis on providing information about postsecondary opportunities is even more troubling.

STUDENT FINANCIAL AID

The evidence reviewed above strongly indicates that student aid was inadequate for low-income students in the late 1980s. Loans clearly helped the middle class, but they did not help low-income students sufficiently. Low-income students had more debt, but the total aid was insufficient. Specifically, grants were insufficient for low-income students and minorities (Kaltenbaugh, St. John, and Starkey 1999; Paulsen and St. John 2002; St. John and Starkey 1995a). This means that the student aid policies of the 1980s helped to expand opportunity for the majority and save taxpayer dollars, but they accentuated inequities.

Conclusion

There were fundamental changes in the rationales used in debates about postsecondary finance after 1980, along with changes in the patterns of funding for federal student aid programs. As funding for grants declined, Reagan administration officials refocused public attention on the educational deficits of minority children and the spending of public and private colleges. These tactics essentially shifted the attention of the press and many analysts away from the consequence of reductions in federal grants and expansion in loans. With a more historical perspective, this chapter has provided insight into the nature and consequences of policy changes.

How did federal financial aid and state finance policies change during the period?

While there was a slight shift in emphasis from grants to loans in the last few years of the 1970s, this shift was massive during the 1980s. By the end of the decade loans had replaced grants as the primary form of student aid. Loans came to represent more than 60 percent of total federal aid dollars available for college students. Further, federal grants declined by more than one-third during the early 1980s. These reductions were more visible than cuts in grants had been in the late 1970s, because of cuts in the Title IV grant programs. However, the amount of reduction in total federal grant dollars was greater in the late 1970s than in the early 1980s. More critically, total federal aid dollars (grants, work-study, and loans) actually declined in the early 1980s, whereas this total increased only slightly in the late 1970s.

The change in philosophy about student aid in the 1980s was nearly as critical as changes in the amounts of federal funds available. The old rationale of using aid dollars to promote equal opportunity was replaced by a new rationale that emphasized academic preparation, a form of reasoning that comes dangerously close to blaming minorities for being the victims of poor-quality urban schools and failed urban school reforms. Further, the new claims that colleges and universities were wasteful and unproductive shattered the old consensus about the investment in higher education being for the general good of society.

During the 1980s, there were incremental reductions in state funding for public universities. Universities responded by raising tuition charges as a means of maintaining their revenues. Thus, changes in state finance policy also had an influence on the access and opportunity patterns during the decade, along with federal student aid. Private colleges adjusted to the decline in federal grants by raising tuition, investing more in their educational programs and in student grants. A new high-tuition, high-loan environment emerged.

How did the key indicators—access, equal opportunity, and efficient use of tax dollars—change during the period?

High tuition and high loans had a substantial and direct influence on student outcomes. Access was maintained because middle-income students used loans to achieve access. Enrollment was higher than NCES's midrange predictions, and overall enrollment rates climbed. However, the disparity in opportunity between Whites and minorities (African Americans and Hispanics) increased during the decade. It appears from the trend analysis that high tuition and high loans did maintain access, but they did not support equal opportunity. However, since the focus of the debate about equal opportunity had shifted from student aid to academic preparation, many analysts overlooked the consequences of the erosion in grants.

Taxpayer costs per FTE declined during the decade. Loans were less expensive for taxpayers than grants. Further, since enrollment remained high, it seemed as though loans were a less expensive way to subsidize access than were either student grants or institutional subsidies. If we examine the relationship between taxpayer costs and equal opportunity, however, we can conclude that the efficiency gains were meaningless and deceptive. So there is reason to explore further how changes in policy influenced students.

Did evaluation studies of students enrolled during the period help explain the apparent relationship between changes in policy and changes in access, equal opportunity, and the efficient use of tax dollars?

The evaluation studies using NPSAS:87 provided substantial confirmatory evidence that the new financial strategies influenced the changes in access and equal opportunity observed during the 1980s. Specifically, student aid was no longer adequate to enable low-income students to maintain continuous enrollment. Low-income students had high loans, but the total of grants and loans left a substantial unmet need for low-income and lower-middle-income students in public universities. Consequently, grant aid was negatively associated with persistence in public colleges. But the investment made by private colleges in student aid paid off. They remained affordable for their students. Grants continued to have a positive association with persistence in private colleges. Private colleges had a competitive advantage because of the erosion in state support for colleges and federal support for student financial aid.

However, loans were also negatively associated with persistence for students in public colleges and for all students. Since loans did not increase in the late 1980s, for some of this period loans were not adequate for the average student. Further, loans per se were not negatively associated with persistence by either low-income or African American students; rather, the deficit in grants was the problem for students with more substantial need. Additionally, loans and grants were adequate for lower-middle-income and upper-middle-income students when these groups were separately examined (St. John and Starkey 1995a). Thus, changes in aid policy do provide at least a partial explanation for the changes in access and equal opportunity observed in the 1980s.

> Did changes in K–12 schools or in postsecondary encouragement influence observed changes in access and equity?

The review of educational reform in relation to changes in enrollment patterns raised more questions than it answered. The new emphasis on outcomes rather than on financial resources may well have had an impact on increased overall participation rates during the decade. But minorities did not benefit as substantially from the gains in participation. Participation rates for African Americans grew slightly, while the gap between African Americans and Whites widened. For Hispanics, there was a decline in college participation rates. Did the new emphasis on testing have a detrimental effect on educational attainment by Hispanics, possibly due to language differences? This is a possibility. The new immigration of language-minority families may have contributed to the problem. But it is just as likely that the emphasis on standardized tests and aligned content standards also had a negative effect, given the disparities in opportunities for African Americans as well as Hispanics. Indeed, evidence suggests that the educational reforms of the 1980s had an especially detrimental effect on urban schools and urban schoolchildren (Miron and St. John 2003), and these schools served predominantly minority populations (Fossey 2003).

Looking back, the 1980s were a period of cruel ironies. The federal grant programs that had provided the foundation for equal opportunity in the 1970s were gutted. New conservative analysts introduced the notion that academic preparation was the cause of the disparity in educational opportunity (e.g., Pelavin and Kane 1988), and at the same time grant programs were being weakened. Then K–12 reforms were introduced, which may have had an unequalizing effect on educational attainment and postsecondary opportunity.

At the start of the 1980s, a small disparity in educational opportunity had already emerged due to the erosion of grants in the late 1970s. A greater emphasis should have been placed on strategies that would equalize opportunity. By the end of the 1980s, the gap had further widened, which was troubling. By 1990 there was a clear need to enhance federal grants to a level of sufficiency; improve K–12 programs, with a focus on minority students; and provide information and other forms of encouragement for first-generation college students. However, the system made more efficient use of taxpayer dollars in 1990, at least from a new conservative taxpayer perspective, than it did in 1980. So, in spite of the new inequality, there was more efficiency. Clearly, American society needed strategies that retained efficiency but equalized opportunity. And the increased emphasis on loans should have occurred alongside a strengthening of federal grant programs for a new generation of low-income students.

7

The 1990s: Justice for Taxpayers?

The policy developments during the 1990s are not easily classified using the traditional terms *conservative* and *liberal*. In January 1993, Bill Clinton entered office with an opportunity to make adjustments to educational policy that would have narrowed the gap in postsecondary opportunity. However, there were ideological tensions that made meaningful change difficult. Whatever actions Clinton chose, he needed support from a majority of Congress. Very little of substance happened in higher education policy in the first two years of the Clinton administration, when Democrats were in the majority in Congress. After 1994, the majority was Republican and held to new conservative tenets. In this environment, pushing major new reforms to enhance equal opportunity would not have been easy. Perhaps Congress could have made incremental changes that emphasized equalizing opportunity, rather than reorienting educational reforms through taxes targeted on the middle-class majority. Instead, higher education policy became a mechanism of shifting the Democratic Party toward the conservative political center. The new Democratic policies were far from the old liberal ideals.

Federal postsecondary policy in the 1990s can be characterized by a question: *did the reform strategy that was chosen (i.e., HOPE Scholarships and related tax credits) improve justice for taxpayers?* At the start of the 1990s, the evidence suggested that a more efficient system of higher education finance had evolved over the prior decade. In the 1980s, loans had allowed an expansion in participation rates at a lower cost to taxpayers. Policies during the 1990s doubled loans, created tax credits, and implemented new default regulations. Of these developments, the legislation on tax credits represents the most visible departure from prior policies, and thus I select as the theme for the decade the question "justice for taxpayers?"

Step 1: Changes in Policy

The Clinton administration initiated new programs, but other than tax credits these programs were largely symbolic, having little cost or impact compared with other forms of aid. The basic pattern of escalating tuition and loans continued and was even hastened by Clinton's policies.

CLINTON'S REFORMS

With the new Republican Congress, coupled with the new conservative Democratic leadership of President Clinton, a new market philosophy took shape. The pattern set in motion during the Reagan years was solidified into a new pattern of federal finance in the 1990s. Clinton also introduced new student aid programs, including:

—*AmeriCorps*, a program that forgives loans for service;
—*Direct Lending*, a program that enables colleges to lend federal dollars directly to college students (an alternative to private loans);
—*HOPE Scholarships and Lifetime Learning Tax Credits*, a set of policies that provides targeted tax relief;
—*GEAR UP*, a program that funds postsecondary encouragement programs.

These programs are essentially middle-class programs. Even though GEAR UP has the potential for improving access for low-income students, it does not provide grants but only provides information about grants. If grants remained as inadequate as they were in the late 1980s (chapter 6), then the program could give false hope. In many respects, GEAR UP is well conceived. It provides information that can help students keep on the right track academically. Yet there is little hope that GEAR UP will help equalize opportunity unless need-based grants are adequate. If a larger percentage of low-income students prepare academically but cannot afford to attend, then, as simple common sense suggests, the new inequality (chapter 6) will increase.

President Clinton embraced these ideas in his second administration with passage of the Taxpayer Relief Act of 1997. HOPE Scholarships provide tax credits of up to $1,500 per year for middle-income families with college students (Brainard, Burd, and Gose 2000; Wolanin 2001). The literature on higher education lobbying paints a picture of a new consensus of large-scale support for student aid (Cook 1998), but the affordability problems increased.[1]

The HOPE Scholarship program, then, allowed students or parents to subtract up to $1,500 in college expenses from their income tax. Since

[1] Perhaps the most complex issue emerging from this new period of consensus was the decline in the proprietary sector, due in part to efforts to regulate loan default rates. The sector has substantially declined; now there are calls to build a new public sector to provide other technical postsecondary education (e.g., Grubb 1996b). This issue is further developed in subsequent chapters.

Pell awards were subtracted from the tax credit, low-income students did not benefit from the HOPE program (Wolanin 2001). Further, there was an upper income threshold. Thus, the program functioned as a tax rebate to middle-income families. Since the "financial" award was rebated after expenses were paid, however, it would not have an immediate enrollment effect. Theoretically, tax credits could affect persistence, but the effect would be difficult to measure since tax records are not accessible to researchers.

In addition, unsubsidized federal loans, created in 1996, extended loan availability. "Unsubsidized" loans had no government subsidy for interest; interest accrued immediately after loans were issued. Many low-income students borrowed unsubsidized loans to meet their educational costs after grants. This dramatic expansion in loans, coupled with income-contingent repayment that extended the time for repaying a loan, caused concern about earnings after education for students in low-earning fields. Unsubsidized loans increased total debt. By 2000, an estimated 39 percent of all students graduated with unmanageable debt: debt of more than 8 percent of monthly income before taxes (King and Bannon 2002).

Despite many changes in the structure of federal loans, the potential improvements in the structure of aid (i.e., improvements in loan administration) were overshadowed by the massive growth in the amounts of federal loans. Total federal Title IV loans increased from $16.4 billion in 1990–91 to almost $46.8 billion in 2000–2001 (table A.2, part A). Grants dwindled to about two-tenths of total federal student aid awarded, while loans comprised three-quarters of federal aid. This massive growth in loans, coupled with the rising cost of attending college, further accentuated high tuition and high loans as a predominant pattern of public finance.

Finally, while only limited data are now available on the use of tax credits (discussed as part of the justice indicators below), this new set of developments represents the symbolic capstone of Clinton's financing strategy. The emphasis of student aid programs (e.g., loans and tax credits) is now on the middle class rather than on equalizing opportunities for the poor. Indeed, it is ironic that during a period of large budget surpluses at the federal level, this new pattern of federal financing was seldom even questioned.

When examining trends in aid awards for the 1990s, we find that Pell grants actually declined in the early 1990s, but increased in the late 1990s (table A.2, part A). The increase in Pell was substantial but did not restore the funding level (chapter 2). There was a modest increase in grants for veterans after the Gulf War (table A.2, part B); consequently, total grants increased slightly (table A.2, part C). Thus, the decline in grants could fuel the new inequality: greater numbers of academically qualified low-income students could be denied financial access if states failed to respond to the challenge.

A TROUBLED PUBLIC SECTOR

Early 1990s

In the early 1990s there was a further shift in the burden of paying for public colleges from taxpayers to students and their families. State and local funding per FTE student decreased even further between 1990–91 and 1995–96, a period during which tuition revenues increased to more than 32 percent of educational and related expenditures (table A.3). There was a nearly direct substitution of tuition revenues for the decline in state subsidies during the same period. The percentage of educational and related expenditures covered from sources other than tuition and state and local appropriations increased slightly (table A.3).

Tuition trends alone may not have been problematic if grants were adequate. Indeed, the notion that a full-time student would pay about $3,141 for college tuition in 1995–96 seems reasonable, especially since the student received an education that cost about $10,000 (the proximate sum of tax dollars and tuition dollars per FTE). However, given trends in total costs of attending and funding for federal student aid, a disturbing new pattern had emerged. In particular, the massive growth in debt reveals that many students borrowed money to pay the high tuition bills. The burden of paying for public college had shifted from current tax revenues to future loan repayments by an indebted generation of students, along with tax deductions for their parents.

Public financing of higher education continued to gain attention as a policy issue in the 1990s, as noted above. However, dramatically different economic conditions existed in most states in the first half of the decade than in the second half, resulting in changes in financing patterns within the decade. In the first half of the decade, state and local funding per FTE declined by 3.78 percent, from $6,243 in 1990–91 to $6,007 in 1995–96 (table A.3). Tuition revenue covered 26.6 percent of educational and related expenses at the start of the decade, compared with 32.2 percent in 1995–96.

Late 1990s

A recent analysis of trends in higher education financial indicators, using information from NCES's Integrated Postsecondary Education Data System, provides more up-to-date information on the state and family shares of educational and related revenue (tuition plus appropriations from state and local governments) in public higher education (St.

John et al. 2002). The state share of the costs of public higher education, as measured by the percentage of educational and related revenues from state appropriations, remained relatively stable in the late 1990s, after declining in the early 1990s. The state share of educational revenue was 57.2 percent in 1994–95 and in 1999–2000. However, revenues and expenditures rose, as did the average state appropriation per FTE, which in public institutions (weighted per FTE in the national system) rose from $5,509 in 1994–95 to $6,119 in 1999–2000.

In contrast, tuition revenue continued to climb in the late 1990s, but not as much as in the early 1990s. Tuition revenues comprised 20.8 percent of educational and related revenues (tuition plus state and local appropriations) within state systems of higher education (two-year and four-year colleges) in 1999–90, 34.1 percent in 1994–95, and 35.2 percent in 1999–2000 (St. John et al. 2002). Tuition grew as a portion of educational revenues in the late 1990s, even though appropriations per FTE increased in real dollars. Some of the growth in tuition revenue was due to growth in out-of-state enrollment in research universities. Looking across the decade, it is evident that public colleges became increasingly reliant on tuition revenue, indicating further movement toward incremental privatization.

State economies were generally better in the late 1990s than in the first half the decade. States maintained relatively stable funding for their public colleges and universities, but the trend toward privatization continued. The economies in many states have taken a recent downturn, and some are again retreating from the support of public colleges, a development that seems to be pushing tuition higher in public colleges during the first few years of the twenty-first century. Given the state of the economy in 2002, it is reasonable to assume that the movement toward privatization of public colleges will continue in the near future.

STATE GRANTS

State funding for student grants also climbed during the decade, increasing from $2.2 billion in 1990–91 to $3.1 billion in 1995–96 and $3.4 billion in 1997–98 (table A.4). Thus, in addition to shifting the burden of college spending from taxpayers to students and their families, states continued to move toward the market model. The debate among scholars about whether states are sufficiently committed to grant programs continues (Mumper 2001; Zumeta 2001), but there is an incremental move toward the market model in states, as illustrated by changing patterns of finance within states. Further, federal grants rose modestly in the 1990s, with federal spending increasing from $8.0 billion in 1990–91 to $9.0 billion in 1997–98 (table A.4), indicating a modest swing back to a market model.

Some analysts argued that the expansion of merit-based programs further undermined the equity effects in the 1990s. A recent trend analysis found that spending on state merit programs increased at an annual rate of 13.6 percent between 1982 and 2000, while need-based programs grew at an annual rate of 7.4 percent (Heller and Rasmussen 2001). While merit programs remain substantially smaller than need-based programs in most states, a few states have started major new programs to reward high-achieving high school graduates. Some analyses of these new merit programs have indicated a modest influence on enrollment (Cornwell, Mustard, and Sridhar 2001; Dynarski 2000), while others indicate no enrollment effects (Binder and Ganderston 2001). The new merit program emphasized subsidies to the middle class rather than promoting equity in enrollment opportunity (Binder and Ganderston 2001; Cornwell, Mustard, and Sridhar 2001; Dynarski 2000; Heller and Rasmussen 2001).

While merit aid might seem more compelling to new conservatives who believe the academic preparation rhetoric, it could fail to meet the challenge created by the decline in federal grants. Given the new inequality (i.e., the lack of opportunity for many qualified low-income students; see chapter 8), advocates of academic preparation must reconsider the role of financial need.

After nearly two decades of shift from a system of direct public subsidy in states to a market model, we should question why better coordination of public finance strategies is not an explicit public goal. More and better coordination of strategies clearly is needed at the state and federal level, and even some continued reinvestment in grants. However, there is reason to strive for more explicit and purposeful coordination, an issue addressed in part II.

ADAPTING TO THE NEW POLICY CONTEXT

Private higher education became more competitive with public colleges in the 1990s. By 1990, a substantially different higher education market had emerged. Private colleges competed better for middle-class students than they had in the prior three decades. Whereas public higher education was the predominant choice of middle-class students in the 1960s and 1970s, because of its lower direct cost, in the 1990s private colleges made a substantial investment in student aid through student aid leveraging (McPherson and Schapiro 1998). Private colleges offered packages that helped attract the types of undergraduates they sought. Their investment in grants increased during the early 1990s (table A.5, part A). They also spent more on educational services and student aid (NCES 2001d).

In the 1990s public four-year colleges also invested more of their revenues in student aid as a means of competing for middle-income students (table A.5, part B). They also increased educational expenditures and services. The concept of "tuition discounting" began to work its way into the financial planning process in the public sector, as public colleges tried to compete with private colleges, especially for out-of-state students. The need for further development in the other postsecondary sector (i.e., technical education, less than one-year programs) also began to gain public attention (Grubb 1996b). The community college movement gained new supporters in the 1990s (Boesel and Fredland 1999), as states began to respond to the demand for the other postsecondary market. Thus, public four-year colleges were squeezed between low-cost two-year colleges and midrange private colleges that used aid leveraging (McPherson and Schapiro 1997). Public four-year colleges lost potential new students to lower-cost two-year colleges, while losing traditional-age middle-class students to private colleges.

Step 2: Changes in Key Indicators

In spite of the new federal programs, the new patterns of injustice and unequal opportunity for poor families continued in the 1990s, as still more questions and concerns emerged. Rather than use his presidency to address the inequities that had developed in the prior twelve years, Clinton developed new policies that accentuated problems inherent in the high-tuition, high-loan environment. Tax credits extended the privileges of the middle and upper classes while constraining choices for the poor in American society.

ACCESS

College enrollment continued to grow in the 1990s. Despite earlier predictions of an enrollment decline (NCES 1990), total FTE enrollment was higher in 1997 than in 1990 (table 7.1). In 1990, NCES predicted an enrollment decline of about 1.53 percent in 1997. However, total enrollment increased by 3.68 percent, from 8.8 million FTE students in 1990 to about 9.1 million in 1997. In 1997, actual FTE enrollment was 5.29 percent higher than NCES had predicted in 1990. There were more substantial increases in percentages and total amounts of FTE in private four-year colleges and public two-year colleges than in public four-year colleges.

Enrollment rates for traditional-age high school graduates increased during the decade, a trend that explains why enrollment was higher than predicted. The overall enrollment rate for traditional-age students in-

UNDERSTANDING THE ACCESS CHALLENGE

TABLE 7.1   Actual FTE Undergraduate Enrollments Compared with NCES Projections, Fall 1990 to Fall 1997

| | FTE Enrollment (Thousands) | | | | |
| | Public | | Private | | |
Type of Institution	Four-Year	Two-Year	Four-Year	Two-Year	Total
1990 Actual	4,015	2,818	1,729	197	8,759
1990 Projection for 1997	3,921	2,754	1,730	220	8,625
Predicted percentage difference	−2.34%	−2.27%	0.06%	11.68%	−1.53%
1997 Actual	4,025	3,026	1,892	138	9,081
Difference (actual minus projected)	104	272	162	−82	456
Percentage difference between actual and predicted	2.66%	9.88%	9.37%	−37.27%	5.29%

Sources: Actual enrollment from NCES 2000c, tables 31 and 32. Projected enrollments from NCES 1990, 46, table 24; 48, table 25. Middle alternative projections were used.

creased from 39.1 to 43.7 percent between 1990 and 1999 (table A.8). More adults arrived on college campuses as an artifact of the baby boom population. The enrollment rates for the nontraditional-age high school graduate did not change substantially (NCES 1998a). Most of the enrollment growth was in public two-year colleges, where enrollment increased by 175,000 FTE between 1990 and 1995 (table A.6), a period when total FTE enrollment increased by only 201,000. Public four-year colleges actually had slightly decreased enrollment in the early 1990s. Within the public sector, there was a redistribution of enrollment to less expensive two-year colleges. Full-time equivalent enrollment in private four-year colleges also increased from 1990 to 1995. In the same period, enrollment in private two-year colleges declined. The prestige pricing strategy of private four-year colleges continued to attract students away from public four-year colleges at the same time that public four-year colleges were losing students to public two-year colleges.

EQUAL OPPORTUNITY

The disparity in educational opportunity also persisted into the early 1990s. Between 1990 and 1999, the overall enrollment rate for traditional-age high school graduates increased by 4.6 percentage points, from 39.1 to 43.7 percent (table A.8). During the same period, the enrollment rate for Whites in the cohort increased by 4.9 percentage points, while this rate increased by 6.5 percentage points for African Americans and by 2.9 percentage points for Hispanics. The opportunity gap between Whites and African Americans decreased during the decade. This may be an outcome of the modest growth in Pell awards during the 1990s (chapter 2).

Thus, while overall opportunity for higher education (or access) expanded during the 1990s, the opportunity for poor and working-class students to attend public four-year colleges declined. The new inequality grew during the decade. The high-tuition, high-loan approach had become even more problematic. The affordability of the nation's public system of four-year colleges for the majority of students declined for the first time in more than a century. The percentage of students who attended public four-year colleges actually declined during the decade, a clear indicator of an affordability problem for low-income students. For the middle class, the pathway to college was paved with loans and tax credits, while low-income families faced increased net costs (chapter 8) and the federal government systematically overlooked these conditions (e.g., NCES 1997a,b, 1998b, 2000b).

TAXPAYER COSTS

The taxpayer benefits provided by the Clinton reforms are the most perplexing part of the developments during this period. Middle-income families with children in college could receive credits of up to $1,500, a targeted reduction. Low-income families could not take full advantage of this opportunity, given constraints in opportunity (noted above), while high-income families were not eligible. It was a targeted reduction in taxes for middle-class families with children in college.

The cost of the HOPE Scholarships was $4.75 billion in returns (i.e., aid for enrolled students), and Lifetime Learning Tax Credits cost $3.496 billion in tax relief (i.e., forgone taxes on savings plans) in 1998, resulting from the education provision of the 1997 tax law (table 7.2). More than 95 percent of the beneficiaries had adjusted gross incomes (incomes minus deductions) exceeding $20,000. Thus, while families with earnings of less than $25,000 faced unreasonable net prices and net costs, the returns to middle-income taxpayers cost more than the Pell grant program. The total cost of $8.25 billion was greater than the expenditure on Pell grants in 1997–98 ($6.3 billion; see table A.2, part A). Unfortunately, as noted above, federal regulations required the Pell award to be subtracted from the HOPE Scholarships (Wolanin 2001), which precluded low-income students from benefiting.

The other substantial change was in grants for the military, a specially directed program. Thus, while there was a small increase in the taxpayer costs for grants per FTE student, most of the increase was attributable to

TABLE 7.2 Who Benefited from HOPE Scholarships and Lifetime Learning Tax Credits in Tax Year 1998?

	Returns		Amount	
Adjusted Gross Income	Thousands	Percentage	Thousands	Percentage
Break-even and loss	0.1	0.0	0.0	0.0
>$0.01, under $10,000	205.0	4.3	46.6	1.3
>$10,000, under $20,000	694.6	14.5	390.5	11.2
>$20,000, under $30,000	655.1	13.7	439.0	12.6
>$30,000, under $50,000	1,208.1	25.3	901.1	25.8
>$50,000, under $75,000	1,201.2	25.2	1,132.7	32.4
>$75,000, under $100,000	808.2	16.9	583.4	16.7
>$100,000, under $200,000	2.9	0.1	2.6	0.1
$200,000 and over	0.2	0.0	0.3	0.0
Total	$4,775.3	100.0	$3,496.2	100.0

Source: Data from Office of Management and Budget, January 21, 2000. Table provided by the Advisory Committee on Student Financial Assistance.

Note: These are preliminary data on usage of education tax credits in the 1998 tax year, including returns processed between January 1, 1999, and November 30, 1999. Amounts are reported in actual 1998 dollars.

policies intended to induce youths into the military, rather than a policy intended to promote equal educational opportunity (table A.2, part B).

Loans also increased substantially in the 1990s. However, as more loan dollars went to students who could afford college and repayment of the debt, repayment rates increased and taxpayer costs per borrower declined. Overall, the student aid system cost average taxpayers somewhat more per student in 2000 and 1995 than in 1990. In 1990, federal student aid cost taxpayers about $1,426 per student, compared with $1,668 in 1995–96 and $1,718 in 1998–99 (table A.9).

If we were to add the costs of the tax credits to this total, the total cost per student in 1998 would be higher than in 1975, a period of much greater equity in opportunity. The increased cost influenced a modest increase in total access, but most of the opportunity gains for low-income students were restricted to two-year colleges, due largely to the high net tuition and net cost in public four-year colleges. At the same time there was a large targeted reduction in taxes to middle-class families with children in college. This reduction, however, was awarded after the money was spent (Wolanin 2001), which could reduce the enrollment effects.

The priority in the use of tax dollars had shifted even more substantially to middle-income students and loans. The average federal tax expenditures on grants per FTE student increased from $801 in 1990–91 to $901 in 1998–99. The expenditures for unsubsidized loans rose from $625 in 1990–91 to $817 in 1998–99 (table A.9). Given the cost of tax credits, federal taxpayers were clearly investing in access for the middle class rather than in equalizing opportunity.

In the early 1990s, state tax expenditures per FTE actually declined. Thus, states had expanded access at a lower taxpayer cost per student. In a sense, states used loans to leverage their investment in public colleges. They had found a low-cost method of financing modest gains in total access, which came at the expense of the poor, who frequently enrolled in two-year colleges or did not enroll. Given the decline in federal grants, state financial strategies played a central role in promoting financial access and maintaining equal opportunity in the 1990s.

Step 3: Evaluation Studies

The trends reviewed above indicate that federal financial aid was inadequate to equalize educational opportunity for low-income students in the 1990s. The purchasing power of Pell grants declined for low-income students in public colleges between 1985 and 1995. Further, national studies indicate that the impact of financial aid on persistence in the 1990s was similar to that in the 1980s. Cofer and Somers (2000) have compared the effects of aid on persistence using National Postsecondary Student Aid Surveys, NPSAS:87 and NPSAS:93. They found very similar patterns in the two periods. While their model differed slightly from the one I reported in chapter 6, they found that low-income students were less likely to persist in both periods and that the negative effects of cumulative debt were more substantial than the slight positive effects of grants.[2] Thus, problems with affordability for low-income students continued into the 1990s.

In this context, states or institutions had to dedicate funds to grant aid to ensure affordability for the low-income students they admitted. Otherwise, these students would be denied financial access (chapter 8). Here I summarize case studies of financial aid programs in two states, Washington and Indiana. These state-level studies used logistic regres-

[2] Cofer and Somers (2000) found not only a negative association between debt and persistence but also a small positive effect of grants on persistence during both periods. The key point here is that the effects of aid were similar during the two periods. The differences in findings between Cofer and Somers (2000) and those reported in chapter 6 are attributable to differences in model specifications.

sion models with appropriate controls to assess the direct efficacy of aid packages. They illustrate the critical importance of the availability of supplemental grants from state or institutional sources.

THE WASHINGTON CASE

Washington is a medium-sized state with two research universities (University of Washington and Washington State University), a state college system, and a well-developed community college system. The National Center for Public Policy and Higher Education report in 2000 gave the state a grade B on affordability. The report indicates that it takes 21 percent of the average family's income to pay for community colleges and 23 percent to pay for public four-year colleges. In contrast, the USA Group Foundation's report (Davis 2000) indicates that Washington is better than average on affordability. It has no state income tax and overall is a relatively low-tax state, which could explain why it is a relatively high-tuition state. The Washington case illustrates how these rankings overlook the central role of grants in equalizing opportunity. In 1998–99, Washington ranked tenth among the states in need-based state grant dollars per resident (DeSalvatore and Hughes 2000).

In 1993 the state of Washington increased its investment in state grants and requested a study of the impact of changes over time. Given that any spending increase on higher education was controversial at the time, the Washington Coordinating Board for Higher Education requested that a study be conducted on the impact of aid. In preparation for this study, the state collected student record information from public four-year colleges, community colleges, and private colleges. Because of differences in the format and content of data, as well as in response rates, the impact of aid on persistence had to be analyzed separately for the three groups of institutions. The analyses of the impact of aid packages on within-year persistence in four-year colleges and a private college are summarized here.[3]

In 1993–94, grants for students enrolled in public colleges increased, to $3,486 from $3,089 per recipient in the prior year (table 7.3), but the percentage of students receiving grants did not substantially change. In addition, there was a substantial increase in the percentage of students who received loans and in the average loan amount per recipient. Indeed, the average loan amount jumped by more than $1,200. Thus, public col-

[3] The analyses conducted for the state were comprehensive (Lee and St. John 1995). We considered both within-year and year-to-year persistence and analyzed three different approaches to assessing the impact of student aid (packages, amounts, and thresholds). I use within-year persistence in this review because it proved to be the best way to assess the effects of student aid.

TABLE 7.3. Trends in Aid Packages and Aid Amounts in Washington State Public Four-Year Institutions, 1991–92 through 1993–94

	1991–92	1992–93	1993–94
Aid Packages [a]			
Grant only	3.2%	3.5%	3.2%
Loan only	8.4%	4.7%	12.3%
Work-study only	0.0%	0.1%	0.3%
Loan/work-study	0.4%	0.6%	0.3%
Grant/loan	1.4%	12.0%	12.8%
Grant/work-study	1.5%	1.4%	1.0%
All three	4.1%	4.2%	4.1%
Aid Amounts for Awardees [b]			
Grant	$3,110	$3,089	$3,486
Loan	$3,225	$3,411	$4,685
Work-study	$1,733	$1,645	$1,656

Source: St. John 1999.

Note: Amounts adjusted to 1997–98 dollars.

[a] Percentage of population receiving each type of aid package.

[b] Actual dollars, inflation-adjusted to 1997–98 dollars.

leges experienced a new context for financial aid, influenced by both the expansion in grants and the expansion in federal loans.

The analyses of the impact of aid packages on within-year persistence (table 7.4) indicate that the increased impact of the investment in grants did have an influence on the opportunity to persist. In 1991–92 and 1992–93, packages that included grants only, loans only, loans/work-study, or grants/work-study were not significantly associated with persistence, indicating an equal probability of persistence compared with students with no financial need. Then in 1993–94—the year the grant increase was implemented and federal loans were liberalized—students with most types of aid packages were more likely to persist than were students with no financial aid.

As these analyses indicate, the increases in both grants and loans had a positive effect on persistence in the public system. Students who received grants only and loans only were more likely to persist after the increases. Students with grants only were 4.1 percentage points more likely to persist than otherwise average students who did not receive aid, and students with loans only were 3.7 percentage points more likely to persist. Thus, students in public colleges in Washington were able to benefit from the expansion of both loans and grants in the early 1990s.

TABLE 7.4 Impact of Student Aid on Within-Year Persistence in
Washington State Higher Education, 1991–92, 1992–93, and 1993–94:
Summary of Delta-p Statistics for Aid Packages

	Delta-p[a]		
	1991–92	1992–93	1993–94
Grant only	NS	NS	0.0411
Loan only	NS	NS	0.0375
Work-study only	NA	NA	NA
Loan/work-study	NS	NS	NS
Grant/loan	0.0417	0.0264	0.0560
Grant/work-study	NS	NS	0.0493
All three	0.0615	0.0401	0.0693

Source: St. John 1999.

Note: Delta-p statistics are given when the beta coefficients are significant at the .01 or
.05 levels. Not significant (NS) indicates equal probability. NA indicates insufficient
cases for analysis.

[a] Delta-p statistics compare receipt of an aid package and no aid.

Two additional findings provide evidence on the relationship between maintaining adequate grants and equalizing opportunity. First,
in the logistic regression analyses (St. John 1999), minority students
(African Americans, Hispanics, and Asian Americans) were less likely
than Whites to persist in 1991–92, and there were no differences in the
probability of persistence for minorities in 1993–94. Second, the within-
year persistence rate increased each year across the three years, as the
amounts of grants increased. These findings show that when grants were
sufficient to be positively associated with persistence, the disparity in opportunities between races was minimized.[4]

THE INDIANA CASE

Indiana, like Washington, has a high-quality system of public higher
education. Indiana is a medium-sized state with three public research universities (Indiana University at Bloomington, Purdue University at West
Lafayette, and Indiana University–Purdue University at Indianapolis). It
also has an urban university that includes the state's research hospital and

[4] Unfortunately, more analysis is needed to confirm this relationship between grants
and opportunity across racial/ethnic groups. Since these analyses did not explicitly
consider minority persistence, we cannot conclude that the investment in grants
actually helped to equalize opportunity. However, this is compelling evidence.

several other state colleges. However, unlike Washington, Indiana has only recently developed a community college system. The National Center for Public Policy and Higher Education report of 2000 gives the state a C+ grade on affordability. The report indicates that it takes 23 percent of the average family's income to pay for community college and 26 percent to pay for public four-year colleges. According to the USA Group Foundation's report (Davis 2000), Indiana is below average on affordability. The state ranks low in its tax burden, which could explain why it is a relatively high-tuition state. It ranks well above average on grants (National Center for Public Policy 2000). The Indiana case and the Washington case illustrate how these rankings overlook the central role of grants in equalizing opportunity.

Indiana has maintained a commitment to providing student aid and expanding access (Hossler and Schmit 1995; Hossler, Schmit, and Vesper 1999). In 1998–99, Indiana ranked seventeenth in population and seventh in need-based grants per resident. It was appropriately classified as a high-tuition, high-grant state. There is a long history of state commitment to need-based grants in Indiana, but state financing strategies have not always been well coordinated. For example, in 1993–94, because of tax-revenue constraints, the state did not fully fund its grant programs. Then, in 1996–97, the state substantially increased its investment in state grants, establishing a more direct link between state grants and tuition. Whether this fluctuation in state funding had an influence on the opportunity to persist in college was an appropriate topic of investigation. In cooperation with the Indiana Commission for Higher Education, some colleagues and I recently completed analyses of the impact of student aid on within-year persistence in 1990–91, 1993–94, and 1996–97 (St. John, Hu, and Weber 2000, 2001).

The analysis considers students in the entire state system, which includes a few two-year programs (in a technical college system, on campuses within the Indiana and Purdue systems, and at one two-year college). The analysis of the state system included full-time students enrolled at four-year campuses.[5]

There was a slight decline in state grant awards in 1993–94 compared with 1990–91, then a substantial increase in 1996–97 (table 7.5). However, the percentage of students receiving state grants remained relatively stable. In 1996–97, the average amount of aid received by recipients of aid

---

[5] This differs from the analysis in Washington, which combined full-time and part-time students (St. John 1999); it represents a refinement in method. For Indiana, it makes sense to examine persistence by part-time students separately since the state has recently implemented a grant program for part-time students.

from state grant programs increased to $1,709, from $1,170 in 1993–94. But the total amount of grant aid awarded per student changed very little in 1996–97 due to the decline in federal grants. The percentage of students receiving federal grants declined (from 31.7 to 25.3 percent) and the average federal grant award was also slightly smaller. The bottom line from the state's perspective was that the substantial increase in state grants merely helped public universities hold ground given the decline in federal grants.

In addition, the trend analysis reveals that the percentage of students receiving loans and the amounts of loans increased dramatically in the state. The average loan per recipient increased from $3,444 in 1993–94 to $5,075 in 1996–97. Indeed, it appears that students were paying for increases in tuition with increased debt. In Indiana, as nationally, a clear transfer occurred in the locus of responsibility for funding higher education, from taxpayers (in the form of institutional subsidies) to students and families (in the form of debt). This further illustrates the pattern of using loans to pay for tuition increases.

In the analyses of the impact of aid packages on persistence,[6] we found that Indiana's investment in grants has kept aid at an adequate level (table 7.6). However, the effects of state grants have eroded, since packages with grants were positively associated with persistence in 1990–91 and not in 1996–97. In addition, while there was a substantial increase in loans, packages with loans remained neutral. These findings confirm that the state's investment in student aid was sufficient to minimize the negative effects of the changes in federal aid strategy—the massive shift from grants to loans.

We also found evidence in the Indiana studies of equity in opportunity across ethnic groups, but opportunity to persist eroded slightly for all groups. Specifically, in the analyses of trends in persistence and changes in the impact of aid (St. John, Hu, and Weber 2001) reviewed above, minorities had the same probability of persisting as all students. Further, in supplemental analyses of persistence by ethnic groups, it is apparent that each group is subject to the same trends (Hu and St. John 2001). Indeed, aid packages were more positively associated with persistence for minority groups than for the whole population, but the persistence rates were declining slightly for each group. Thus it appears that when states provide sufficient grants they can maintain equity, but, at the same time, higher tuition might also contribute to an overall decline in persistence rates. Students who do not receive aid may also be negatively

---

[6] We used the aid packages approach in Indiana, as we did in Washington, because institutions reported aid received rather than aid awarded.

TABLE 7.5 Trends in Student Aid in Indiana's Public Colleges and Universities in the 1990s

Variable and Coding	1990–91		1993–94		1996–97	
	Percentage	Mean	Percentage	Mean	Percentage	Mean
Aid Packages						
Grants only	25.6		25.4		16.9	
Loans only	4.7		8.6		15.0	
Grants and loans	16.0		20.3		24.5	
Other	3.8		4.3		4.1	
No aid[a]	49.9		41.4		39.3	
Aid Amounts (by type)						
Grant						
All		1,234		1,392		1,386
Recipients	45.2	2,728	49.7	2,799	45.0	3,065
Loan						
All		675		1,098		2,174
Recipients	23.4	2,889	31.9	3,444	42.8	5,075
Work-study						
All		51		59		56
Recipients	3.8	1,359	4.3	1,368	4.1	1,367
Aid Amounts (disaggregated)						
Federal grant						
All		617		684		543
Recipients	28.8	2,142	31.7	2,156	25.3	2,746
State grant		347		322		445
All						
Recipients	24.8	1,402	27.5	1,170	24.9	1,709
Other grant						
All		269		388		397
Recipients	20.4	1,319	23.4	1,656	23.4	1,695
Subsidized loan						
All						1,425
Recipients					37.3	3,822
Unsubsidized loan						
All						749
Recipients					17.6	4,257
Tuition						
Full tuition		2,435		2,823		3,354
Net tuition		1,200		1,436		1,968

TABLE 7.5 *Continued*

Variable and Coding	1990–91		1993–94		1996–97	
	Percentage	Mean	Percentage	Mean	Percentage	Mean
Persisting	91.5		90.6		89.9	
(N)	(3,939)		(3,890)		(3,772)	

Source: St. John, Hu, and Weber 2001, with CPI-U adjustment.

Note: Amounts adjusted to 1997–98 dollars using the CPI-U. Income was classified according to a statewide sample of students who reported income. Some columns may not total 100% due to rounding.

[a]The uncoded comparison variable in the sets of design variables used in the logistic regression models.

influenced by tuition increases. Indeed, the research indicates that high-income students are modestly influenced by tuition (St. John 1990a; St. John and Starkey 1995a).

UNDERSTANDING THE NEW CONTEXT

These studies illustrate that states now play a crucial role in keeping public colleges affordable for low-income students (chapter 8). When states invest substantial sums in their grant programs, they can either improve affordability or maintain affordability in the face of declines in federal student aid and rising tuition. However, most states do not invest sufficiently in student aid (Hossler et al. 1997; Paulsen and St. John 1997; see also chapter 8), and thus they need to consider ways of coordinating their financial strategies to ensure affordability. State grant programs can also keep private colleges affordable. In the Washington case, students in private colleges also benefited from state grants (St. John 1998). The direct investment in grants either adds to the total amount of grant aid students receive when they attend private colleges or reduces the average tuition for all students.

Step 4: Possible Explanations

In the early 1990s there were modest gains in total access for a majority of students, but gains in opportunity for low-income students were largely limited to two-year colleges. There were also modest increases in costs to the average taxpayer and targeted tax reductions for middle-class families with children in college. Thus, a substantial gap in opportunity opened as the taxpayer cost per student incrementally increased. Before

TABLE 7.6 Impact of Student Financial Aid on Persistence in Indiana's Public System of Higher Education in the 1990s: Summary of Delta-p Statistics for Aid Packages

Packages	1990-91		1993-94		1996-997	
	Delta-p	Sig.	Delta-p	Sig.	Delta-p	Sig.
African Americans						
Grants only	NS		0.068	***	0.090	***
Loans only	NS		0.066	*	0.108	***
Grants and loans	0.060	*	0.100	***	0.110	***
Other package	NS		0.109	***	0.111	***
Hispanics						
Grants only	NS		0.063	*	0.073	*
Loans only	NS		NS		0.082	*
Grants and loans	NS		0.091	***	0.102	***
Other package	NS		0.072	*	0.115	***
Whites						
Grants only	NS		NS		0.032	
Loans only	NS		NS		0.031	
Grants and loans	0.048	*	NS		0.046	*
Other package	NS		NS		0.060	*
All Students						
Grants only	0.051	**	NS		NS	
Loans only	NS		NS		NS	
Grants and loans	0.053	**	0.061	**	0.059	**
Other package	0.077	**	0.060	*	0.091	***

Sources: Statistics for all students from St. John, Hu, and Weber 2001. Statistics for racial/ethnic groups from Hu and St. John 2001.

Note: * Significant at the .05 level; ** significant at the .01 level; *** significant at the .001 level, *NS;* not significant.

reaching conclusions about the impact of changes in federal student aid policy, we need to consider other possible explanations.

SCHOOL REFORM

In the 1990s, the dominant pattern of school reform—an emphasis on national standards linked to increased use of standardized tests—continued. Many states engaged in high-stakes testing, requiring students to pass tests to graduate from high school. Recent research indicates that implementation of high-stakes graduation tests increased dropout in urban schools (Clinchy 2001). Using an NCES database, Jacobs (2001) found that dropout rates increased for low-income students in states that implemented high-stakes graduation tests. Minorities, poor students, and mainstreamed special education students fail these tests at high rates (Manset and Washburn 2003). States attempted to promote school improvement through high standards and professional development (St. John, Ward, and Laine 1999). These state strategies provided opportunities for schools to focus on improvement of educational outcomes. Although these reforms could be a contributing explanation for the overall increase in college participation rates by high school graduates, the opportunity gap between Hispanic and African American students and White students was not resolved by these strategies. If we use high graduation rates as an indicator of the efficiency of high-stakes testing, there is reason to question further the efficiency of such testing. In 1999–2000, only 70.6 percent of the high-school-age population had graduated high school, compared with 73.2 percent in 1990–91 (table A.7). The reform strategies of the 1980s may have contributed to this decline. There was some reduction for African Americans in the gap in college enrollment rates compared with Whites, but not for Hispanics. Given these trends, it simply is not possible to attribute gains in postsecondary access in the 1990s to school reform. But there is a compelling reason to conclude that the decline in federal grants was the reason for this new inequality.

Some evidence suggests that the new effort to promote research-based reading reforms and comprehensive school reforms (St. John, Manset, Chung, Musoba, et al. 2003; St. John, Manset, Chung, Simmons, et al. 2003) could eventually help reduce the opportunity gap, especially since several of these reforms have a history of success in schools that serve low-income students. It is too early to know whether these reforms will eventually influence postsecondary opportunity for low-income students.

POSTSECONDARY ENCOURAGEMENT

In the 1990s there were hopeful new developments in encouraging postsecondary education. The Indiana Career and Postsecondary Advancement Center began to provide information to high school students in the late 1980s (Hossler and Stage 1992; Stage and Hossler 2000), and by the middle of the decade these programs had apparently helped improve postsecondary participation rates in Indiana (Hossler and Schmit 1995). In spite of limited evidence that these new programs influenced changes in college choices by minority youths (Hossler, Schmit, and Vesper 1999), the state has maintained adequate aid to equalize opportunity for persistence by minority students (Hu and St. John 2001). Thus, there is compelling evidence that postsecondary encouragement coupled with adequate student aid can improve and help equalize opportunity.

More recently, the federal government has promoted postsecondary encouragement across the United States through GEAR UP. It is still too early to assess the impact of this new program. However, unless states invest sufficiently in their grant programs, there is reason to question whether this new program will actually improve equity in postsecondary opportunity. Preliminary research (Hossler, Schmit, and Vesper 1999; Perna 2000) does indicate that information could make a difference.

STUDENT FINANCIAL AID

Reductions in federal grants for low-income students help explain why the new inequality persisted through the 1990s. Growth in loans enabled more middle-class students to attend despite tuition increases, but there was restricted opportunity for low-income students, many of whom could not afford college even after taking out loans.

Has the high-tuition, high-loan environment plateaued in effectiveness? In the evaluation studies reviewed above, it was apparent that substantial state investments in grants kept colleges affordable in this new environment. Specifically, state grants helped equalize opportunities in Washington (St. John 1999) and Indiana (Hu and St. John 2001), two states that continued to expand their grant programs during the decade. These findings parallel the pattern observed in private colleges, where increased institutional investment in grants helped to maintain opportunity (McPherson and Schapiro 1997; Paulsen and St. John 1997).

Although too early to assess the impact of tax credits, there is reason to question whether they will have an impact on enrollment. They should be evaluated using frameworks similar to those used in the studies for other types of aid, reviewed above. Whether tax credits could directly influence postsecondary opportunity for low-income students is questionable, because families must spend the money before they can claim credit for the expenses. However, the primary benefit of tax credits may be that they provide targeted tax relief to middle-income families. This benefit should be weighed against general tax relief, not against grant aid. Indeed, it is despicable that low-income families were not even eligible for this targeted tax relief.

The two state cases illustrate the challenge that states face as they attempt to balance the interests of taxpayers and diverse college students. Indiana and Washington ranked relatively low on affordability and are low-tax states. Students and their families paid larger portions of college costs in these states than in the "average" state. Both states have substantial state grant programs. Indiana ranked seventh and Washington ranked tenth in total need-based grants per student in 1998–99 (DeSalvatore and Hughes 2000). Further, the evaluation studies show that these states managed to keep their investments in grants at a sufficient level to equalize opportunity for low-income students, in relation to students who did not need financial support. These case studies illustrate that a balance between the interests of conservative taxpayers and the goal of equal opportunity is possible. It takes a substantial state investment in grants, in addition to Pell grants, for states to equalize opportunity. Yet states can maintain this threshold of equal opportunity if they maintain a sufficient commitment to state grants.

Lower taxpayer support for institutions meant higher tuition in the 1990s. But if state grants are sufficient, affordability can be maintained at a lower cost to taxpayers than was evident in the 1970s. Average middle-income students may pay more, but their burden is mitigated by tax credits. In this environment, it is crucial that college-qualified low-income students have an opportunity to attend four-year colleges in their states.

Conclusion

The Clinton years did little to reduce the opportunity gap that emerged during the Reagan years. The introduction of tax credits did nothing to reclaim the emphasis on equal opportunity. Indeed, the review in this chapter adds to the chorus of voices that have questioned the achievements of the Clinton years (e.g., Schneider 2001; Talbet 2001).

How did federal financial aid and state finance policies change during the period?

The Clinton administration expanded loans, introducing new loan programs that included direct loans and unsubsidized loans. These changes substantially changed the use of loan capital. In addition, the new policy on tax credits changed the way student aid was financed. The direct effects of tax credits are not well understood and merit further study. The Clinton administration did not refocus student aid on equal opportunity.

Many states added merit-based grant programs. These programs did not address the new inequality in postsecondary opportunity.

How did the key indicators—access, equal opportunity, and efficient use of tax dollars—change during the period?

Access continued to improve in the 1990s, as indicated by higher-than-expected enrollment and increases in the participation rate for traditional-age high school graduates. Further, unlike in the 1980s, minorities and Whites improved their enrollment rates. But enrollment in public four-year colleges declined and was substantially below NCES's predictions, indicating that affordability had become especially problematic for this sector. The gap in opportunity compared with Whites declined slightly for African Americans but widened slightly for Hispanics. The new pattern in inequality persisted.

Taxpayer costs and benefits are especially difficult to untangle. The costs of student aid programs per student grew because of the growth in loans. Further, the impact of targeted tax relief for middle-income families is not yet visible. At the very least, these changes in policy indicate a tradeoff between the efficient use of tax dollars and the targeted relief of some taxpayers.

> Did evaluation studies of students enrolled during the period help explain the apparent relationship between changes in policy and changes in access, equal opportunity, and the efficient use of tax dollars?

The evaluation studies provided further insight into the consequences of the new financing strategies. The adequacy of financial aid was variable and depended largely on colleges' financial strategies and the amounts of government grant aid available to their students. The two state case studies illustrate that state grants were crucial in maintaining financial access in public four-year colleges.

> Did changes in K–12 schools or in postsecondary encouragement influence observed changes in access and equity?

Student financial aid was directly linked to the observed patterns of change in total enrollment. It appears that improvements in K–12 schools also contributed to the gains in access by improving college qualifications of high school graduates. However, the percentage of high school graduates declined slightly. Given the few changes in postsecondary encouragement that could have influenced enrollment during the 1990s, there is substantial evidence that student aid is central to financial access. Providing adequate grants for low-income students remains central to equalizing postsecondary opportunity once again. Loans and tax credits apparently increased the choices available to middle-income students, but did nothing to remedy the new opportunity gap.

While a number of high-profile federal student aid programs were introduced in the 1990s, new tax credits and expansion of loan programs failed to deal with the new inequities in postsecondary opportunity.

However, evidence did grow from evaluation studies during the decade that student grants were essential for equalizing opportunity (McPherson and Schapiro 1991, 1997; St. John 1990a,b, 1994, 1999). Yet there was an insufficient investment in grant aid. As is evident from these case studies, states can equalize opportunity if they make sufficient investments in grants.

The analyses of changes in access to higher education during the past three decades of the twentieth century (chapters 5–7) confirm two essential understandings about the role of finances. First, changes in federal student aid and state finance policies correspond with trends in access to higher education (i.e., participation rates) and equal opportunity (i.e., the gap in participation across income and racial/ethnic groups). Second, evaluation studies that examine the direct effects of aid packages confirm conclusions about the inadequacy of aid for low-income students since the late 1980s. There are sound reasons to argue that raising educational standards may have enabled more high school graduates to enroll in college, but the academic preparation rationale does not explain the new inequality. We need a more balanced approach than the one used by the National Center for Education Statistics (1997a,b) to build an understanding of the root causes of the new inequality.

The findings thus far do not resolve the dispute about the causes of the new inequality in access, the opportunity gap that opened after 1980. Critics of the efficacy of student aid could conclude that low-income students enroll at lower rates because they are not academically prepared (Finn 2001; NCES 1997a). Unfortunately, these analyses were based on a logical model that overlooked the role of finances. NCES finds a correlation between academic preparation and college enrollment but does not consider how finances influenced the marginal differences in enrollment rates reported in its own studies of access.

To further demonstrate that finances are the root cause of the new inequality, this chapter reexamines analyses reported by NCES in a study of the high school class of 1992. First, I propose a new logical model that carries forward the NCES's "academic pipeline" model but also considers the direct and indirect effects of financial aid. Second, I reexamine the statistics in the NCES report (1997a) using a balanced logical model. I conclude with some intermediate understandings of the role of finances.

A Balanced Logical Model

In efforts to untangle the relative effects of finances and academic preparation, we need to consider the dual nature of access. Studies that examine the causes and cures of the opportunity gap should examine two types of access—academic and financial (chapter 3):

—*Academic access* is determined by institutional admissions decisions, which are based on a review of students' academic qualifications and applications for admission.
—*Financial access* is the ability to afford initial and continuous enrollment; it can be influenced by governmental and institutional aid subsidies, college costs, and family incomes and savings.

This distinction helps clarify the role of family finances and student aid in the academic pipeline to college. The *balanced access model* (fig. 8.1) provides a more complete way of viewing financial and academic access that is consistent with the two main streams of prior research.

First, the definition of academic access is conceptually aligned with the criteria NCES uses to determine qualification. NCES's pipeline model (NCES 1996a, 1997a,b, 2001a,c) is integrated into the logic of the balanced access model. The new model adapts the NCES pipeline but recognizes that family finances and concerns about college costs have an influence on academic preparation. The reconstructed pipeline is as follows:

—Family background and income influence student expectations and plans.
—Student expectations and plans influence course-taking in high school.
—Taking college preparatory courses in high school influences students to take college entrance exams and to apply for college.
—Planning for college, taking preparatory courses in high school, and applying for college influence college enrollment (and destination).

This reconstructed pipeline is consistent with other, more balanced research on the college enrollment process (e.g., Hossler, Schmit, and Vesper 1999). In addition to acknowledging the role of this academic pipeline process, the balanced access model expands the logic of the NCES model to include the role of family finances, consistent with the definition of financial access given above.

Second, the balanced access model recognizes that tuition and financial aid both directly and indirectly influence enrollment decisions,

FIG. 8.1 The balanced access model.

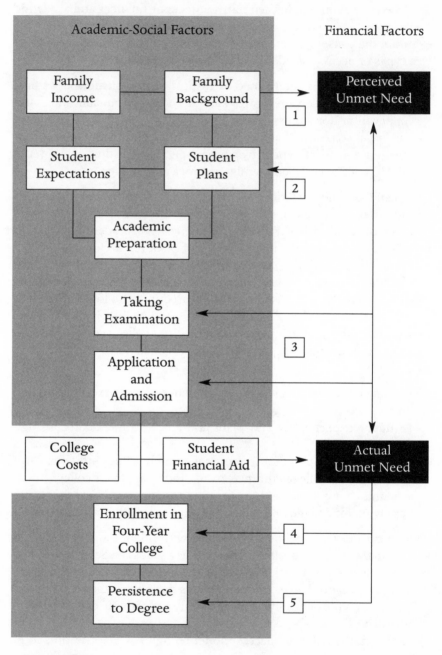

Source: St. John 2002.

UNDERSTANDING THE ACCESS CHALLENGE

consonant with the new definition of financial access. Consistent with more recent research on the role of finances (St. John, Cabrera, et al. 2000), the new model specifically recognizes the following linkages between family finances, financial aid, and college enrollment:

— Family income influences a family's concerns about college costs and ability to pay for college (linkage 1).
— Family concerns about finances, including concerns about costs after student grants (i.e., perceptions of unmet need), can influence college plans (linkage 2).
— Family concerns and postsecondary plans and expectations can influence which courses are taken in high school (academic preparation) (linkage 3).
— Unmet need, as measured by students' costs after student aid (net prices), can influence students' decisions to enroll (or not enroll) in four-year colleges after they have applied for and received aid offers (linkage 4).
— Inadequate aid (and unmet need) can influence continuous enrollment (persistence or dropout) by undergraduates (linkage 5).

Thus, the balanced access model offers a more complete way of viewing the effects of policy on academic access and financial access. This way of conceptualizing the role of finances is consistent with economic research on human capital, which shows that students consider their potential earnings, their potential debt, and their forgone earnings when they make educational choices (Becker 1964; Paulsen 2001a,b). By examining these linkages, we can untangle how finances influence academic preparation, college enrollment, and persistence.

The balanced access model identifies linkages between family finances and enrollment—parents' and students' perceptions of need and how these perceptions relate to the academic preparation process, as well as how aid might have a direct effect on student enrollment. Below I reexamine a recent NCES report (1997a) on college access by the high school class of 1992. By dissecting the analyses reported by NCES, we can see how its method—and the conclusions cited above—overlook evidence related to the role of finances that was present in NCES's own analyses.

The reexamination carries forward NCES's method of defining college qualification, an approach consonant with the concept of academic access used above. Since this reexamination focuses on students who met the commonly accepted criteria for access to four-year colleges, as defined by NCES, I did not examine the influence of perceptions of finances on academic preparation.[1] Instead, the reexamination focuses on *the influences of perceptions of finances on the academic pipeline for students who took the steps necessary to prepare for college.*

The influence of family finances on persistence (linkage 5) could not be examined using these reports, but the reviews of evaluation studies (chapters 5–7) provide confirmation of this proposition. Thus, due to constraints in prior analyses, only four of the linkages noted in the balanced access model were examined and are presented below.

This chapter reexamines statistics reported by NCES but does not reanalyze the impact of parental and student concerns about finances on academic preparation in high school; nor does it assess the impact of financial aid on access, controlling for academic preparation (as measured by NCES). A further reanalysis of NELS:88 would be needed to provide a more complete analysis of the impact of student aid.

Reexamination of NCES Analyses

In *Access to Higher Postsecondary Education for the 1992 High School Graduates*, NCES provided a thorough descriptive analysis of NELS:88, using its academic pipeline model to analyze the sequence of educational choices made by students in the high school class of 1992.[2] This section starts with a reexamination of NCES's analyses that defined the populations of college-qualified students from high-, middle-, and low-income families who were college qualified, using the logic of the balanced access model. Finally, I make a few observations about the status of academic and financial access for the high school class of 1992.

THE BOUNDARIES OF ACADEMIC ACCESS

In its comparisons of students in the high school class of 1992, NCES divided the population into three income groups and in each group differentiated students by academic qualifications. Its analyses treated students from families with incomes below $25,000 as low-income and students from families with incomes above $75,000 as high-income. The group between the two extremes, the middle half of the high school population in 1992, was treated as middle-income. NCES also developed

[1] Family concerns about finances could have discouraged some low-income students from preparing for college. And fewer low-income students may have taken college preparatory courses because they were aware of the inadequacy of financial aid and knew they could not afford to attend a public four-year college in their state.

[2] Throughout this section, all discussion of the NCES study refers to this NCES 1997a report.

a "college qualification index" (adapted from Adelman 1995) computed from five sources: combined SAT score, class rank (percentile), GPA from academic courses, percentile of NELS test (administered by the survey contractor), and the ACT composite score.[3] It divided the population into three groups: not college qualified, minimally/somewhat qualified, and highly/very highly qualified. My reanalysis uses these basic population breakdowns.

Combination of the middle two quartiles of the population into a single group artificially limits the analyses in some critical ways. Analyses of prior NCES surveys reveal substantial differences between lower-middle-income and upper-middle-income students (Paulsen and St. John 2002; St. John 1990a; St. John and Starkey 1995a). Students from lower-middle-income families made choices in what can be characterized as a working-class model—they were more likely to work longer hours than to use loans as a means of paying for college. Consequently they were disproportionately represented in community colleges, given the modest Pell grants after 1980 (Paulsen and St. John 2002). In contrast, the upper-middle-income group was more substantially influenced by loans (Paulsen and St. John 2002; St. John and Starkey 1995a). By combining the two "middle" income groups, the NCES report obfuscates the substantial difference in educational opportunities between working-class families and upper-middle-income families.

When the three income groups were compared on the college qualification index (fig. 8.2), there were differences in qualification by income group, as would be expected. About 86 percent of the high-income group was college qualified, compared with 68 percent of the middle-income group and 53 percent of the low-income group. Conversely, about one-half of the low-income group was not qualified for college (48 percent), compared with about one-third of the middle-income group (32 percent) and a lower proportion of high-income students (14 percent). This means that nearly one-half of the low-income population was not considered in the analyses of financial linkages below, since this reexamination controls for the influence of academic preparation. It is entirely possible that concerns about finances influenced many of these students to prepare for employment after high school (i.e., to take vocational courses) rather than to prepare for college while in high school.

[3] NCES (1997a) provides great detail on the methods used to calculate the index, including how it treated missing data. This reexamination of NCES's reported statistics uses, and therefore implicitly accepts, NCES's index. A reexamination of this index may be needed, but it is important to report analyses using this index so as to build an understanding of the role of finances, controlling for academic preparation as defined by NCES.

FIG. 8.2 College qualifications of the high school class of 1992, by income group.

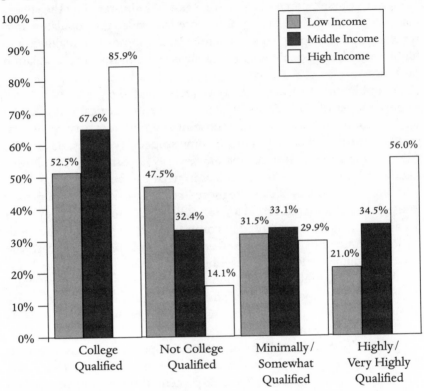

Source: NCES 1997a, 29, table 15.

The extent of college qualifications also differed across the three income groups. Most of the high-income students who were qualified were actually highly qualified (56 percent of the high-income group), while nearly equal portions of those in the middle-income group were minimally/somewhat qualified and highly/very highly qualified. In contrast, more of the low-income group who were college qualified were minimally/somewhat qualified (32 percent) than highly/very highly qualified (21 percent). However, since college entrance exams were included within this index, failure to take entrance exams could explain why some low-income students were grouped in the minimally prepared group rather than in the highly/very highly prepared group.[4] In the analyses

[4] Further, if some low-income students who were otherwise prepared did not take entrance exams because of concerns about finances, then NCES's analyses and interpretations have even more logical problems.

UNDERSTANDING THE ACCESS CHALLENGE

FIG. 8.3 Enrollment of college-qualified students in four-year college, by income group and race/ethnicity.

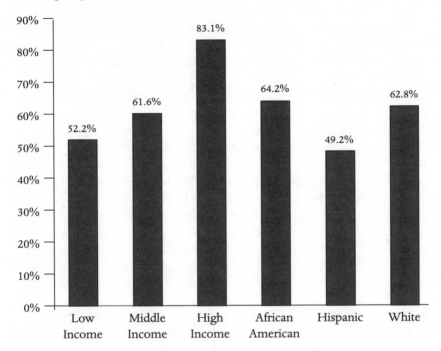

Source: NCES 1997a, 37, table 20.

below I explore whether these decisions were related to family concerns about college costs, an explanation overlooked in the NCES analyses.

For students who have prepared to go to college, the extent of college qualification should influence destination and especially the selectivity of colleges they attend, but not *whether* they attend. Indeed, as the trend analysis above reveals, there was once near-equal opportunity for college participation by high school graduates across racial/ethnic groups. However, for college-qualified students in the high school class of 1992, race/ethnicity played a major role in determining college destination (fig. 8.3). About one-half (52 percent) of the low-income college-qualified students attended four-year colleges compared with more than three-quarters (83 percent) of the high-income group. The percentage of college-qualified African Americans who enrolled in four-year colleges (64 percent) was slightly higher than the percentages for Whites (63 percent) and substantially higher than the percentages for Hispanics (49 percent) and low-income students (52 percent). In spite of having lower incomes on average, African Americans were more likely to take advantage of opportunities for college. The new inequality for college-qualified students appears to be directly related to income and unrelated to race/ethnicity. However, since larger percentages of African Americans and Hispanics than Whites are from families with low incomes, they are disproportionately affected by the decline in student aid.

If our purpose is to estimate the impact of family finances on the pipeline to college for students who prepared for college, it is appropriate to limit the analysis to college-qualified students. Therefore, the remainder of this section considers college-qualified students by income group. It is also appropriate to compare college-qualified students from low-income families with college-qualified students from high-income families, because low-income students have substantially higher unmet need than do high-income students. While the figures below represent the three income groups, we are most concerned about the disparity in opportunity between low-income and high-income students,[5] because the middle-income group includes some students with unmet financial need (i.e., lower-middle-income students) and the high-income group includes very few students with unmet need. This approach—comparing high-income and low-income students—provides insight into the effects of family income and perceptions of college affordability on enrollment by students who meet generally accepted criteria for academic access.

In its analyses, NCES did not consider the possibility that perceptions of financial problems could affect a family's decision about academic preparation or college enrollment. Instead, NCES considered the steps in the academic pipeline process, observing only slight erosion in the percentages of students who took the exams and applied and then actually attended college, from 91 to 83 percent of the high-income group and from 62 to 52 percent of the low-income group. NCES concluded that to expand access, more students should be encouraged to take the right courses in high school and to take the entrance exams and apply for college.

FINANCIAL ACCESS FOR LOW-INCOME COLLEGE-QUALIFIED STUDENTS

The information reported by NCES allows a reexamination of the role of parents' concerns about college costs, as an indicator of family perceptions of unmet need. First, I examine the relationship between income and

[5] Low-income students have a high average amount of unmet financial need after grant aid, while high-income students, on average, have little or no unmet need. Middle-income students also have unmet need after grants, but they can use loans to pay for these costs. NCES (1997a) did not report the unmet need for the three groups. However, it did report that low-income college students had substantial costs after grants and loans, a compelling indication of financial problems that were overlooked as a possible cause for the disparity in access.

concerns about finances for low-income students; then I try to untangle the effects of these concerns on subsequent steps in the academic pipeline for college-qualified students in the three income groups. This examination provides insight into the limits of financial access for some students who have achieved the generally accepted standards for academic access. Evidence related to four of the five specific linkages is reexamined below.

Linkage 1: Family Income and Concerns about Financing College

Other researchers using NELS:88 found that family resources had a substantial effect on who took responsibility for saving for college (Steelman and Powell 1993) and subsequent educational outcomes in high school (Downey 1995). Similar findings are evident from studies using state databases (Hossler, Schmit, and Vesper 1999). This linkage between family financial means and concerns about finances is central to the logic of the balanced access model, but was completely overlooked by the NCES model of academic access. If concerns about financing college are greater among parents in low-income families, then these concerns may affect preparation for college.

The NCES report included analyses of parental concerns about finances but failed to consider whether these concern could have influenced any subsequent educational outcomes. Parental and family concerns about college costs varied substantially across the three groups (fig. 8.4). Most college-qualified children from low-income families were very concerned about college costs and financial aid (79 percent), but only a small percentage of children of parents with high incomes (16 percent) shared these concerns. Similarly, most children from low-income families were concerned about financing college (69 percent), but only a few of their peers with low financial need shared these concerns (20 percent). These results indicate that both parents and children in low-income families were concerned about college costs. NCES attributed these concerns to poor information, despite reporting information on substantial net cost after student aid for low-income students (reviewed as part of linkage 4 below).

More than half (52.7 percent) of the middle-income parents of college-qualified high school students were also concerned about finances, as were about half of their children (47.1 percent). Recent research (e.g., Paulsen and St. John 2002) suggests there would also be substantial differences in parental concern between lower-middle-income and upper-middle-income families, but it is not possible to test this proposition because NCES analyses aggregated these groups.

Thus, while the low-income students in the high school class of 1992 were seniors in high school, aware of constraints of government student aid, they shared concerns with their parents about financing college.

FIG. 8.4 Concerns about college costs and financial aid among college-qualified students and their parents, by income group.

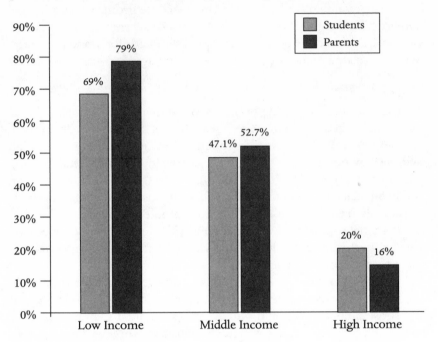

Source: NCES 1997a, 54, table 27.

Given recent research on the impact of perceptions of finances (Cabrera, Nora, and Castaneda 1992; Paulsen and St. John 1997, 2002; St. John, Cabrera, et al. 2000), there is reason to expect that parents' concerns about finances would influence students' plans and expectations in eighth and twelfth grades.

Linkage 2: How Do Family Income and Concerns about College Costs Relate to Postsecondary Expectations/Plans?

One way in which concerns about finances influence the new inequalities is that some children with these concerns reduce their expectations. From prior analyses of longitudinal databases, there is little doubt about a relationship between expectations and college enrollment by minorities (Carter 1999; St. John 1991b). It is also clear that high school students from low-income families fall short of their aspirations compared with students from wealthier families (Hanson 1994; Hearn 2001a; Hossler, Schmit, and Vesper 1999). A reexamination of college expectations in eighth grade and college expectations in twelfth grade reveals a

UNDERSTANDING THE ACCESS CHALLENGE

FIG. 8.5 Expectations and plans about college attendance among college-qualified students, by income group.

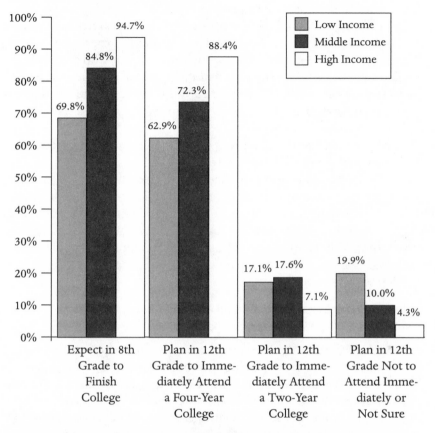

Note that for students planning to attend four-year and two-year colleges, percentages are adjusted from the original report to take into account the percentage not planning to attend immediately after high school.
Source: NCES 1997a, 36, table 19.

relationship between these intermediate outcomes and family income (fig. 8.5).

We see differences across groups in the level of postsecondary expectations, especially for students planning four-year degrees. Nearly equal percentages of middle-income and low-income college-qualified students planned in twelfth grade to attend two-year colleges (17.1 and 17.6 percent, respectively), with relatively few high-income college-qualified students making these plans (only 7.1 percent). Only slightly fewer of the low-income students in the college-qualified group planned in twelfth grade to attend college than expected in the eighth grade to finish college. A substantially larger percentage of middle-income students changed their plans: 84.8 percent expected in eighth grade to complete college, compared with 72.3 percent who planned as twelfth graders to attend four-year colleges. Thus, academic experiences in high school were not a deterrent for low-income children who took college preparatory courses. This suggests that the emphasis on academic preparation that was already in place in the early 1990s had a positive influence on the expectations of low-income students who followed the narrow academic path.

Unfortunately, nearly 20 percent of the low-income college-qualified students when seniors did not plan to attend college. However, only 69.8 percent expected as eighth graders to complete four years of college. There was no drop in expectations for these children. Instead, they took the steps to prepare for college even if they feared they could not afford to go. Given this situation, it is remarkable that the NCES study suggested that if these students had only paid for expensive applications while in high school and had paid to take entrance exams, the access problem would be solved.

Linkage 3: How Does Family Income Influence Students' College Entrance Testing and College Application Behavior?

Much of NCES's misinterpretation of the descriptive data of academic access results from placing too much emphasis on entrance examinations and college applications in twelfth grade (i.e., applying to college in advance). Many two-year and four-year colleges do not require students to make applications in advance. Some do not require college entrance examinations. This limitation of the higher education market was completely overlooked in NCES's analysis. Indeed, in many states, less selective, essentially open-door colleges are located within driving distance of most urban centers. Since these colleges cost less to attend, it is reasonable to consider whether students who are concerned about college costs would decide to attend local colleges that did not require advance applications. Indeed, considerations of location close to home and close to work are central to the college choices made by many low-income and lower-middle-income students (Paulsen and St. John 2002). Since NCES's pipeline criteria treated entrance exams and applying for college as central to access, we need to consider how family finances interacted with these steps in the pipeline to college.

The NCES statistics on the relationship between family finances and test-taking and college application by college-qualified students (fig. 8.6) reveal a substantial differential between low-income and high-income

FIG. 8.6 Variability in test-taking and application among college-qualified students, by income group.

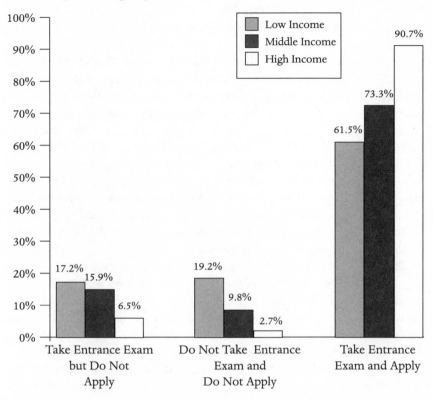

Source: NCES 1997a, 42, table 22.

students in the percentages who took entrance examinations and applied for college. College-qualified students from high-income families were more likely than similarly qualified low-income students to take entrance exams and apply (91 percent vs. 62 percent). However, the percentage of low-income students who met these criteria was substantially lower than the percentage planning in twelfth grade to attend college. Readers of the NCES report must ask themselves: if low-income college-qualified students paid the advance application fees required by these colleges, would they have received the financial support they needed to support continuous enrollment? When arguing that inducing more students to apply in advance was the answer to the opportunity gap, NCES essentially assumed that finances were adequate.

The statistics reviewed thus far seem consistent with a sequential student-choice process that was realistic and aware of college costs, especially for the low-income college-qualified group. Making an advance college application is not a sorting criterion for who goes to college, but rather an indicator of which students are willing to pay the extra costs of institutions that require advance applications after paying for the entrance exams. Not only must students pay a fee to take these exams, but the more selective colleges that require the exams also charge higher prices. Thus, students who are concerned about college costs (i.e., most low-income students) would be less likely to go through these steps. This conclusion is confirmed by the analysis of application and exam-taking as distinct behaviors. Fully 17 percent of low-income students took the exams but did not apply in advance. These students made a realistic assessment, one consistent with the cost information reported below. Moreover, 16 percent of middle-income students took the exams and did not apply in advance. In contrast, only 7 percent of high-income students took the exams and did not apply in advance—and they could afford to do so. It appears that college costs may have influenced where students concerned about costs actually applied.

In combination, these findings document that family finances were associated with students' decisions to apply to colleges that required applications before enrollment. College-qualified low-income students were cautious about taking the exams and still more cautious about applying for college after they took exams. It appears these students made prudent decisions, given family finances and expected costs after student aid. These statistics indicate that test-taking and especially advance college applications are constrained by finances. It would be shortsighted to encourage low-income students to pay for entrance exams and for applications to four-year colleges when their realistic assessments of college costs would lead them to believe they could not afford to attend these colleges.

This reexamination of the final two steps in NCES's pipeline raises serious questions about whether advance college applications should be viewed as a "necessary step" for access. Rather, this appears to be a financial barrier related to the costs of attending the expensive colleges and universities that require advance applications. Recall that this measure is derived from a question posed to high school seniors. There is good reason to eliminate this measure as a sorting criterion for the measurement of "college qualification." This huge misconception about college choice was deeply embedded in NCES's pipeline model and further illustrates how NCES's analyses obfuscated the relationship between student aid and college destination—the most appropriate indicators of whether students who are qualified academically can afford to attend four-year colleges.

FIG. 8.7 Average college costs for low-income 1992 high school graduates, by type of postsecondary institution.

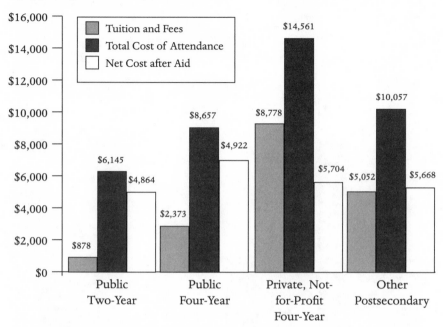

"Other postsecondary" means other than a four-year college.
Source: NCES 1997a, 13, table 6.

Linkage 4: How Does Unmet Need Relate to Enrollment (and College Destinations)?

The analyses using the NCES access model overlooked the question: *did family finances—low incomes and the prospect of high costs after student aid—influence enrollment behavior?* The balanced access model, consistent with economic theory, assumes that prices and subsidies have a direct influence on college enrollment. To test the direct effects of student aid on financial access using the definition above, one would have to analyze the effects of aid offers on enrollment and the effects of aid on continuous enrollment. However, NCES did provide information that can be used to build an understanding of the direct effects of student aid.

The NCES analyses failed to consider whether student aid had a direct effect on enrollment when they concluded that not taking entrance exams and not applying to college in advance were the primary reasons for low college attendance for low-income college-qualified students. However, NCES did present information on the net costs of attending after student aid for low-income students (fig. 8.7). The average net cost

FIG. 8.8 Enrollment behavior (type of college selected) by college-qualified students, by income group.

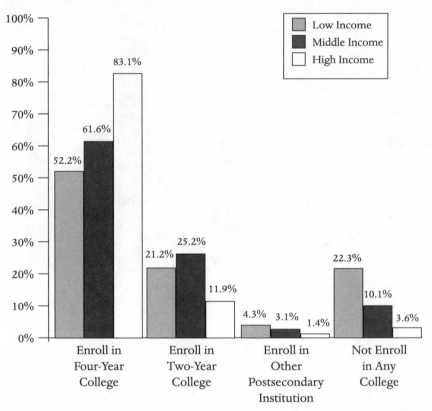

"Other postsecondary" means other than a four-year college.
Source: NCES 1997a, 37, table 20.

facing low-income students at a public four-year college, after grants and loans, was $4,922. Further, low-income students consistently faced costs after grants and loans that were higher than the tuition charges of the colleges they attended. Parents who were concerned about costs were well informed indeed.

The cost after aid varied from $4,864 in public two-year colleges to $5,704 in private four-year colleges. These costs are extremely high, given that these students were from families with a total income of $25,000 *or less*, mostly less. According to the NCES report, even after borrowing an average of $3,455, these students faced, on average, an annual cost that was more than 20 percent of family income. Thus, parents had valid reasons for concern about college costs. There is also reason to expect that knowledge of net cost could deter enrollment by college applicants and reduce persistence rates by students who did enroll.

The NCES report also provided an analysis of the enrollment rates for students in the three income groups (fig. 8.8). College-qualified high-income students were much more likely to enroll in four-year colleges. Substantially more of the qualified high-income students (83 percent) than either middle-income or low-income students (62 and 52 percent, respectively) enrolled in four-year colleges. In contrast, college-qualified middle-income students were substantially more likely than either low-income or high-income students to enroll in two-year colleges. Twenty-five percent of the middle-income students attended two-year colleges, compared with 21 percent of low-income students and only 12 percent of high-income students.

In contrast, college-qualified low-income students were substantially less likely to attend four-year colleges (52 percent vs. 83 percent for high-income students). Indeed, fully 22 percent of the low-income students who took the courses necessary to attend college had not attended by two years after high school, compared with only 10 percent of the middle-income and 4 percent of the high-income group.

This reexamination indicates that family income and the inadequacy of financial aid both had an influence on college destinations. Since a larger percentage of the high-income students were in the most highly qualified group, achievement in high school probably also had an influence. Yet, the quartiles for college qualification used by NCES included college entrance exams as a measure in the index. Given the costs associated with entrance examinations and advance applications—coupled with the high cost after aid for low-income students attending four-year colleges—these criteria seem biased toward the upper class, toward those who can afford college without student aid. By including these measures in its pipeline criteria, NCES obfuscated the detrimental effects of college costs and unmet need on students' enrollment patterns.

In its report, NCES argued for encouraging more low-income students to take (and pay for) college entrance exams, a view that seems misguided given the net costs facing those students who did eventually attend. Many low-income and lower-middle-income students attend less expensive colleges that do not fit the analytic model used by NCES's studies of college access using NELS:88. Fully 81 percent of the college-qualified low-income group took the exam, but this reanalysis reveals that 22 percent of this group did not attend any institution. Further, many low-income students met the qualifications and took the entrance examination but decided they could not afford to attend any college. The pipeline analysis led to fundamentally misleading conclusions about access, conclusions that entirely overlooked the role of finances.

Understanding the Role of Finances

In this reexamination I have reviewed the statistical analyses of the NELS:88 cohort previously reported by NCES (1997a). Fortunately, NCES provided statistical analyses of sufficient detail to permit this reexamination. It leaves little doubt about the central role of financial aid in promoting and prohibiting equal opportunity. Finances have both direct and indirect influences on enrollment behavior. The most substantial effects of finances are indirect. Low-income families—parents and children—are concerned about college costs. In eighth grade, many of these students expect they will not be able to afford college, yet they take the steps to prepare. In twelfth grade, 20 percent do not expect to go to college. Those students who do go to college face costs that are in excess of 20 percent of their families' total income. Yet NCES concludes that if more of these students paid the fees required to apply to college in advance and to take college entrance exams, there would not be an access problem. Something is seriously wrong with this narrow interpretation of the data.

There is substantial evidence of a correlation between the types of courses taken in high school and college enrollment (e.g., Adelman 1999; NCES 1997a,b, 2000; Pelavin and Kane 1990). However, as this reexamination reveals, this correlation was greater for high-income students than for low-income students. A substantial percentage of low-income college-qualified students did not attend college. During the 1990s, more than fourteen hundred thousand low-income students who took the right courses in high school were not able to attend college.[6]

If analysts fail to consider the role of finances, as was the case with the NCES analyses reviewed above, they can reach false conclusions about the causes of the opportunity gap. In fact, NCES has consistently focused on the role of academic preparation in college enrollment, using a narrowly conceived pipeline model that overestimates the role of aca-

---

[6] In a reanalysis of NELS:88, John B. Lee (2001) estimated that 140,606 college-qualified low-income students in the class of 1992 did not attend for financial reasons. Given the increased size of high school classes during the decade and the decreased purchasing power of Pell grants, it is reasonable to assume that this is the annual number of low-income college-qualified students who could not enroll. Using Lee's estimate as a base, 1.4 million is a conservative estimate of the number of low-income college-qualified students who did not enroll in the 1990s due to inadequate grant aid.

demic preparation and ignores the role of student financial aid. Since the federal government's primary role in higher education is to fund student grant programs that promote equal educational opportunity, it is crucial that policy researchers consider the role of finances. Given the serious deficiencies in the analyses of NELS:88 to date, this database should be reanalyzed,[7] with a focus on the influence of finances and academic preparation.

In conclusion, the evidence that changes in federal and state finance policies induced the new disparity in postsecondary educational opportunity seems beyond dispute. The facts are as follows:

—Changes in state and federal finance policy after 1980 correspond with the opportunity gap between high-income and low-income students (and between Whites and minorities) that opened after 1980 (chapters 6 and 7).
—Evaluation studies that assess the effects of aid packages on enrollment persistence confirm the inadequacy of student aid for low-income students in the late 1980s (chapter 6) and 1990s (chapter 7 and this chapter).
—Improvements in academic preparation since 1980 may explain increased enrollment rates by high school graduates since 1985 (chapters 6 and 7), but, due to the inadequacy of financial aid, not all groups of prepared students benefited from these gains (chapters 6 and 7 and this chapter).
—A reexamination of NCES statistics of the high school class of 1992 reveals that more than 22 percent of the college-qualified students could not enroll, probably because of family concerns about finances and larger levels of unmet need after grants and loans (this chapter).

These analyses, in combination, provide clear and compelling evidence of greater inequality in postsecondary opportunity than in prior decades and evidence that this new inequality was caused by the decline in need-based grants rather than by a failure of school reform. A better coordination of public financial strategies is essential to address the new inequality.

---

[7] This chapter reexamines statistics reported by NCES. However, NCES did not consider the impact of family concerns about finances on academic preparation, nor did it examine persistence during the two years of college for which it had data. A more complete reanalysis should use the balanced access model to assess the impact of concerns about finances and financial aid on college destination and persistence.

PART II   Meeting the Access Challenge

A second purpose of *Refinancing the College Dream* is to inform policy-makers about refinancing and educational reform strategies that can improve access and equalize opportunity. The current patterns of finance are simply no longer viable if our goals are to expand postsecondary access and close the opportunity gap. To resolve the new inequality in postsecondary opportunity, we must expand opportunity for college-qualified students from low-income families. The evaluation of the effects of policies adopted during the past three decades, presented in part I, built an understanding of how changes in financing strategies influenced financial access for the majority, equality of opportunity across groups, and taxpayer costs. These analyses also provide a basis for identifying educational reforms that might expand academic and financial access, moving American society toward a more balanced approach to educational policy and finance.

In part II, I develop the contingency theory of higher education finance and use it to examine refinancing and educational reform strategies for expanding access to higher and other postsecondary education. Chapter 9 examines changes in the rationales for public funding and introduces the contingency theory of finance. Chapter 10 further explains how institutions and states can use the contingency approach to refine financing strategies and recommends a federal strategy to facilitate this process. Finally, chapter 11 analyzes and recommends strategies for improving academic preparation, enhancing postsecondary encouragement, and expanding public systems to improve access.

How can American society expand opportunity for more students to attend higher education institutions, in a way that is *equitable* for low-income students and *just* for students from middle-class families and for taxpayers? While this question may seem straightforward, it is actually quite complex. The answer requires balancing the interests of three very different groups: taxpayers, the majority of students (traditional-age, middle-class), and students with substantial financial need. The interests and needs of these groups vary from state to state, which complicates efforts to achieve a balanced approach to higher education finance. And these groups have different values, concerns, and interests.

The strategies used by states to address the interests of the three groups have changed over time. The low-tuition philosophy widely used through the 1960s provided access at high taxpayer costs per student. In the past three decades, a few states moved toward high tuition and high grants, an approach that expands access and maintains equity at a lower cost to taxpayers than the traditional low-tuition approach (chapter 6). However, most states moved incrementally toward high tuition and did not make sufficient investments in grants to maintain equity, given the decline in federal grants. While federal need-based grant aid once equalized postsecondary opportunity for students from low-income families, federal grants are no longer sufficient to meet this goal (Advisory Committee 2001a,b; Kane 1999, 2001; McPherson and Schapiro 1997).

This affordability crisis comes at a time when higher education in the United States is facing another challenge: to substantially expand access to postsecondary education, many study groups argue, about 90 percent of the population should have at least some college education (Boesel and Fredland 1999; Council for Aid to Education 1997; McCabe 2000). Not all analysts agree that access should expand this extensively (e.g., Finn 2001; NCES 1997a), but, in either case, we remain a long way from the goal. Further expansion of postsecondary education is still needed for economic development in many states. In 1999, about 45 percent of college-age high school graduates attended an institution of higher education (NCES 2001b). This percentage would have to grow to about 75 percent to reach the goal of 90 percent of the college-age population with at least some college education. There would also need to be increased college participation by adults who have an inadequate education. Expanding access would challenge the capacity of taxpayers to fund public systems of higher education at current rates and to provide student aid for students in both public and private colleges. It could require a near doubling of the nation's postsecondary funding, unless taxpayer dollars are used more efficiently.

Even for those who do not argue that the college participation rate should be substantially increased, it is beyond dispute that opportunity should be equalized for low-income students who are academically prepared for college (chapter 8). Currently, given the unmet needs for financial aid, the price of attending public four-year colleges in most states is too high to ensure financial access (chapters 7 and 8). Increased public investment is needed to rectify this injustice, even if the public lacks the will to expand college participation beyond the current level.

The goal of expanding access comes at a time when the structure of public finance has broken down. There are many academically qualified students who cannot afford continuous enrollment (chapters 7 and 8). Ironically, public four-year colleges are now less affordable for low-income students than at any point in the past half-century. As stated in a recent report by the Advisory Committee on Student Financial Assistance, *Access Denied: Restoring the Nation's Commitment to Equal Educational Opportunity*, "The opportunity gap for low-income students that exists today stands in stark contrast to the unparalleled prosperity of many American families and the large budget surpluses of the nation. In order to address the current opportunity gap and avoid a potential access crisis in the future, the federal government must renew the nation's commitment to a *broad access strategy*" (2001a, vi; emphasis added).

Financing Transitions in Access

This is the third time in its history that the United States has faced a challenge to substantially expand access to higher education. The first of these transitions took place in the late nineteenth century. After the Civil War, the federal government provided incentives for states to fund colleges as a means of expanding access to technical and professional education. The Land Grant Acts set in motion a pattern of funding universities with state tax dollars (Jencks and Riesman 1968; Johnson 1989), a pattern of public finance that has enabled state universities to educate a professional middle class in all states in the union. Over time, the middle class expanded and demands arose to invest in teachers' colleges and, later, in comprehensive colleges that educated students across the middle-class professions.

After the land grant colleges were created, the United States had an oversupply of higher education opportunity, since the private universities were already well developed (Johnson 1989; Marsden 1994). At the time, some economists argued that funding students was more appropriate than funding institutions, but the basic strategy of funding institutions was chosen (Marsden 1994). Both public and private colleges adapted to the shortfall in demand by providing student grants from their own resources (Johnson 1989; Marsden 1994). Thus, funding of students and institutions has a long history, but the prevailing approach to funding access was direct subsidies to public institutions. However, institutional subsidies were not extended to previously existing "private" colleges, as they eventually were in Canada (Lang 2002).

The second major transition in access occurred in the middle of the twentieth century: the transition to mass higher education (Trow 1974). This movement was accompanied by another transition in financial strategies. After World War II, American society responded to new pressures to expand, again through a pattern of federal incentives and state responses. The federal government funded the GI Bill, the first major student aid program (Finn 1978). States taxed their citizens to build mass systems of higher education that helped expand the American middle class. Then, with the National Defense Education Act of 1958 and the Higher Education Act of 1965, the federal government developed a role of funding students and making strategic investments in areas of high national priority. Through these new student aid programs, the federal government provided funding to low-income students to equalize opportunity and provided incentives for states to start need-based grant programs. In particular, the Education Amendments of 1972 created a State Student Incentive Grant program, providing matching funds for states' need-based grants (Gladieux and Wolanin 1976).

The structure of public finance used in the 1970s was remarkably successful at equalizing opportunity for low-income and middle-income students (chapter 5). While a "low tuition" philosophy was adhered to in most states through 1980, before the 1970s a large number of potential students could not afford the direct costs of attending (i.e., tuition, books, room and board). The federal student aid programs started in the 1960s and expanded in the 1970s used needs-analysis methods to assess the extent of student need (Hearn 1993; see also chapter 5). When the federal programs were adequately funded, they provided sufficient aid to equalize the opportunity for college-qualified low-income students to enroll, which had become a goal of federal student aid programs (Gladieux and Wolanin 1976; Finn 1978; National Commission on Financing 1973). However, this basic structure of public finance eroded after 1980 (McPherson and Schapiro 1997; St. John 1994; see also chapters 6 and 7). States reduced their subsidies to institutions at the same time that the federal government reduced its investment in need-based grants. Thus, the commitment of states and the federal government to ensuring equal access to the nation's system of higher education eroded, contributing to the new affordability crisis confronting American society.

Now, in the early twenty-first century, states and the federal government are faced with new calls to expand access to higher education. However, there is no political consensus about what the state and federal roles should be in expanding access and keeping colleges affordable. For the last half of the nineteenth century and first three-quarters of the twentieth century, there was a broad consensus that taxpayers should fund higher education. Initially, states taxed their citizens to subsidize colleges, which provided educational opportunity at a low cost. This was similar to the way in which states and local governments taxed citizens to pay for public K–12 schools (Theobald 2003). The old consensus was held together by complementary beliefs in economic development (a conservative political interest) and expanding opportunity (a liberal political interest). This consensus was forged during the progressive period in the late nineteenth century and continued through the creation of mass public systems in the middle of the twentieth century (Becker 1964; Blau and Duncan 1967). Ironically, the old consensus broke down in the 1980s, before this most recent call to expand access.

In the twenty-first century, a broad access strategy must include a commitment to subsidize college-qualified students who cannot afford the direct costs of attending, or *financial access*, and a commitment to provide adequate academic preparation for all students, or *academic access*. However, there is currently no rationale for public funding that is broadly accepted by both conservatives and liberals. All too frequently the debate is framed by juxtaposing the interests of wealthy taxpayers against the interests of low-income students (e.g., Finn 2001). The policy battles in the past two decades have been over which coalition will attract middle-class voters. In fact, the focus of federal student financial aid has shifted to the middle class. In the 1980s the Republicans emphasized loans, a form of aid that appealed to middle-class families (chapter 6). Then, in the late 1990s, the Clinton administration used tax credits to appeal to middle-income families (chapter 7). Neither strategy adequately addressed the financial needs of low-income families. In the 2000 presidential election, the Al Gore campaign argued that expanding tax credits for the middle class was the best way to expand access, but this argument ignored the real access problem.

In this context, a new rationale is needed to build a new consensus. Rawls's theory of justice provided a starting point for examining the interests of the middle class, the poor, and the wealthy in American society, as they relate to the current rationales for public funding of higher education. My argument is that a broad new coalition of interests will be needed—one that balances the interests of diverse economic groups in American society—if this country is to solve the financial dilemma facing higher education: the new inequality in postsecondary opportunity. If we have a rationale that can hold a new consensus together, then it should be possible to develop new, more workable financial strategies. Toward this end, in this chapter I propose a contingency theory of finance, which requires analysts and policymakers to work cooperatively, in a political policy environment, to craft new policies that create a broad access strategy. But first, I examine how we reached the point where the rationales for public funding were reduced to appeals to the self-interest of the middle class.

Changing Rationales for Public Funding

Through most of the twentieth century, the argument that funding for public higher education would both educate professionals (in engineering, education, law, and other professions) and fuel economic development provided a rationale for taxpayer support in states. The priority in most states was clearly placed on educating elite professionals (Halstead 1974). The argument that "investment" in higher education stimulated economic development helped maintain conservative support, while the argument about expanding opportunity to new generations of students helped maintain liberal support. The theory of human capital (Becker 1964) supported both rationales. Before 1980, conservatives tended to favor more limited spending, while liberals tended to argue for more rapid expansion of opportunity and public spending (St. John 1994). Thus, the old common ground held together through the movement to mass higher education in the 1960s, much as it did when public systems were first created nearly a century earlier. In the 1970s, state spending on public colleges continued to expand, providing low-cost opportunity to attend a mass public system, while federal spending on student grants also expanded rapidly and more diverse groups gained access to higher education. This rationale for investment is frequently expressed along the lines used by Lombardi and Capaldi: "Given the almost universal recognition that university education and research produce a high return on the aggregate investment society makes in them, we should accept the proposition that the individuals and political units and subunits that pay for higher education receive a high return on their private or public investment" (1996, 87).

During the expansion in opportunity in the 1960s and 1970s, most states held to a low-tuition philosophy, making an adequate "investment" in higher education based on this rationale (chapter 5). In this same period, the federal government held to a strategy of providing aid to students with substantial financial need. However, in the late 1970s, the middle class began to argue that they, too, deserved financial relief. Many Republicans and conservatives of that time supported tax credits for higher education, basing their argument on conservative economic theory (Friedman 1962). Instead, Jimmy Carter promoted extending access to grants and loans to middle-class students, an argument that became the foundation for the Middle Income Student Assistance Act of 1978. Had it been fully funded, MISAA would have stimulated massive expansion of spending on student aid programs. But the new provisions for student aid programs were never fully funded.

THE CONSERVATIVE CRITIQUE

In 1981, Ronald Reagan came into office with a "new conservative" philosophy. The new conservatives argued that spending on social programs, including student grant programs, had gone too far, that it was fairer to taxpayers to reduce spending and taxes than to continue funding these programs at historical levels. As the Reagan years proceeded, leaders in the Reagan administration argued that colleges were greedy (Bennett 1986, 1987; Finn 1988a,b) and that they raised tuition to increase the amount of student aid they received (Bennett 1987; Carnes 1987). There was a large reduction in federal grants and a massive expansion in loans during the decade (chapter 7). Given these developments, we could ask: *was the attack on colleges mounted to disguise the retreat from the federal commitment to equal opportunity?* While this question merits thought, reflecting on it feeds into the class warfare that prevails in policy debates about higher education.

As the analysis in chapter 6 illustrates, the efficiency of the national system of higher education did improve in the 1980s, at least if we use tax dollars per student as a measure of efficiency. In addition, access expanded (i.e., participation rates rose) during both the 1980s and 1990s. Thus it is possible to expand access *and* make more efficient use of tax dollars. However, this new strategy also created a new inequality that must be addressed.

States, too, responded to the new conservative arguments, as criticisms of higher education excess grew in severity. Faced with troubled state economies and expectations of reductions in enrollments, many states adopted strategies that curtailed the percentage of educational costs in public colleges that was subsidized by taxpayers; but student costs began to rise. National lobbying organizations developed new guidelines to inform lobbyists how to respond to the new criticisms (Eiser 1988; State Higher Education 1988), but their arguments did nothing to change the new pattern that was developing. The new rationale, that colleges were greedy and that federal aid fueled price increases, was widely accepted in the popular press (Brimelow 1987; Putka 1987), and legislators responded to the concerns that were being raised by cutting back on their financial commitments to higher education.

These policy shifts coincided with growth in tuition charges in private colleges. At the same time that conservative analysts were arguing that institutions were greedy and trying to optimize government aid, private colleges were dedicating growing portions of their revenues from gifts and tuition to student grants (Hauptman 1990; McPherson and Schapiro 1998; NCES 2001d). The institutional lobbying community argued that cuts in federal grants had caused tuition to climb (Council for Advancement and Support 1987). However, these counterarguments were not widely reported by the press. Reductions in public funding continued.

In the 1990s, concerns about affordability grew as the Democratic and Republican parties took positions that seemed to contradict those they had historically held. The Clinton administration promoted targeted tax relief for the middle class through the Taxpayer Relief Act of 1997, while letting federal grant aid dwindle. Indeed, given the dramatic expansion in loans during the 1990s, coupled with the recent creation of tax credits, it would appear that the focus of federal student aid had shifted from the poor to the middle class.

The excesses of the 1990s—the dramatic expansion in (often unsubsidized) loans and the creation of middle-class tax credits—decreased the efficiency of the student aid, increasing taxpayer costs per student (chapter 7). However, the new strategy did not address the new inequality—the gap in participation rates that developed after the 1980s and persists until the present time.

In the 2000 presidential campaign, George W. Bush's platform argued for expansion of the Pell grant program, the major federal need-based program. In contrast, the Gore campaign argued for expansion of tax relief for the middle class. As the agenda for the new Bush administration unfolds, it is possible that his argument for more support for the Pell program will be taken seriously. After his election, Bush introduced a new budget with an additional $1 billion for the Pell grant program, the major federal program for providing access to higher education. The language of his first budget proposal indicated an intent of providing more need-based grant aid to low-income college students. However, the budget language did not explain how the funding would be allocated to students, and the push to return taxes to taxpayers constrained the prospect of increasing grants. And, while the recent reports of the Advisory Committee on Student Financial Assistance (2001a, 2002) support arguments for reinvesting in Pell grants to improve access, it is not clear that front-loading new Pell grant dollars would be the way to achieve this goal. So the question remains whether additional funding will be spent on first-year students (front-loading) or spread across students at all levels (increasing the maximum award).

Given these shifts in federal student aid policy and conservative arguments about affordability, we should also examine how liberal policy analysts now conceptualized "affordability." With the increased emphasis on loans and tax credits, it is important that we develop methods for evaluating the effects of these policies. The analytic methods most liberal analysts use to assess the effects of student aid programs focus almost exclusively on grants, an approach that limits insight into the impact of loans and tax credits. Loans may be necessary because they are a less expensive way for the federal government to expand opportunity for the majority. Loans cost taxpayers less than subsidies to institutions, grants for low-income students, or tax credits for middle-income students. More recently, liberal analysts have argued that affordability, as measured by family ability to pay, should be a major concern to states.

NEW POLICY ARGUMENTS ABOUT AFFORDABILITY

Most of the economic research on the financing of higher education has used the concept of *net price* as a basis for investigating college affordability (Paulsen 2001a,b). This approach involves subtracting the average grant from the price charged for higher education to estimate the net cost. Two recent national studies have recognized that to expand access again, it will also be necessary to improve affordability. Both studies used "indexes" to rate states on the affordability of college for their students. These studies have refocused attention on affordability as it was conceived when states expanded public systems in prior decades. This rationale implicitly argues for reducing the price paid by the "average" student rather than for equalizing the opportunity for financial access.

The National Center for Public Policy and Higher Education's *Measuring up 2000: The State-by-State Report Card for Higher Education* ranked states on preparation, participation, affordability, completion, and benefits, and gave states a grade on affordability. It is important to consider how this national study group conceptualized "affordability." The National Center's report gave "the percent of income needed to pay for college minus financial aid: at community colleges, at public 4-year colleges/universities, at 4-year private colleges/universities" (2000, 186). It also considered the percentage of costs paid by the "poorest families" at low-priced colleges, as well as the average loan amount students borrowed each year.

This rating approach assumes that affordability can be measured by family income minus net costs (tuition minus grant aid). An attempt was made to adjust for the needs of low-income families, which would seem to be sensitive to the interests of the average student in a state system of public and private colleges. However, this type of rating does not provide insight into how well the state finance systems equalize opportunity for students from poor families compared with students from middle-income families. In these grading systems, a low-tuition state can be ranked as affordable even if it does not provide sufficient aid to be affordable for low-income students. Thus, we should question whether this approach even considers equity for low-income students.

Another recent report, prepared by Jerry Sheehan Davis of the Lumina Foundation (2000), used a similar method for rating states on affordability, but Davis tried two variations on the affordability index. One method simply ranked states on the prices charged by colleges (the "gross"), and the other subtracted grant aid (the "net"). Both indexes focused on the number of working days needed by the average family to pay for a year of college. He used this measure to consider both trends in affordability nationally and differences in affordability across states.

Davis's analysis of trends in affordability reveals more change in the gross costs of attending than in the net costs. Between 1970 and 1980, the gross cost of attending a public college dropped from 27 to 23 days of work for the median-income family; by 1997 it had risen to 32 days(Davis 2000, 11). In contrast, the median net cost of attending a public college was 26 days of work in 1970, 22 days in 1980, and 28 days in 1997. Davis also found great variations across states on both affordability indexes. Indeed, the actual rankings of states on affordability was similar in both approaches, illustrating rather conclusively that these indexes measure charges relative to income for the entire population in a state, rather than measuring equity across diverse economic groups. "Regardless of whether 'gross' or 'net' charges are used," Davis observed, "the data show there are substantial differences among states in the affordability of their public colleges. There are substantial differences, at least 29 percent, in the amounts of effort required to pay for college expenses.

The seven additional days required in the more expensive states [the difference between the average of the more expensive states and the average for the less expensive states] could be considered a kind of 'public college tax' of about 2.8 percent of family earnings (7 days is 2.8 percent of the 250 working days in the year)" (2000, 39).

Davis also observed that this geographic difference in the costs of attending college (the variation in costs between high-cost and low-cost states) was greater than the "temporal" increase in average costs across the United States between 1985 and 1997. Thus, while college costs have risen for families, the variations in costs across states are greater, in an absolute sense, than the increase in costs over the recent period.

In these reports, both Davis and the National Center for Public Policy and Higher Education argue for a shift in the focus of debates about affordability, from affordability as a national policy issue to affordability as a state policy issue. Thus, they implicitly recognize that the federal government is unlikely to generate the additional grant dollars needed to reverse the trend toward high tuition in public colleges. Since states remain primary sources of support for public higher education, this shift in focus makes sense at a prima facie level. However, there are some underlying problems with these indexes.

First, these affordability constructs do not consider the diverse economic perspectives of those who have an interest in higher education. The notion of net price that underlies these analyses of affordability does not provide a fair basis for assessing equal opportunity. Nor does it value the interests of conservative taxpayers who are concerned about spending on education. It is merely another liberal rationale for keeping public colleges affordable for the middle class, an approach considered problematic for decades (Hansen and Weisbrod 1969; Hearn and Longanecker 1985). As states attempt to expand access in the twenty-first century, they should consider opportunity for the majority of students (and especially the large middle class), equity in opportunity for the poor, and taxpayer costs. While the net-price approach may be an appropriate way of measuring affordability for the majority of students, it does not adequately consider equality in opportunity for students from poor families.

Second, the family ability to pay does not adequately consider the effects of loans and tax credits on the educational choices of middle-class students. With the shifts in political arguments about affordability, it is crucial that we not overlook whether the claims made by those who advocate loans and tax credits hold up to empirical evidence. Since this approach does not consider loans and tax credits, we need another way of assessing the effects of changes in public policy over time.

The analyses in part I illustrate the limitations of the net-price concept. Analyses of the impact of aid illustrate that two states with moderate ratings on these affordability indexes—Washington and Indiana—maintained equal opportunity for enrollment across income groups in the 1990s (chapter 7). During the same period, public colleges were not affordable for low-income students nationally (chapters 6–8). In the high-tuition context of the late 1980s and 1990s, a substantial reinvestment in grants was needed to maintain financial access. Net price overlooked the central role of state grants in equal opportunity (e.g., National Center for Public Policy 2000; Davis 2000).

The Contingency Theory of Higher Education Finance

The changing rationales used in the financing of higher education in the late twentieth century necessitate a rethinking of the assumptions used in higher education finance. I propose the *contingency theory of higher education finance* as a practical approach to policy analysis and development, one that can be used to reconstruct the state and federal roles in the financing of postsecondary education in the early twenty-first century. The key elements of the contingency theory are a workable set of goals for public finance, a differentiated approach to price response that can help us better understand the consequences of the new pattern of higher education finance, and an approach to refinancing that encourages adaptation to new conditions soon after they develop. If we can balance the interests of three groups (the middle-income majority, low-income families, and taxpayers) as policy changes are debated, evaluated, and refined, then it may be possible to evolve a more just system of public finance.

COMMON BUT PRAGMATIC GOALS

During the progressive period of higher education finance—the late nineteenth century and most of the twentieth century—states promoted access and economic development by subsidizing public institutions and developing public higher education systems. However, it has become questionable whether subsidizing institutions is the most appropriate way to promote the public interest. Before we can assess alternative strategies, we need to define what the public interest is. In the new political context of higher education finance, the following goals seem to be emerging:

—*Improve access by improving academic preparation.* During the past two decades, states and the federal government have made a substantial investment in K–12 schools to raise standards. This reform strategy enabled more high school graduates to attend college but failed to increase graduation rates. Improvement in early reading programs, comprehensive school reform, and improvements in family income can improve academic preparation, but not all students who prepare can afford to attend college.

—*Equalize opportunity by refocusing on meeting financial need.* With the decline in need-based student aid, a new inequality has emerged: well-prepared students from poor families lack the opportunity to attend college, a situation that does not confront students from upper-middle-income and upper-income families. There is also now a greater disparity in opportunity between African American and Hispanic families and White families than in the 1970s. Whether economically diverse students have the same opportunity to enroll and persist, controlling for academic preparation and college grades, provides a good indicator of whether the goal of equal opportunity is being achieved. States and the federal government should monitor the impact of student aid on persistence by students from low-income families and should continue to refine their financial strategies to reduce the inequality in postsecondary opportunity.

—*Improve productivity by refining the incentive structures embedded in public financing schemes.* When states provided more of the funding for public colleges, there was a potential for promoting productivity through direct governance processes. Indeed, expenditures per student in public colleges rose after 1990 as states reduced their spending per student. In this new financing context, states and the federal government should reexamine how their programs and funding schemes provide incentives or disincentives for constraining educational expenditures that are passed on to college students.

Strategies that encourage movement toward any one of these goals can affect the other goals. For example, in the last two decades of the twentieth century, the federal government changed the way it financed access and promoted academic preparation. These changes created the new inequality. In addition, college costs have also risen, because efficiency is not valued within academe. Therefore, a more balanced approach to public finance is needed, one that reemphasizes equity but does not once again push up taxpayer costs.

EVALUATING THE EFFECTS OF FINANCE POLICIES

A new understanding of price response—especially one that explicitly recognizes the role of loans and leaves room to incorporate a research-based understanding of tax credits—can help states and the federal government develop more workable financing strategies. The older notion of net price, which assumed that students responded to a single price (tuition minus grants), is not adequate in this new context.

The central assumption of the contingency theory of higher education finance is that *students respond to prices and subsidies based on their situated circumstances*. This differentiated view of price response emerged as a research-based understanding of price response (St. John and Starkey 1995a). It has five subsidiary assumptions:

1. *Students respond differently to subsidies (grants, loans, and work) than to the costs of attending (tuition, books, housing, and other living costs)*. This means that we need to examine the effects of costs and subsidies separately (independent of each other) rather than using a single metric (tuition minus grants). This differentiated approach should include statistical controls for other factors that influence student outcomes. At a minimum, evaluations of the effects of aid on enrollment should control for the influence of background (including family income) and academic preparation/achievement. In evaluating the effects of student aid on persistence, we need to control for college experience variables that influence persistence (e.g., grades), as well as for background (including family income). Such evaluation studies are adequate to assess the impact of student aid (St. John, Cabrera, et al. 2000).

2. *Students' responses to prices and subsidies in persistence are independent of their responses to prices and subsidies in first-time enrollment*. During the past few decades, it has become apparent that students often enroll in college even when they do not have enough money to persist. Student aid offers can be adequate to enable initial enrollment but insufficient to ensure students can afford continuous enrollment. Therefore, we must examine the adequacy of aid in promoting persistence, as well as consider whether low-income and middle-income students have an equal opportunity to persist, controlling for grades and other factors that influence this outcome.

3. *Students' responses to prices and subsidies change over time, as a result of changes in governments' financing strategies and the labor market*. Assessing how price response changes as a result of major policy changes provides a means of evaluating the effects of current and historical policies on equal opportunity and opportunity for the majority. Over the past twenty years, enrollment patterns have been substantially altered by changes in federal, state, and institutional aid policies (McPherson and Schapiro 1991, 1997; St. John 1993, 1994).

4. *Students with different financial means respond to changes in prices and subsidies in different ways, depending on the combination of costs and subsidies they face.* Specifically, packages with grants have different effects on enrollment by middle-income students and by low-income students (St. John 1990a,b; St. John and Starkey 1995a). Therefore, we need routine assessments of the impact of prices and subsidies on diverse groups to determine whether the dual goals of financial access and equal opportunity are being met. By comparing evaluation studies for diverse groups conducted during different time periods, we can untangle how policy changes influence the various groups.
5. *Frequent evaluations of the effects of student aid are needed to inform policy development.* If the effects of student aid change over time (as an outcome of policy changes), we need to evaluate the impact of policy changes. Research on the effectiveness of federal student aid has been largely ignored for the past two decades.

While this way of viewing evaluation is not as clear-cut as the net-price logic more frequently used in policy studies, it provides a better way of evaluating the impact of policy changes. Part I presented an evaluation of the effects of changes in state and federal policy. As shown in chapters 7–9, in the late 1980s and early 1990s student aid was inadequate for low-income students. This finding is crucial if we are to develop finance policies that are more just.

REFINANCING STRATEGIES

In the context of the new inequality challenge, the differentiated concept of price response can be used to inform strategies for refining state and federal policies toward the common goals outlined above, as well as provide a basis for informing government decisions about financial strategies within colleges and universities. At each level in this refinancing process—federal, state, institutional, and family—it is important to evaluate the impact of current and past policies and to use information from these evaluations to inform new policies. In chapter 11, I recommend refinancing strategies for institutions, states, and the federal government.

First, institutions can use an inquiry-based approach to envision new financial strategies and to evaluate and adapt these strategies to move toward institutional goals (chapters 10 and 11). Over the past decades, private colleges have developed sophisticated tuition discounting and aid leveraging strategies (McPherson and Schapiro 1997) through research based on net-price assumptions. Given the impact of rising public college prices on financial access, more public colleges and universities will need to adopt new financial strategies.

Second, it will be increasingly important for states to assess how their financing strategies influence both public and private institutions, as well as how they influence students. They need to assess the impact of tuition increases in public colleges, especially increases attributable to a shift in the burden of college support, on access and persistence by diverse groups; they should assess the impact of both current and historical strategies. This information can be used to guide refinements of policies toward these common goals. States should also assess how their finance policies influence the productivity of public and private colleges and the supply of mid-skilled workers. States need to find better ways to coordinate their financing strategies so that colleges have adequate resources and students can afford to attend in this new market. As they attempt to adjust to new conditions and to refine their financing strategies, states and the federal government should balance the interests of diverse economic groups. It is crucial to examine the taxpayer costs associated with different methods of expanding and equalizing postsecondary opportunity.

Finally, the federal government shares responsibility with states for promoting equal opportunity. However, to refocus attention on low-income students, a consideration of taxpayer costs and access for the majority of students will be essential. Based on this assessment of the impact of changes in federal policy over the last three decades of the twentieth century, the final chapters suggest new directions in state and federal policy for improving social justice in postsecondary finance in the early twenty-first century.

A Contingency Approach to Refinancing

Different constituents have different visions for the future of higher education. Advocates of public institutions will probably continue to develop new rationales for more substantial direct funding. Advocates of private institutions will probably continue to argue for student aid as an alternative to institutional subsidies. The new conservative argument for less public spending will also continue to evolve. In spite of these competing rationales, there is an ongoing need to analyze outcomes and adapt policy. This chapter recommends a contingency approach to public finance that policymakers in states and institutions can use to guide and inform the evolution of their financial strategies. Further, based on the evaluations in part I, a new federal financial strategy is recommended.

Improving access and equal opportunity involves a set of decentralized decisions within many colleges and universities that essentially compete with each other for students, along with well-coordinated decisions by legislators and chief executives in the many states and at the federal level. The expectation that such a coordinated effort can be achieved through rational planning is unreasonable. Nevertheless, a combination of financial strategies and communicative, action-inquiry processes could be used by institutions, states, and federal officials who are seriously interested in improving affordability; these processes are outlined below. I also suggest an approach that the federal government might use to transform the incentive structure for states and institutions in ways that could improve affordability and reduce the gap in opportunity.

Institutional Financial Strategies

A new institutional financial strategy was embedded in prestige pricing—a strategy implemented by private colleges in the 1980s and 1990s. Before the 1980s, when institutions used a structural, incremental approach to financing decisions, pricing decisions were mostly made after budget plans had been developed. College officials decided how much they would need to raise tuition to meet their budget totals at a projected enrollment level. However, as prestige pricing emerged, more college executives and board members began to consider tuition charges and allocations to student aid as an integral part of annual budget-making. Prestige pricing provided a way to generate sufficient funds to make the educational improvements considered necessary for institutions to remain competitive in the academic marketplace. Pricing decisions became an integral part of the construction of institutional budgets. This new pricing approach had complex consequences for affordability. However, institutions can use *action inquiry* to rethink and refine pricing strategies (St. John 1995). The five basic elements of this approach are outlined here.

BUILD AN UNDERSTANDING OF THE CHALLENGE

Each college and university needs to assess its own financial challenge related to access and equal opportunity. Some colleges still have room to increase prices,[1] if they also increase investments in grants, while others do not. Colleges should systematically evaluate the effects of current strategies for the diverse groups who apply and enroll. Do all qualified students have an equal opportunity to enroll and persist? If not, then a challenge exists. It is important to assess how past pricing strategies influenced students' enrollment and persistence across income groups. The information on specific challenges facing the institution should be shared with budget-planning committees as they deliberate on alternative pricing and student aid strategies. And as part of these deliberations, decision groups must also consider the costs of educational processes and services in relation to the costs of student aid programs. In the process, these groups will gain insights into the linkages between educational costs (productivity) and prices—and thus will learn about the consequences of current pricing strategies.

IDENTIFY POSSIBLE SOLUTIONS

Each institution will have a range of alternatives that merit consideration. Some alternatives, such as raising or lowering tuition (or holding tuition constant), may be possible in the short term. Others may take longer to implement and should be considered as longer-range possibilities. The crucial issue is to think critically about the types of outcomes that can be expected from the various alternatives. Key decision groups

[1] Having room to increase prices does not mean campuses *should* increase prices. Historically, American colleges and universities were priced substantially below students' ability to pay (Garvin 1980). In the current context, colleges should ponder the merits of further increasing tuition.

on campus need to have some insight into the alternatives being debated as well as an opportunity to suggest new alternatives (or hybrid solutions). The alternatives should be assessed relative to the status quo (and to analyses of the effects of past policies on first-time enrollment and persistence).

ANALYZE POSSIBLE SOLUTIONS AND SYNTHESIZE INTO AN ACTION PLAN

Financial plans should treat new strategies as "experiments." Strategic enrollment management typically involves estimating the enrollment effects of pricing alternatives, such as tuition discounting (e.g., DesJardins, Ahlburg, and McCall 2002; Singha 1997). But while these analyses can inform the choice of strategies, it is also important to evaluate the effects of tuition and institutional grants on financial access (i.e., the ability of low-income qualified students to enroll and persist). And these strategy "experiments" require periodic evaluation. Each year, as new approaches to aid awards and price increases (or decreases) are implemented, planners should consider how students respond, taking into account not only student price response but also the implied contract with students (Paulsen and St. John 1997). Action plans should consider methods for evaluating the impact of new policies on first-time enrollment and on persistence. Further, policymakers should think through the entire marketing, admissions, and retention cycle when developing annual financial plans. Communication with students, parents, and faculty about financial strategies and what to expect in the future is also important.

TREAT NEW STRATEGIES AS LEARNING OPPORTUNITIES

The implementation of new pricing strategies—annual decisions about tuition and student aid—should be treated as learning opportunities. In the budget process, it is important to consider the linkages between educational expenditures, tuition charges, and student aid. Each campus should routinely evaluate the effects of student aid on enrollment and persistence.[2] In colleges and universities that use decentralized budgeting, different academic units should perhaps be prepared to coordinate their academic and budget strategies with the pricing and aid strategies. In many instances, some experimentation with different pricing strategies in different academic units may be appropriate, an approach that has proved successful in at least one research university (Singha 1997).

[2] St. John and Somers (1997) and Somers and St. John (1997a) suggest workable models for assessing the impact of financial aid on enrollment and persistence.

MEETING THE ACCESS CHALLENGE

Given the dynamic nature of pricing processes and students' decision-making, it is crucial for campuses to make routine assessments of the consequences of their action strategies. Some strategies can be monitored as an integral part of implementation. In these instances, aid administrators and admissions officers can have some discretion when making awards. Other action strategies are best evaluated a year or two after implementation; for example, one cannot assess the effects of aid on persistence until a year after the award is made. However, colleges should plan for routine assessments of the effects of their pricing strategies and the ways in which the institution communicates with students.

A REFLECTION

It may seem odd, at least on an initial reading of this text, that I have recommended a process approach to solving the affordability problem, rather than a specific set of strategies. However, few solutions to the pricing puzzle have not been tried somewhere at some time. Scanning what has been done elsewhere and then applying it locally would not be sufficient. Such an adaptive, incremental approach ignores the extent to which local circumstances—the financial means and expectations of current and prospective students and their families—influence the success of new strategies. The alternative is to turn the process of finding better financing methods into a learning opportunity for the college community. This does not presuppose a specific solution; rather, it suggests a path to finding locally situated solutions that work.

State Strategies

The state role in financing higher education has usually been characterized as one of two conflicting, ideal types: high subsidies and low tuition at public institutions (the old public institution "ideal") and a high-tuition, high-grant strategy that includes government grants for students in public and private colleges (the private institution "ideal"). What has evolved is an unexpected hybrid—a high-tuition, high-loan model—that includes some of the worst features of both: high tuition and low grants have constrained financial access in many states. Here I suggest a fourth approach: strategic use of student grant aid coordinated with other strategies for promoting marginal reductions in educational expenditures. This approach builds on lessons learned from the Minnesota financing experiment (Hearn and Anderson 1995; St. John 1995).

The institutional argument for funding frequently carries forward the old assumptions about affordability: that the funding institutions would ensure access and affordability. However, as the examination of trends and evaluation studies in part I of this book reveals, levels of funding declined but enrollments climbed. Clearly, this old argument did not hold up well, as illustrated in chapters 6 and 7.

In the second strategy frequently advocated for the state financing of higher education, higher tuition and higher grants, states would reduce the percentage of educational costs they funded directly with increases in tuition and increases in need-based grants. However, few states followed this path. Loans were used extensively, because they provided a way for families to pay their increased share. The consequence of this development was limited access for low-income students, especially to four-year colleges, while four-year colleges remained affordable for the middle class. Indeed, federal expansion of loans disguised the crisis in financial access for the poor.

States should provide adequate support to maintain financial access for state residents. Growing evidence suggests that public colleges are no longer affordable for low-income students (Paulsen and St. John 1997, 2002; St. John 1999). There are two traditional paths for providing adequate support: increasing student grants to ensure the emergence and maintenance of a high-tuition, high-grant environment; or increasing institutional support as a means of returning to low tuition, and lobbying the federal government to increase Pell grants. Both paths have a high cost for states. Providing adequate support to ensure access presents a substantial financial challenge for most states.

The alternative approach is for states to coordinate institutional and student subsidies to ensure affordability within the traditional public system. Once these strategies are set in motion, the annual budget process can focus on how much to subsidize public institutions so the subsidies can be balanced by an explicit consideration of affordability. If the institutional subsidy per student declined, sufficient new grant support would be needed to ensure that students could afford to attend and persist. Maintaining a stable, balanced funding approach is essential.

Financial restructuring, or refinancing, should include a focus on curtailing the escalation of costs. It is rare for states to systematically evaluate their financing strategies and to maintain coalitions that support these processes. Even states that have put together the coalitions to do this have found them difficult to maintain (Hearn and Anderson 1995). I recommend three strategies for states to consider: establish a systematic approach to assessing the effects of prices and subsidies, develop a coordinated statewide financial strategy, and promote an open dialogue about financial strategies.

First, *establish a solid baseline of information about the consequences of state financing strategies.* Unless college officials, public administrators, and legislators all have valid information about the consequences of public financing strategies, it is extremely difficult to contend with arguments that advocate reducing support for higher education. In most states there is little coordination between tuition and state grants. When tuition is held in check, due to generous institutional subsidies, state grants usually also increase. But the reverse is also true: when institutional subsidies go down, tuition rises. If grant aid also goes down, opportunity is threatened. States need a systematic approach to measuring the effects of tuition and student aid if they are to maintain affordability and efficient use of tax dollars. There are now sound, proven approaches that can be used to assess state pricing and aid strategies (St. John 1999), and they should be used routinely.

Second, *establish a method for coordinating state financing strategies.* This involves coordinating institutional subsidies with allocations to state grant programs. When systematic processes have been established for this purpose, it is possible to inform legislators about the consequences of past financial strategies. However, the process of establishing a coordinated strategy involves holding together a political coalition (Hearn and Anderson 1995).

Finally, *set up regular meetings among senior analysts within the state bureaucracy to consider evaluative information.* Having good information about the effects of aid and prices is essential. Lobbyists for institutions, state agency officials, and legislators from different parties may disagree on specific strategies, but if they share an understanding about the consequences of current strategies, it is easier to assess the consequences of the alternatives being promoted in the political process. Routinely sharing information on the results of evaluations may be the best means of achieving this end.

Again, open inquiry processes must be created. States need to promote financial access more actively, whether or not they are able to provide generous institutional subsidies. States must coordinate their financing strategies and hold together a political coalition that understands the importance of the affordability goal.

Federal Strategy

In the 1980s and 1990s, there was a widening gap between the ways that the middle class dealt with the dilemma of paying for college and the theory economists used to analyze access. Specifically, net-price theory, as most economic analysts used it, underestimated the value of loans in promoting educational choice for the middle class. Loans had a more substantial influence on enrollment decisions by the middle class than could be measured using net-price assumptions to evaluate the effects of aid. After the federal aid strategy shifted its emphasis from grants to loans, enrollment climbed while the price tag for federal student aid declined. Net-price theory simply broke down. An opportunity gap emerged, but this received too little attention in the federal policy discourse. A contingency approach to financial issues can be integrated into and facilitated by federal policy. I suggest specific steps for the ongoing reconstruction of the federal grant and loan program. Then I consider how this approach can help states and institutions address the specific challenges they face.

The current federal aid programs have evolved since 1975 without serious review (Hearn 1993, 2001b); St. John 1994). Based on the review in part I of this book, it is possible to suggest specific steps to reform federal programs.

FEDERAL GRANTS

The erosion in federal need-based grants led to changes in the entire structure of higher education finance. The effects of reductions in federal grant aid and escalation of tuition were mitigated by the availability of loans. Even if loans continue to be central to public finances, we need to ensure financial access. A three-step strategy is needed, as outlined here.

Create a First-Tier Grant to Ensure Financial Access

A minimum standard for federal support of access requires a rethinking of the formulae used to calculate Pell program awards. If Pell maximums were restored to historical levels, focusing exclusively on financial need would provide an incentive for public institutions to raise tuition.[3] At the very least, the Pell grant maximum should equal half the average cost of attendance at public four-year colleges. A new Pell maximum should be indexed for inflation, but not to college prices. With adequate grant aid there should be an added incentive to constrain tuition increases. *To ensure financial access, the first tier of federal grants (basic grants) should be sufficient to enable continuous enrollment by low-income and lower-middle-income students in low-cost public institutions.* This minimum standard is necessary, but has not been met for two decades.

---

[3] By 2002 the George W. Bush administration had increased the Pell maximum to $4,000, taking an important step toward restoring Pell grants.

Establish a Second-Tier Grant That Encourages Coordination of
Federal, State, and Institutional Grants

The college-choice process also needs to be considered in the construction of a second tier of federal student aid. *Because federal aid can escalate with tuition in a purely need-based system, the allocation formula for the second-tier grant program must include incentives to constrain increases in educational expenditures per student.* The maximum for the second-tier grant should also equal half the cost of attending the average public college. Students in both public and private colleges should be eligible. The maximum federal share should be 30 percent of the second-tier grant.[4] This approach would provide an incentive to constrain unnecessary costs in colleges that choose to participate.

The second-tier grant program could be integrated with state policies in ways that both encourage academic preparation and ensure equal opportunity. For example, states might want to link eligibility for second-tier grants to students who meet certain admissions standards (i.e., certain grade point averages, or even grades in specific courses). This approach would be consistent with the definition of academic access developed in part I of this book, and it leads to three further recommendations:

1. In the second-tier grant program, states should have an option of limiting eligibility to students who meet specified standards of academic preparation, possibly consonant with admissions standards at elite public universities.
2. Second-tier grants should be awarded based on need, even if academic criteria are used for eligibility.
3. Institutions should have the option to participate in the second-tier grant if they are not covered in an eligible state program.

Further, *institutions (or states) should not be eligible for the second tier unless they agree to provide their share (the other 70 percent) of the second-tier grant.* This approach not only would ensure an enhancement of college choice but for the first time would provide a mechanism for constraining increases in college costs. The federal government would share a portion of the cost of need-based grants for poor students to attend college. Cooperating states or institutions would subsidize the remaining portion of these grants. Further, the institution would be responsible for any additional grant award over the ceiling of the second-tier grant.

---

[4] The 30 percent (thirty cents per dollar of grant) of the second-tier program should make this program more economical for the federal government than loans: grants could replace loans. The 30 percent federal subsidy for the program encourages states to rethink their financial strategies.

Establish Reasonable Cost Controls

Finally, *the upper limit of the second-tier grant should be capped at an amount equal to the first-tier grant.* All grants above this upper limit would be entirely an institutional responsibility. This would provide an incentive for institutions to assess whether and how to use prestige pricing to enhance their development. With this reconstructed approach to awarding grant aid, ensuring adequate funding to equalize the opportunity to persist could become the standard for measuring the adequacy of federal (and state) student aid. Indeed, recent analyses (Hu and St. John 2001; St. John 1999) indicate that persistence research can be used for this purpose.

This two-tier federal grant strategy merits serious consideration and debate. It would help bring more stability and balance to the system, ensuring adequate funding of aid, facilitating cooperation among partners in the postsecondary system, and providing mechanisms for constraining the escalation of college costs and possibly improving productivity.

This strategy has two advantages over the simpler strategy of restoring need-based grants to historical levels (e.g., Advisory Committee 2001a; Mumper 1996; National Commission on Responsibility 1993). First, the new strategy would be less costly to the federal government than the approach used in the 1970s, because it would share costs for a second-tier grant with states and/or institutions. Second, this strategy would create incentives for institutions to control their costs, and thus it provides a clear alternative both to the current situation of inadequate federal grants and to the older pattern of liberal grant awards with inadequate cost constraints.

FEDERAL LOANS

Loans played a vital role in the financing of higher education in the latter half of the twentieth century. As American higher education moved toward a high-tuition approach in the 1980s and 1990s, students increased their reliance on loans. Loans enabled more students to attend private colleges, but excessive loans may have inhibited persistence in these institutions. Loans can influence students to reevaluate their decisions based on the quality of their experiences in relation to their debt burden (Paulsen and St. John 1997; St. John 1998). Before wrestling with the excessiveness of loan programs, we need to consider recent changes in the ways that loans have been used.

A fundamental shift in the underlying assumptions about loans occurred in the 1980s. Loans had been considered a means for families and students to make contributions to costs after their calculated needs were

MEETING THE ACCESS CHALLENGE

met with grants. Then, in the 1980s, loans became part of the packages offered to meet need. Initially the Reagan administration proposed "self-help"—loans plus work-study—as the basic initial component of aid packages, even before grants. The self-help approach was rejected (Hearn 1993), but because of the decline in grants coupled with the rise in tuition, loans became part of the basic aid package. Thus, even though self-help was rejected as a logical part of the aid foundation, loans became central to student aid; a de facto high-tuition, high-loan strategy developed, making loans a more integral part of federal student aid.

This increased reliance on loans had two benefits. First, loans were less costly to the federal government than grants, which is the real reason for the shift to loans: it saved taxpayer dollars. Second, loans had a positive influence on enrollment levels, especially for middle-income students, a development that was not expected and was initially overlooked (McPherson and Schapiro 1998; St. John, Kirshstein, and Noell 1991).

Nevertheless, overreliance on loans has created new problems, especially for low-income students. States and the federal government should monitor the effects of debt on persistence and life choices after college. They also need to explore ways of expanding grants and other forms of federal aid to bring more balance back into the overall federal student aid system.

A great deal is known about loan defaults. Defaults are linked to unemployment, employment in fields unrelated to the student's field of study, and low earnings (Flint 1997). The single biggest challenge facing the federal government regarding its loan programs is to revise the way debt is managed. There has been a gradual movement toward increased flexibility in repayment. However, the entire system of repayment merits comprehensive study, if not comprehensive revision. More generally, we need to know more about the ways in which the loan burden influences graduates' choices after college. Given the high levels of college debt now held by many graduates, it is important to explore how debt influences subsequent life choices. Indeed, we need to explore how debt affects subsequent economic choices (i.e., home and car purchases and career decisions), as well as citizens' views on taxation, having children, and so forth. These unintended consequences of debt are important subjects of study, because they have long-term economic and social consequences, especially for low-income students (U.S. General Accounting Office 1998; King and Bannon 2002).

Thus there are serious problems with federal loan programs, especially with respect to debt burden for low-income students. The U.S. General Accounting Office (1998) argues that grants and loans do not have equivalent effects on low-income students, a view consistent with the findings of this study. The second-tier grant program would provide a clear and distinct alternative to loans. If the federal government covered 30 percent of the cost, second-tier grants would be more economical than loans for federal taxpayers. They would provide a means for states to finance access to elite public colleges and to private colleges that compete with them for qualified students in their states. This would stimulate market forces while providing an incentive for efficiency.

FEDERAL WORK-STUDY

Before the 1980s, work-study was a relatively small program that seemed to have a positive influence on student outcomes, apparently because this program promoted academic integration. However, when work-study was expanded in the 1980s as part of the initial push for a self-help approach to federal student aid, some problematic aspects of work-study surfaced.

When work-study was overemphasized as part of a basic aid package, two new issues emerged. The low hourly pay rate often required excessive work time to earn aid awarded on "need." In addition, *work-study* lost its meaning; it became a social stigma, more identifiable with low income. Recent research indicates that the work-study program now has a negative influence on persistence for many students.

Three approaches could be used to correct these problems: (1) use work-study exclusively as an option for students to pay for their expected contribution (not as part of basic need); (2) increase the hourly rate for work-study; and (3) improve the quality of jobs available to work-study students. More attention should be given to this issue in an effort to improve the quality of work-study jobs.

TAX CREDITS

The political push for tax credits in the 1990s was probably influenced by the growth in debt burden among middle-income students, coupled with rising tuition. Now that tax credits have been enacted, it is crucial that analysts examine their effects and costs relative to the effects and costs of other forms of aid. Indeed, the new logic of differentiated price theory creates a new, different vantage point from which to analyze the effects of tax credits.

Tax credits, like loans, could expand college choice and improve two-year persistence for middle-income and upper-middle-income students. However, tax credits cost substantially more than loans: a dollar of tax credit costs at least a dollar, compared with about fifty cents per dollar of loan. And it is exceedingly difficult to measure the economic value of forgone tax revenues awarded for savings plans (Wolanin 2001). Therefore, the cost-benefit ratio for tax credits is substantially lower than for loans. Such differences need to be further investigated and documented. We should ask the question: *does the targeted tax relief provided by tax credits offset the disadvantage of their high cost (compared with other forms of aid)?* Put another way: *should lower taxes be targeted to middle-income families with students in college, or should tax cuts be spread across all taxpayers?* An efficient system of public finance benefits all taxpayers, while the HOPE Scholarship and tax schemes benefit only some taxpayers.

An even more critical issue emerging from tax credits is that they could further shift federal student aid from the poor to the middle and upper classes. This is especially problematic with the growing opportunity gap. Research on tax credits must be carefully constructed to discern the effects of the economic impact on student choice.

CREATING MORE JUST INCENTIVE STRUCTURES

The strategies outlined above are intended to put in motion a new set of incentives. The recommendations for refining the use of loans, work-study, and tax credits are modest and involve primarily the use of evaluation to guide policy development. However, I recommend a bold new approach to federal grants. The intent of the recommended program is to create a set of incentives for improving access, equalizing opportunity once again, and increasing efficiency in the use of tax dollars for higher education. The two-tier structure of the proposed grant strategy deals directly with the dual goals of access and equal opportunity.

The basic grant, the first tier, focuses on ensuring financial access to low-cost public two-year and four-year colleges. As is evident from the analyses presented in part I, federal grants were not adequate to ensure access for low-income college-qualified students in the late twentieth century. The first tier of federal grants should provide this support. However, these recommendations also recognize that not all the nation's public colleges are no longer low-cost: tuition charges rose substantially over the past two decades. Therefore, to make efficient use of federal tax dollars, the first-tier grant should be set at the minimum threshold for financial access. In the early history of the Pell program, the half-cost provision limited this federal grant to half the cost of attending public colleges. Setting the threshold for the first-tier grant at the level of attending public colleges raises the combined grant to a level that ensures college choice for students with financial need. However, limiting the total grant to this threshold ensures that the costs of the program will not rise with college tuition. The new basic grant should be sufficient to allow enrollment of qualified low-income students who could not otherwise afford continuous enrollment, but it should not be prone to misuse. Putting an upper limit on funding constrains the potential misuse of the program and defuses claims that institutions could raise tuition to maximize awards.

The second tier of the proposed grant strategy involves putting incentives in place that encourage higher-cost institutions to constrain future tuition increases. By limiting the maximum award to the level of the first-tier grant, the program encourages cost competitiveness in a market with government (state and federal) subsidies to lower-income and lower-middle-income students with financial need. Thus, the second-tier grant ensures equal opportunity to enroll in moderate-cost to high-cost colleges. Of course, the colleges themselves could use their own internal allocations for grant programs to create a third tier of aid. But the second-tier grants encourage the market to develop in ways that promote equity.

Limiting the federal share of the second-tier grant to about 30 percent of program costs is responsive to the interests of conservative taxpayers. At this level, the second-tier grant would have a lower cost than subsidized loans. Thus, the program is more economical than loans, creating an economic incentive to reduce debt burden—a crucial aspect of the proposal. The injustices created by heavy debt burdens are not yet well understood. Putting a substantial grant program in place creates a new incentive to adapt state financing systems in ways that ensure adequate funding and equal opportunity.

Currently, there is a great deal of ambiguity in state grant programs, with a growing emphasis on quasi-merit grants that seem to be oriented toward keeping middle-income, middle-ability students in state (chapter 7). While the idea of coupling merit (i.e., grade point and course requirements) to grant aid is antithetical to the historical intent of federal student aid, such mechanisms are not incongruent with the historical state role in funding public systems of higher education. In a sense, states taking this path are choosing to shift their funding strategy from funding all students (i.e., institutional subsidies) to funding students who meet certain desirable admissions criteria. Such approaches are not inconsistent with mission-oriented planning: rather than restricting admissions and providing subsidies to students who meet the admissions requirements, these programs direct the subsidy to students who meet desirable admissions criteria. If a foundation grant is in place to provide equal access to public colleges, then this strategy has a certain type of fairness to it, especially if financial need is part of the award criteria. By limiting eligibility for these second-tier grant programs to students with need who meet eligibility criteria, the new federal program encourages the linking of equity considerations to mission-oriented planning in states.

In fact, the second-tier grant strategy would encourage states to refine and coordinate their financing strategies with their mission-oriented planning. The two-tier strategy recognizes the two markets functioning within most state systems of higher education. Community colleges and low-cost four-year colleges provide academic access to a quality higher education that enables students to enter local labor markets. Encouraging these institutions to maintain relatively low costs for students makes sense, because for many students who prepare for work in local labor markets, their earnings potential is lower than that in national labor markets. A very basic function of public colleges is to provide the labor force of teachers, nurses, business people, technicians, and other expert and skilled professionals who work in local economies. Many comprehensive public colleges and community colleges continue to have local missions, much like the older teachers' colleges, nursing schools, and junior colleges from which they evolved. A first-tier federal grant program should ensure financial access for low-income students who qualify to enter these public institutions. As the history of Pell and other federal grant programs shows (chapter 5), providing this type of subsidy is an important federal role.

The new, more competitive higher education market of elite public and moderate-priced private colleges evolved in the last two decades of the twentieth century. In 1980, economists pointed out that colleges— public and private—were priced lower than their value (e.g., Garvin 1980). After twenty years of adaptive behavior, enrollment management, and prestige pricing (chapters 6 and 7), many colleges now compete in new ways for high-achieving students. They are higher priced, and they have found a way to provide grant aid to ensure access for some students who meet their admissions standards. However, this market is far from equitable (McPherson and Schapiro 1997; see also chapter 8). The second-tier grant would create a more equitable finance structure in states that adapted their grant programs to take advantage of the incentives embedded in the proposed program.

The second-tier grant program could potentially bring a new rationality to state markets. At one extreme, states could choose to move substantial portions of their investment from elite public institutions to state grant programs. This would reduce taxpayer costs per student enrolled in the state system while relying on market forces to redistribute revenues. At the other extreme, states could create more modest second-tier grant programs that ensured financial access to public research universities and provided modest market stimulus for private colleges. The second-tier strategy would leave these decisions to states, where they appropriately belong. The 30 percent subsidy for the program would provide ample incentive for states to refine their financing strategies, if not to seek better coordination of their mission-oriented planning and financing strategies.

Thus, the proposal for the two-tier grant program provides an alternative way to structure the federal and state roles in higher education finance. It encourages more explicit consideration of three goals: access for all who are prepared academically, equal opportunity to attend for low-income students, and efficient use of tax dollars in support of the nation's system of higher education. Further, the proposed strategy recognizes that states are central to higher education finance, but that the federal government has responsibility for guiding the development of the nation's system of higher education in ways that are both fair and just.

Conclusion

Improving access and equalizing opportunity are major challenges that will probably grow in importance with increased demand for access in the early twenty-first century. Improving financial access is a complex process. It requires coordination of institutional, state, and federal financing strategies. The contingency approach to finance, developed in this chapter, provides a method for addressing this important challenge. However, the challenge posed by the decline in college affordability for low-income students should be more openly discussed. Strategies for remedying this social injustice merit systematic analysis and discussion by Congress and state legislatures.

Reform strategies should focus on both financial and academic access. Improving financial access requires better coordination of public financing strategies within states and between states and the federal government. However, coordination without a commitment to improving financial access will not solve the affordability problem for low-income students: in the past two decades, there were gains in access but increased inequality. Academic access is also a growing challenge. Better K–12 education would prepare more students. Improvement in postsecondary encouragement would motivate more students to take college preparatory courses. However, unless states meet the financial access challenge, improvement in K–12 education and postsecondary encouragement will have only modest impact.

11   Improving Access and Equalizing Opportunity

A major new challenge confronting the American educational system is how to expand postsecondary opportunity to reach virtually all college-age students. In the late 1990s, the Council for Aid to Education, a RAND subsidiary, described this challenge as a ticking time bomb: "What we found was a time bomb ticking under the nation's social and economic foundations: *At a time when the level of education needed for productive employment is increasing, the opportunity to go to college will be denied to millions of Americans unless sweeping changes are made to control costs, halt sharp increases in tuition, and increase other sources of revenue*" (1997, 1; emphasis in original). More recently, access has become a focal point for national groups engaged in assessing state higher education systems. In a commentary on the state "report card" on higher education, McCabe described the access challenge as follows: "Eighty percent of new jobs will require some postsecondary education, but unfortunately, only 42 percent of today's students leave high school with the necessary skills to begin college-level work. America's greatest strength is its commitment to the value and importance of every individual; the nation benefits when everyone's talents are fully developed" (2000, 180).

These two statements provide different views on the challenge we now face. As the RAND statement communicates, part of the challenge is financial. States and the federal government need to find the means and the will to support an expansion in the nation's system of postsecondary education; most of the new students will have greater financial need than do current students. McCabe's statement communicates the academic aspect of the challenge: meeting this challenge will require reforms in the K–12 system and expansion of the postsecondary system.

Both aspects of the access challenge merit serious consideration by educators, as well as by taxpayers. To address the challenge—a near doubling of postsecondary opportunity in the United States—we need not only a substantial expansion of postsecondary education systems but also a rethinking of the relationships between K–12 education and postsecondary education. This chapter takes a closer look at the challenge of expanding postsecondary opportunity as a problem confronting the entire system of education (especially K–16), then recommends strategies for expanding the postsecondary system, focusing on three goals:

1. improving access to postsecondary education;
2. equalizing opportunity for low-income students to attain a postsecondary education;
3. increasing efficiency of tax expenditures.

Understanding the New Access Challenge

With insights from the review of the impact of higher education finance presented in part I, and other recent studies using a similar framework,[1] it is possible to reframe the access challenge. The three major components of the problem—academic preparation, postsecondary transition, and expanding state systems—are reexamined below.

ACADEMIC PREPARATION

Too frequently, advocates of school reform have not viewed educational improvement as having the goal of improving access to postsecondary education (e.g., Finn 2001; Finn, Manno, and Ravitch 2001). Rather, school reform has more frequently been framed as an issue of improving quality, as measured by scores on standardized tests. The emphasis on algebra and conventional high school honors courses further obfuscates the issue (e.g., NCES 1997a; Pelavin and Kane 1990) by suggesting that a college education is the goal for all students. There is little reason to doubt that encouraging more students to take algebra and other advanced math courses can prepare more students for four-year colleges, but the effect on equalizing opportunity will be limited. Changing high school graduation requirements may increase college enrollment for high school graduates by five or ten percentage points over the next two decades, much like the impact of the educational reform movement of the past two decades. But the problem with academic preparation is more substantial than stiffer standards alone can address. In fact, the enrollment increase in the 1990s was in two-year colleges (Kane 2001), where advanced math courses are not crucial for admission. As the analysis in chapter 8 indicates, the opportunity for low-income students to at-

---

[1] During the past three years I have been conducting evaluation studies of reading reforms, comprehensive school reforms, and school choice (e.g., Miron and St. John 2003). This section uses insights gained from these studies, along with studies of the effects of student aid (summarized throughout part II).

MEETING THE ACCESS CHALLENGE

tend four-year colleges is constrained by finances. A large percentage of college-qualified low-income students lack the opportunity to enroll.

The framework developed in chapter 4 (see fig. 4.1) suggests that we need to focus on attainment/equity outcomes of K–12 reform, along with achievement-related outcomes. If more students complete a high school education (an attainment goal) and pass standardized tests (an achievement outcome), then there is a greater likelihood that K–12 schools will double their capacity to prepare students for postsecondary opportunities. However, if testing and higher standards force more people out of the K–12 system, then we need to rethink school reform. More attention should be given to high school graduation rates as an outcome of school reform. Three types of reforms—literacy and reading reforms, comprehensive school reform, and improved school choice—are frequently advocated and merit our attention here.

Literacy and Reading Reforms

Learning to read and comprehend is the first challenge everyone faces in school. During the middle to late 1990s, early reading emerged as a major policy concern nationally and in many states. Before society can reach the goal of 80 or 90 percent of the college-age population having at least some postsecondary education, it will need to expand literacy. This issue involves both school reform and efforts to expand family literacy.

The National Research Council recently undertook a comprehensive review of the research on reading, concluding that early literacy required approaches focusing on early phonics instruction (Snow, Burns, and Griffin 1998), an *explicit/direct* approach to instruction. However, recent studies of state reading interventions in Indiana suggest the problem is far more complex. Using the framework for assessing the impact of policy reforms on early reading to measure the impact of early reading interventions in Indiana's elementary schools, several colleagues and I uncovered a couple of seemingly contradictory findings (St. John, Manset, Chung, Simmons, et al. in press):

—*Explicit/direct approaches*, combining the practices of phonics instruction, basal readers, and worksheets/workbooks, were associated with higher pass rates on reading tests but also with higher failure rates in K–3 classrooms.
—*Text-connected approaches*, combining independent reading, cooperative learning, creative writing, invented spelling, paired reading (student-to-student), and reading aloud, were associated with lower failure rates in K–3 grades.

In one sense these studies confirm that *explicit/direct approaches* help improve achievement on tests. But if these approaches also increase the number of students who are retained in grade level—and if being retained increases the chances of subsequent failure and dropout—then they have clear limitations. Further, given the finding that *text-connected approaches* improved the percentage of children who made normal progress, then a balanced approach to early reading education may be needed.

Educators, researchers, and the general public need to exercise caution when using research to inform policy development. Any change in one aspect of educational practice, like requiring phonics instruction for elementary students or algebra for middle-school students, will have unintended as well as intended consequences. The study cited above (St. John, Manset, Chung, Simmons, et al. in press) confirmed a link between explicit approaches and pass rates on tests, but the results suggest that overemphasizing such strategies can reduce the percentage of students who remain in the educational mainstream. This illustrates the vital importance of continually assessing the impact of reading reforms on both attainment outcomes and achievement outcomes.

Comprehensive School Reform

Over the past four decades, the federal government has promoted improvement in education for "disadvantaged" students through the Elementary and Secondary Education Act Title I program. Early reform efforts emphasized pulling out special needs children from their classrooms and providing supplemental instruction. Over time, the federal government and some states have promoted schoolwide reforms. Most recently, the Comprehensive School Reform Demonstration, a component of Title I, has encouraged schools to adopt comprehensive schoolwide reform models. These models include Success for All, Accelerated Schools, and other reform models developed by university educators and other independent reformers in collaboration with schools.

Initial studies of the effects of comprehensive reforms in states indicate that these models can improve attainment/equity outcomes. For example, a study of teachers in Wisconsin found that some of these models enabled teachers to reduce failure rates, an important finding given that Wisconsin does not permit social promotion—passing students who fail to the next grade level, because of their age (St. John, Manset, Chung, Simmons, et al. 2003). However, while one reform model (Accelerated Schools) was more substantially associated with reductions in retention in Wisconsin, in the Indiana studies of reading reforms other models were associated with this outcome (St. John, Manset, Chung, Simmons, et al. 2003). Thus, the success of different reform models can vary across contexts.

While it is too early to judge the success of comprehensive reform, we can conclude that the study of school reform requires a sophisticated approach. Several reports that compare the impact of reform models with "control" schools indicate that reforms can improve student learning outcomes (Ross and Smith 1994; Knight and Stallings 1995). However, most studies focus on single reforms. More recently, a few studies have begun to examine the large-scale impact of comprehensive reforms in states and to compare the effects of features of different reforms on similar outcome measures. One study has found that political forces in school districts have influenced the choice of models (Datnow 2000). Further, state-level studies of reforms, controlling for the characteristics of schools and patterns of classroom practices, have found that some reforms do reduce grade-level retention (St. John, Manset, Chung, Simmons, et al. 2003). Other forces, however, such as the extent of implementation and availability of support from reform-model experts, seem to influence the efficacy of these models. So, although preliminary research is promising, we need more extensive efforts to test different approaches to reform. There seems to be little doubt that these reforms can have a substantial effect on improvement in students' academic preparation for college.

School Choice

For the past decade, two types of reforms have enhanced the school choice opportunities for schoolchildren: charters for public (or quasi-public) schools and scholarships for low-income students. Both of these efforts can potentially influence student outcomes.

Two forms of charters are being used in states. The most common form involves giving public schools charters that release them from many of the district and state requirements. This reform strategy functions something like a comprehensive reform, since schools can develop their own reform model or adopt a proven model. Less commonly, a few states (e.g., Arizona) also allow charters for private and religious schools, an approach that functions like a voucher. There is very little research on the effects of these reforms on achievement or attainment outcomes. However, this movement enjoys the support of teachers' unions, especially when it is limited, as it typically is, to public schools (Rosenberg 1989), and therefore is likely to continue. These reforms are clearly in need of further study.

The scholarship approach has been more widely studied. Both Milwaukee and Cleveland have implemented public scholarships for students to attend private schools. The studies of these reforms indicate a modest impact on student achievement (Metcalf et al. 1998; Witte 1998). No studies have systematically examined the effect on attainment outcomes, retention in grade level, or special education referral.

Several cities have also had private scholarship programs, including New York, Washington, San Antonio, Indianapolis, and Dayton. Analyses of test scores, or "effect sizes," reveal a modest effect on achievement in some of these efforts (Peterson 1998). There have also been a few qualitative studies of the impact of these reforms on schools, or the "school effect." These studies indicate that both public and private school systems rapidly adapt to these programs (St. John and Ridenour 2001), but that there are substantial constraints (i.e., accountability and testing) on teacher innovation within public schools (Ridenour and St. John 2003).

Many questions are raised by the new school choice initiatives. However, it is important to acknowledge that a majority of parents and the general public favor more opportunity to choose schools (Rose, Gallup, and Elam 1997). But polls also reveal that public school teachers do not favor these initiatives. Thus, these reforms remain contested but merit further study. Many questions remain about how increased opportunities for parental choice of schools would influence college enrollment.

Improving Academic Preparation

While increasing the requirements for high school graduation can potentially improve the percentage of high school graduates enrolling in college, there is little hope that these reforms can effect a doubling of enrollment. The review of changes in participation rates in the 1990s (chapter 7) showed that these reforms could have had a modest influence. But more substantial reforms in schools would be needed to increase the high school graduation rates and improve academic preparation. The more substantial systemic reforms hold greater potential in this regard than merely changing graduation requirements or encouraging more students to take algebra.

Improving teachers' capacity to teach children to read seems to hold the greatest potential in the long term. However, since a decade passes between the acquisition of reading skills in early primary grades and college enrollment, improvement in all levels of schooling is also crucial. Comprehensive reforms also have the potential for improving postsecondary participation. If more students achieve at grade level, then more students will probably go on to college. Comprehensive school reforms can increase the chances that students who have learned to read will continue to progress at grade level. These reforms often also include a capacity to "double dose" in reading and math for students who are having

MEETING THE ACCESS CHALLENGE

trouble (St. John, Loescher, et al. 2000), an approach that can bring more students up to grade level without the stigma of pull-out programs that take a "remedial" approach. More research is needed on this to inform practice.

School choice remains an enigma in the policy arena. It has become an ideological issue for political conservatives and many parents. As a reform strategy, however, it raises issues about the relationship between church and state as well as educational questions. The more serious issue, from the perspective of meeting the new postsecondary access challenge, is to improve the existing educational system in ways that improve students' learning, as measured by achievement and attainment/equity. In fact, to the extent that family choice of schools does increase as a result of changes in public policy, it will be important to provide more information to parents about the efficacy of different types of educational practices, so they can make more informed educational choices for their children.

To achieve these ends, we need more cooperation between policymakers and educational researchers. Historically, educational researchers have tended to use "experimental" designs in research that are essentially advocacy oriented. People who promote a specific reform conduct studies that compare the reform with "control" schools (Peterson 1998; Madden et al. 1991). These studies hold to the tenets of natural experiments but lack both controls for changes in the day-to-day practices of teachers and sophisticated statistical controls. Communication about the effects of reforms should be carried out in ways that can lead to more informed choices by educators about reform strategies, as well as more informed decisions by policymakers about frameworks to guide reform (St. John and Miron 2003). In examining the impact of reforms on schools and students, we need more sophisticated statistical models. Policymakers and researchers should collaborate on assessment of reform models and development of new reform strategies. This new generation of collaborative reforms should focus on improving attainment, including an examination of the ways in which school reforms improve postsecondary opportunity.

POSTSECONDARY TRANSITIONS

More attention must be given to strategies that could influence college transitions. Recent efforts to promote "postsecondary encouragement" provide movement in this direction, but probably do not sufficiently address the depth of the access challenge. The movement to mass higher education, increasing participation rates to about 45 percent of high school graduates, took more than a century. A substantial increase in high school graduation rates and college participation rates in the first two decades of the new century will require a massive change in perceptions and expectations for high school students and their parents.

Postsecondary Encouragement

In the past few years, a number of new efforts have been instituted to provide information on postsecondary opportunities to high school students, and even to students in middle schools. A new federal program, GEAR UP, has provided opportunities for states and universities to experiment with new approaches to providing information about postsecondary opportunities.

The research to date (e.g., Hossler and Schmit 1995; Hossler, Schmit, and Vesper 1999; Perna 2000) indicates that postsecondary encouragement can improve participation. Recently, newspapers have even begun to carry stories about the ways in which these efforts have influenced college participation rates in Indiana, a state whose college participation rates rose from fortieth place in the United States in 1986 to seventeenth place in 1998 (Wilson 2001). That newspapers have begun to document the success of postsecondary encouragement efforts is heartening, but there is also a need for more systematic research aimed at informing policy.

Far more research is needed on the ways in which different types of information influence students' aspirations and parents' perceptions, as well as on how these interventions influence transition into college and persistence in college. The perceptions of parents are important, because college attendance and college choice are essentially family decisions. Indeed, to increase the percentage of families who send their children to college, families need more information about the value of education, options for postsecondary education, and the types of school experiences that will prepare students for college.

Similarly, to benefit from the opportunity, students themselves must aspire to a postsecondary education. In this sense, educational reforms are crucial because they can influence aspirations. More requirements for graduation can negatively affect aspirations for some students. If the goal is to expand postsecondary participation, schools and families need more information on how different types of courses in middle and high schools affect aspirations for college.

Admissions

Admissions practices remain the missing link in the debate about postsecondary access. There is little doubt that the families who do not anticipate sending their children to college are those that are more disadvantaged economically. Their children are more likely to attend low-quality schools. However, little is known about ways of adjusting admissions processes so as to equalize opportunity to attend high-quality colleges. If large segments of the population feel that they lack the opportunity to send their children to good colleges because of the quality of their high schools, this will constrain the effect of encouragement strategies.

For a substantial part of the late twentieth century, affirmative action was used to equalize opportunity in college admissions. Now that some federal courts have taken the position that racial preferences can no longer be used, more research is needed on fair and equitable ways of equalizing opportunity to attend high-quality colleges.

An approach taken in a few states—including California, Texas, and Florida—has involved using class rank to adjust admissions practices. This helps equalize opportunity because schools remain racially isolated, more so than before the *Brown* decision (Fossey 1998 in press). However, more research is needed to determine how well class rank predicts persistence in college. A closely related approach involves creating indexes to adjust admissions criteria so as to take diversity and quality into consideration (Goggin 1999), an approach that has been referred to as "merit-aware" admissions.

A few studies have tested the assumptions of merit-aware admissions. One study found that indexing SAT scores to the high school average—by imputing a difference between the student's score and the average for his or her high school—provides a more equitable approach to admission (St. John, Simmons, and Musoba 2002). A second study found that this type of merit index predicted college persistence about as well as did the SAT (St. John et al. 2001). Indeed, a systematic improvement of equity in college admissions is possible. Bernal, Cabrera, and Terenzini (2000) have examined the influence of variables related to socioeconomic status on opportunity to attend different types of colleges. They found that emphasizing SES variables in admissions did not increase diversity. Colleges have historically tried to use these variables in awarding aid after admission (i.e., to meet need), and it is clear that academic merit (i.e., grades and test scores) is increasingly being used in the awarding of aid in private colleges (McPherson and Schapiro 1997). However, since adjusting admissions criteria for school quality can improve equity in college admissions, the prospect of adapting admissions strategies in ways that adjust for high school quality (St. John, Simmons, and Musoba 2002) should be seriously considered.

Creating fairer and more just approaches to college admission is crucial. In the recent past, the opportunity to attend public four-year colleges has declined (chapter 7), due in part to changes in the financial strategies used by states and the federal government. With the current need to expand postsecondary opportunity, there is reason to question whether four-year colleges will continue to be available for students who aspire to attend them. For several decades, racial preferences were used to avoid making critical judgments about the allocation of opportunity to attend public colleges. If we are to meet the challenge of expanding opportunity in the next few decades, admissions strategies must be developed over next few years that increase social justice.

Student Aid

The systematic review of the effects of policy changes on postsecondary outcomes should leave little doubt of the link between financial aid and equal opportunity in postsecondary education. Furthermore, finances influence *perceptions* of affordability, as well as financial access. If families perceive that they cannot afford to send their children to college, a substantial expansion of opportunity will be difficult.

A new generation of research has begun to examine the influence of perceptions of affordability. In particular, Cabrera, Nora, and Castaneda (1992, 1993) have documented that perceptions of the ability to pay directly influence persistence by undergraduates. Sandler (1999) found that adults are especially sensitive to concerns about affordability. Further, research studies using the financial nexus model have documented that expectations, formed in the college-choice process, have a sustained impact on persistence (Paulsen and St. John 1997, 2002). The influence of perceptions of debt on early careers has seldom been investigated but merits further study, especially given the current challenge to double postsecondary opportunity.

Improving Postsecondary Transitions

More can be done to facilitate the transition of economically diverse groups into postsecondary education. The role of policy is only moderately well understood and has not been sufficiently studied. It is clear that "postsecondary encouragement," as currently defined, can influence students' behavior (e.g., high school courses taken), but it does not sufficiently deal with the underlying problems related to financial access. In addition to improving academic preparation, efforts must be made to improve equity in college admissions and to rectify injustices in college affordability. Maintaining financial access is crucial.

A generation of students has left college—as graduates and dropouts—with high levels of debt. Low-income students were more likely to drop out and default. And recent research indicates that low grades and high debt influence freshman dropout rates (St. John et al.

2001). This means that debt and poor achievement contribute to dropout. If low-achieving students are more likely to drop out, then debt could be a factor that inhibits academic access.

EXPANDING STATE SYSTEMS

Achieving the goal of doubling postsecondary access would require a doubling of the capacity of the postsecondary system. There are several different approaches to system expansion, as detailed below.

Postsecondary Opportunities

There is compelling evidence to suggest that the greatest challenge is to expand education for mid-skilled workers (Grubb 1996a,b). Grubb's argument that educational programs need to blend traditional academic courses with technical courses is also compelling. This is essentially the strategy that was used in proprietary schools, a sector of education that declined as a result of efforts to reduce loan default (St. John 1994). There is also a push to expand community colleges to meet this challenge (Boesel and Fredland 1999).

Whether other postsecondary education (i.e., education that blends academic and technical courses) is offered by private corporations or by public two-year colleges, the rapid development of this sector could accentuate class differences within American society. There is a substantial difference in earnings potential between completion of high school and some postsecondary attainment (two years or less), as there is between some postsecondary attainment and a four-year degree (Grubb 1996a,b; Leslie and Brinkman 1988; Pascarella and Terenzini 1991). Almost one-third of the high-school-age population does not graduate from high school and therefore enters the college-age population underprepared. Two-year colleges must face the challenge of providing adequate academic support if the United States is to meet the academic access challenge.

Academic access to four-year colleges may be limited by prior achievement, especially when merit consideration influences admissions, but economic privilege should not be the primary determinant of access to four-year colleges. It is crucial to maintain financial access to four-year colleges for all students who are academically prepared. Resolution of questions about justice in admissions to four-year colleges is certainly part of the process of achieving equity in opportunity (e.g., Bernal, Cabrera, and Terenzini 1999, 2000; St. John et al. 2001) and can help minimize the potential for injustice across economic groups. But as policymakers make decisions about how to expand state postsecondary systems, they must understand the tradeoffs associated with emphasizing other postsecondary opportunities.

Better articulation between two-year and four-year systems can also help mitigate the potential for injustice. As individuals gain experience after completing other postsecondary programs, they may increase their aspirations. If they choose to go on to four-year colleges, they should not be penalized for their prior educational choices. If academically prepared students are forced to start in two-year colleges for financial reasons, they should have the same chances of graduating in four years as similar students who go directly to four-year colleges. States should have statewide agreements about the transferability of college courses between systems.

Expanding Public Four-Year College Systems

During the twentieth century, the expansion of public four-year systems closely paralleled expansion in opportunity. However, in the 1990s, the opportunity to attend four-year colleges declined, and the gap in opportunity between Whites and minorities widened. Thus, in the decades ahead, ample opportunity to attend public four-year college systems should be made available. Private colleges certainly have a role, but the challenge remains to ensure adequate opportunity within public four-year systems.

Two-year colleges cost less than four-year colleges not only for students but also for taxpayers. The emphasis on efficiency in two-year colleges (Voorhees 2001) is unlikely to fade away in the near future. As states attempt to expand postsecondary opportunity, they will probably continue to develop two-year colleges as a low-cost alternative. If most students who attend two-year colleges have high levels of financial need, little is gained from high tuition and high grants in this sector unless a basic commitment to efficiency is maintained. Employment options for some postsecondary graduates continue to pay less than employment options for four-year graduates, so it is unlikely that the labor market will push up faculty salaries in the two-year sector. In fact, there is a surplus of professionals prepared to teach in this sector, as evidenced by the extensive use of part-time faculty.

Four-year college systems are more expensive for states to operate. Universities must compete with industry for faculty with a Ph.D., and the private sector can pay substantially greater salaries. While scientists in industry will probably continue to earn more than college professors, four-year colleges must be somewhat responsive to these pressures. Thus, four-year colleges will probably continue to require more tax dollars (either for direct subsidies or student aid) than two-year colleges. The option of financing "two plus two" programs, which provide the second two years of college on two-year campuses only, partially resolves this problem. Offering only two-year completion programs on two-year campuses constrains the educational options available to students. It simply is not possible to replicate the educational and social opportunities provided by a four-year college when four-year programs are developed as add-ons to two-year programs. Thus, the decision to maintain access to four-year systems remains a challenge for states.

Privatization

During the last two decades of the twentieth century, there was a gradual movement toward privatization of public four-year college systems. The percentage of educational revenues derived from tuition increased as the percentage from state appropriations declined. This type of privatization will probably continue in the next few decades, increasing the competitiveness between public and private colleges for four-year college students.

A lesson of the 1990s is that there are limits to the efficacy of high loans as the primary means of providing student aid as part of the privatization process. Clearly, affordability within public systems is an important issue for states (Davis 2000; National Center for Public Policy 2000). As the analyses in part I indicate, maintaining equity in opportunity is closely linked to making a sufficient state investment in government need-based grants. Therefore, as states move toward increased privatization of public colleges and increased competition between public and private colleges, it is essential that they maintain adequate state grant programs.

Questions about the extent of expansion of four-year systems and the extent of privatization of these systems are inexorably linked, especially given the need to expand other postsecondary opportunities. As they attempt to respond to the new access challenge, states need to closely monitor the impact of their financing strategies.

ELIMINATING THE NEW INEQUITY

Now that states are confronted by a challenge to expand their public systems, coordination and planning are important again. Most states need a new vision of postsecondary education, as well as a new generation of planning for state systems, a topic considered below.

Recommendations

No single optimal strategy or blueprint can fit all states in their efforts to expand postsecondary access and equalize opportunity. However, examining strategies from the three perspectives on justice might help states develop workable approaches, addressing the needs of their populations and their economies. States should strive for a balanced approach to expanding access, equalizing opportunity, and maintaining low taxpayer costs.

RECOMMENDATIONS FOR EXPANDING ACCESS

1 Educational reforms should be evaluated based on attainment/equity outcomes and achievement outcomes.

By emphasizing attainment/equity outcomes, including high school graduation and college enrollment, along with improvements in achievement tests, states can target school reforms on improving postsecondary opportunity. The choices of which combination of reform strategies to emphasize—for reading improvement, schoolwide improvement, and enhancement of parents' involvement in their children's learning (e.g., school-choice schemes, including charters)—should be guided in part by assessing the impact of these reforms on educational attainment. Strategies that increase the percentage of K–12 students who stay in the mainstream (i.e., those that reduce retention and referral) will improve graduation and enhance college access. Assessment of reforms along these dimensions may be more important, in the long run, than whether reforms improve test scores per se, although the two outcomes are obviously related.

2 Postsecondary encouragement for students in middle and high schools should emphasize taking courses that help prepare them for college and should provide information that helps families with their financial planning.

Systematic outreach to students is crucial and has not been implemented in most states. Most states have not made the commitment to ensure adequate aid for low-income students or adapted their admissions processes to optimize opportunity for all. However, for the admissions aspect of postsecondary policy, even more than for postsecondary encouragement, it is important to balance the goal of expansion with the goal of equity in opportunity.

The need to provide adequate student aid not only is crucial in efforts to promote and expand financial access but also is central in reaching a threshold of college affordability within states. Thus, the affordability aspect of postsecondary encouragement has implications for the entire system of state finance. At the very least, states should routinely assess whether their colleges are affordable for diverse students and should communicate information about college affordability with parents and students.

MEETING THE ACCESS CHALLENGE

3 If states plan for expanding community colleges as a means of providing more postsecondary opportunity, they should ensure that admission to four-year colleges is equitable and that academically prepared undergraduates have opportunities for transfer.

Questions about how to expand public systems—including whether to emphasize two-year or four-year college systems—are among the most important issues for states. A better balance between the two types of opportunities will be needed and, in most states, the greater growth probably should be in two-year college opportunities. However, maintaining equal access to four-year college systems is essential. And given the eroding access to public four-year colleges, states must also find better ways to ensure that graduates of two-year colleges gain access to the second two years of their undergraduate education.

4 The proposed first-tier federal grant (the basic grant) should be sufficient to promote financial access for low-income students to the average public four-year college.

Erosion in the purchasing power of Pell grants is a major reason for the financial aspect of the access challenge. As discussed in chapter 10, the first tier of federal student aid should be adequate to enable low-income students to attend low-cost public four-year colleges. Providing a basic grant sufficient for this purpose will expand access for low-income youths.

RECOMMENDATIONS FOR ELIMINATING THE NEW INEQUALITY

1 States should routinely assess whether middle schools and high schools adequately prepare all children and whether colleges provide adequate academic support for students they admit.

States should strive to expand and equalize the opportunity to attend college across diverse groups. Simple comparisons of rates of postsecondary participation across diverse groups provide one indicator. However, equalization of opportunity must also be assessed by "controlling" for differences in academic preparation and achievement. Using statistical analyses that control for both students' preparation for college and their achievement in college has several advantages over simple comparisons of participation rates. It provides an analysis of the relative effects of academic preparation, college achievement, and finances:

—If poor academic preparation inhibits equality of opportunity to enroll or persist, the state should put more emphasis on K–12 reforms.
—If poor academic achievement in college inhibits equality in persistence rates, the state should emphasize improvement in academic support for college students.

—If financial aid is inadequate to equalize the opportunity to enroll or persist, controlling for students' preparation for and achievement in college, states should provide more financial aid to equalize opportunity, given the costs of attending.

2 Admissions standards for four-year colleges should reward academic merit, controlling for the quality of high schools that students have attended.

Given the great disparity in the quality of K–12 schools, states should routinely assess whether diverse groups have equal opportunity to attend more elite institutions, controlling for the quality of the high school attended. College admissions policies should not penalize students from low-income communities because they attended low-quality K–12 schools. The quality of K–12 schools is the responsibility of the state and local communities, as much as or more than it is the responsibility of parents in a school's attendance area. College admissions policies are unjust if they prevent children from attending college because of the poor quality of the K–12 schools they attended. However, it is also important to reward achievement, controlling for school quality. This means that admissions to elite public universities should take school characteristics and quality into account. One method of doing this is to use high school rank instead of test scores (as in Texas, California, and Florida, for example). Another method is to adjust test scores for school characteristics (e.g., Goggin 1999; St. John, Simmons, and Musoba 2002).

3 States should fund need-based grant programs at a level sufficient to equalize opportunity for persistence between low-income students and middle- and upper-income students, controlling for academic preparation and performance.

The drift toward high tuition in public colleges and universities has contributed to the growing gaps in opportunity between students of low-income and middle-income families and between Whites and people of color. If states choose to let tuition rise rather than provide adequate subsidies to institutions, they should also provide adequate state grants to equalize opportunity for low-income students to persist, controlling for academic preparation and performance. It is also appropriate to subsidize the opportunity to attend private colleges as an integral part of state programs. States should also periodically evaluate the adequacy of grant aid as a means of determining whether this goal is being met.

4 The federal government should institute a second-tier grant that includes incentives to states and private colleges to provide adequate grant aid to enable college choice within state systems of public and private colleges. States should have discretion to set merit-related criteria for second-tier awards, but aid should be awarded based on need.

A cost-sharing approach should be developed for the second-tier federal-state grant program. The parameters for developing such a program were discussed in chapter 10. The second tier of grants should provide incentives for achieving greater efficiency for institutions and states that choose to be part of this program.

RECOMMENDATION FOR INCREASING TAXPAYER JUSTICE

1 States should routinely monitor taxpayer costs per student enrolled in state systems of higher education (institutional subsidies plus student grants), but the efficiency goal should be balanced with both access and equity considerations.

Different strategies for expanding opportunity, including decisions about whether to expand two-year systems or emphasize grants, influence taxpayer costs per student, and these costs merit consideration when plans are developed for expanding postsecondary systems. However, the process of developing a system of public finance that is efficient for taxpayers involves more than reducing taxes for families with children in college. The efficiency goal of maintaining modest tax expenditures per student needs to be balanced against the equity goal—both equal opportunity to attend and equal opportunity to attain a four-year degree.

During the progressive period in the United States (1880s through 1970s), two sorts of rationales were frequently used to argue for taxpayer funding: (1) promoting economic development, a conservative rationale, and (2) expanding social opportunity, a liberal rationale. By the middle 1960s, the theory of human capital provided a general rationale that integrated both liberal and conservative arguments. Advocates used this human capital rationale to argue that more spending on higher education would improve the economy and increase individual opportunity. However, the credibility of this long-standing rationale broke down. It was possible to spend less on higher education for the majority of students and still expand access, as was the case in the 1980s and 1990s.

Cost-benefit ratios were also frequently used to construct arguments for public funding; this involved analyzing spending and returns. When this approach was used to examine the impact of the federal investment in student aid, it became evident that student aid had a high return rate (St. John and Masten 1990). However, when the federal role changed in the 1980s, the idea that a single ratio could be used to rationalize funding seemed to break down. If loans had lower costs than grants, and if enrollments increased when high tuition and high loans were used, this strategy had a high cost-benefit ratio (i.e., more access for less money per student). But this approach overlooked the consequences of reductions in grants for low-income students.

An alternative approach is to construct a set of indicators that can be used to assess the effects of aid. This book has related the interests of majority (traditional-age and middle-income) students, minority (nontraditional and low-income) students, and taxpayers. The analyses provide a basis for rethinking financial strategies. However, more research is needed to develop a workable set of indicators.

> **2** The federal government should evaluate the efficacy of targeted tax credits as a means of funding higher education in relation to the goal of maintaining lower tax rates for all taxpayers.

The Economic Growth and Tax Relief Reconciliation Act of 2001 both extended federal tax credits for higher education and reduced overall tax rates. A parallel can be drawn between this recent effort to extend targeted tax credits and efforts to extend student grants to middle-income students in 1978. In retrospect, it is now clear that the guidelines for federal grant programs were liberalized too much after 1978. The refinancing of the 1980s showed that loans were a more economical way to expand postsecondary opportunity for middle-income students. Did the most recent liberalization of tax credits take a similar turn, liberalizing the program too extensively? Are loans a more efficient way than tax credits to finance middle-class access?

The role and impact of tax credits should be systematically evaluated as a form of targeted tax relief. We need to ask questions about the relative cost burden to low-income and middle-income families. Is it just to reduce taxes for middle-income families while their children are in college, when low-income students face excessive unmet need? The effects of targeted reductions in taxes should be evaluated relative to their impact on college participation and equal opportunity to participate in college across diverse groups.

Conclusion

Policymakers concerned about postsecondary access and the new inequality face a major new challenge. For the next two decades, states will need to address the challenge of expanding their capacity for postsecondary opportunities. This could include an increased emphasis on grants and loans as a means of expanding opportunities within private colleges and private corporations that provide postsecondary training (i.e., proprietary schools). However, a substantial percentage of the expansion should be in low-cost postsecondary institutions. At the same time, it is crucial to maintain equal opportunity for access to moderate-cost public four-year institutions. Finding a balanced approach to expansion, one that considers the interests of diverse racial/ethnic and economic groups, will not be easy.

The political nature of this new financial access challenge is not diminished by other types of interventions that can expand demand. Improvements in K–12 schools can influence students' preparation for college. Postsecondary encouragement can increase the percentage of students who aspire to attend college. But these strategies essentially expand demand and increase the political pressure to make wise decisions about the development of postsecondary educational systems within states. Decisions about how to expand public systems of higher education are political, but research can help inform these decisions. To maintain an open debate about alternative paths through this puzzle, it is important to conduct policy studies that can inform legislators and other policymakers in states and at the federal level.

Trends in Finances and Outcomes

Eric H. Asker

The trends in finances and the key indicators of outcomes are presented in nine tables. We chose to place these tables in an appendix because they are referred to in several of the chapters. After summarizing the approach used for the trend analyses, I describe the sources for each table.

The Trend Analyses

The methods used to calculate and present trends are consistent with St. John's earlier trend analyses (1991a, 1992a; St. John and Elliott 1994; St. John and Noell 1989). The data from generally available sources were used to present trends in key financial indicators and outcomes.

First, the trend analyses consider national statistics reported by the National Center for Education Statistics and the College Board, because these are routine and relatively standardized data collections. The NCES data collections—the Higher Education General Information Surveys (HEGIS) and its successor, the Integrated Postsecondary Education Data Education System (IPEDS)—are the primary sources of information for most of the enrollment and finance information reported here. The structure of the data elements collected in HEGIS and IPEDS has changed over time, but the primary categories of revenue and expenditure have been maintained, thus making it possible for us to report trends. In a few instances, the NCES data reported here were from sources other than HEGIS/IPEDS. For example, NCES summarizes Current Population Surveys to report on trends in college participation. Further, NCES's K–12 data collections were the source for information on high school graduation and college enrollment by high school graduates. The College Board collects information from the U.S. Department of Education and other federal agencies that administer student financial aid programs. The board's data collection is the only consistent source of information on the amount of aid awarded. There is no consistent source of information for the actual costs of student aid programs.

The method we used for estimating financial amounts per FTE is the best available method for calculating from NCES's statistical reports. However, the method has some limitations. Over time, the universe of institutions that report to NCES on HEGIS/IPEDS has changed. Specifically, a number of private proprietary schools did not report to HEGIS, but better efforts were made to include these institutions in IPEDS. Therefore the statistics on private two-year colleges do not capture the entire universe of institutions. Further, not all institutions report on all forms and all data elements each year. Given the nature of the IPEDS/ HEGIS forms, it is difficult to control for this problem, even as the actual data files are reanalyzed. The effects of the missing data on the aggregate numbers reported by NCES are difficult to estimate. However, the large aggregate numbers imputed by NCES are the most accurate information available and therefore are used as a basis for these tables. In general, NCES does an exceptional job of collecting detailed information from thousands of colleges and universities.

Second, we examined changes in five-year periods, from 1970 until the most recent year reported by NCES or the College Board. Had every year been reported here, the trend tables would have been overly lengthy, elaborate, and difficult to interpret. But ten-year trends would be too long to capture the consequences of changes in policy. The half-decades, often used in trend analyses in student aid (e.g., Hearn 1993; St. John 1994; St. John and Elliott 1994), provide a reasonable basis for capturing the consequences of changes in policy that correspond to changes in national leadership.

Third, for most of the financial indicators, we converted to dollars per FTE student when appropriate. Dollars per FTE were calculated by summing the number of total full-time students and an FTE calculation for part-time students, obtained by dividing the total number of full-time students by three, an approach used by NCES in its annual reports (*The Condition of Education, Digest of Education Statistics*, and so forth). In this method, three part-time students are assumed to be equal to one full-time student in terms of revenue contribution and/or consumption of resources. When calculating and comparing financial amounts across sectors, we used total FTE in a sector as the denominator (graduate and undergraduate) and the total amount of funds as the numerator (for revenue or expenditure categories).

Fourth, the dollar amounts in the trend tables were converted to 1997–98 dollars using the Consumer Price Index for All Urban Consumers (CPI-U). The conversion to a common, inflation-adjusted amount provides a basis for comparisons of dollar amounts. All dollar amounts reported in tables throughout the book were also converted using this method.

Fifth, we examined the accuracy of NCES's enrollment projections, reported annually in the *Projections of Education Statistics.* We also examined the accuracy of enrollment predictions made in 1970, 1980, and 1990, estimating the difference between predicted and actual enrollment. These tables show the difference between actual enrollment and the estimates made in 1970, 1980, and 1990.

The Trend Tables

Trends in price and cost of attendance (table A.1) were taken directly from NCES's *Digest of Education Statistics* (1999a, 2001b). The numbers reported by NCES were converted to 1997–98 dollar amounts (Amt.) using the CPI-U, and the percentage change (% Ch.) was imputed for each five-year period.

Trends in federal aid awarded to postsecondary students (table A.2) are from the College Board's *Trends in Student Aid* (1998, 2000). We adjusted these numbers to 1997–98 dollars using the CPI-U and calculated the five-year change percentages; a total amount of federal student aid was imputed by adding specially directed and generally available aid within aid categories (grants, loans, and work-study).

Trends in educational and related revenues per FTE in public institutions (table A.3) were calculated using multiple tables in NCES's *Digest of Education Statistics* (1999a, 2001b), as indicated in the source note for this table. The gross expenditures by category were divided by total FTE, using similar categories of institutions across NCES's tables. Total educational and related revenue was calculated by adding revenues from tuition and fees and revenues from state and local sources. The percentage of revenues from each source was calculated using the same method.

Trends in total student aid (table A.4) used the College Board's *Trends in Student Aid* (1998, 2000) as the primary source. The "total student aid" category includes the total aid (from table A.2) along with state aid, institutional aid, and other loans. Five-year change percentages were calculated for each category of award.

Trends in educational expenditures per FTE (table A.5) were calculated from information reported in NCES's *Digest of Education Statistics* (1999a, 2001b), as indicated in the footnotes. We calculated the expenditures per student by dividing the total reported expenditures for each category, by the total FTE in the respective sector (private sector in part A, public sector in part B). We calculated total educational and related expenditures by adding expenditures on instruction, academic support, student services, institutional support, and operations and maintenance. After calculating expenditure categories per FTE, we calculated the five-year change percentages.

Trends in FTE undergraduate enrollment (table A.6) are from NCES's *Projections of Education Statistics* (1980, 1989, 1999b, and 2000c). Trends in the percentage of high school graduates (table A.7) and college enrollment rates of high school graduates (table A.8) are from NCES's *Digest of Education Statistics, 2000* (2001b). No additional calculations were made from the data reported by these primary sources.

Calculations of trends in tax expenditures per FTE (table A.9) were drawn from the multiple sources reported above (see the table source note). We abstracted trend data from NCES's *Digest of Education Statistics* (various years) and the College Board's *Trends in Student Aid* (various years). Consistent with prior research (e.g., McPherson and Schapiro 1997), we assumed that it cost fifty cents to subsidize one dollar of loans. This method probably overestimated the taxpayer cost of loans, given the lower default rates in the 1990s. Also, no costs were attributed to unsubsidized loans.

TABLE A.1 Trends in Price and Cost of Attendance

	1970–71 Amt.	1975–76 Amt.	70–75 % Ch.	1980–81 Amt.	75–80 % Ch.	1985–86 Amt.	80–85 % Ch.	1990–91 Amt.	85–90 % Ch.	1995–96 Amt.	90–95 % Ch.	1999–2000 Amt.	95–99 % ch.
Cost of Attendance (one undergraduate year)													
All 4-yr.	—	—	—	10,450	—	13,722	31.31	15,990	16.53	18,440	15.32	19,871	7.76
Private													
Universities	12,892	13,021	1.00	12,271	−5.76	16,408	33.71	19,936	21.50	23,560	18.18	25,341	7.56
Other four-year	10,594	9,867	−6.86	9,805	−0.63	12,715	29.68	14,762	16.10	16,959	14.88	18,368	8.31
Two-year	8,571	7,903	−8.04	8,038	1.71	9,683	20.47	11,237	16.05	12,106	7.73	13,150	8.62
All four-year	—	—	—	4,763	—	5,738	20.67	6,346	10.60	7,344	15.73	7,894	7.49
Public													
Universities	6,020	5,641	−6.30	5,066	−10.19	6,165	21.69	6,747	9.44	7,798	15.58	8,512	9.16
Other four-year	4,916	4,830	−1.75	4,522	−6.38	5,408	19.59	6,045	11.78	7,046	16.56	7,484	6.22
Two-year	4,068	4,040	−0.69	3,786	−6.29	4,433	17.09	4,188	−5.53	4,415	5.42	4,510	2.15
Tuition and Fees (one undergraduate year)													
All four-year	—	—	—	6,757	—	9,102	36.70	10,972	20.54	12,818	16.82	14,031	9.46
Private													
Universities	8,070	8,398	4.06	7,986	−4.91	10,965	37.30	13,746	25.36	16,338	18.86	18,445	12.90
Other four-year	6,534	6,075	−7.02	6,333	4.25	8,388	32.45	10,134	20.82	11,828	16.72	12,862	8.74
Two-year	4,520	4,160	−7.96	4,507	8.34	5,450	20.92	6,729	23.27	7,427	10.37	7,743	4.25
All four-year	—	—	—	1,502	—	1,960	30.49	2,281	16.38	2,982	30.73	3,201	7.34
Public													
Universities	1,948	1,871	−3.95	1,709	−8.67	2,284	33.65	2,608	14.19	3,299	26.50	3,605	9.28
Other four-year	1,353	1,367	1.03	1,349	−1.32	1,720	27.50	2,062	19.88	2,785	35.06	2,951	5.96
Two-year	762	714	−6.30	730	2.24	953	30.55	995	4.41	1,297	30.35	1,276	−1.62

Sources: NCES 1999a, 334–35, table 311; 2001b, 345, table 313. Data converted to 1997–98 constant dollars using CPI-U.

Note: All dollar amounts in constant 1997–98 dollars, converted using CPI-U.

TABLE A.2 Trends in Federal Aid Awarded to Postsecondary Students

	1970–71 Amt.	1975–76 Amt.	70–75 % Ch.	1980–81 Amt.	75–80 % Ch.	1985–86 Amt.	80–85 % Ch.	1990–91 Amt.	85–90 % Ch.	1995–96 Amt.	90–95 % Ch.	1999–2000 Amt.	95–99 % ch
1. Grants													
Pell Grants	—	2,701	—	4,457	65.01	5,347	19.97	5,961	11.48	5,728	–3.91	6,331	7.62
SEOG	670	701	4.63	689	–1.71	612	–11.18	553	–9.64	610	10.31	583	–4.43
SSIG	—	57	—	135	136.84	113	–16.30	71	–37.17	67	–5.63	50	–25.37
Grant subtotal	670	3,459	416.27	5,281	52.67	6,072	14.98	6,585	8.45	6,405	–2.73	6,964	8.73
2. Work													
CWS	816	860	5.39	1,233	43.37	975	–20.92	879	–9.85	799	–9.10	906	13.39
3. Loans													
Perkins Loans (NDSL)	979	1,342	37.08	1,295	–3.50	1045	–19.31	1,051	0.57	1,077	2.47	1,062	–1.39
Guaranteed (FFELP)	4,133	3,695	–10.60	11,581	213.42	13,138	13.44	15,301	16.46	19,820	29.53	22,048	11.24
Income cont. loans								7					
Ford Direct Loans										8,848		10,874	22.90
Loan subtotal	5,112	5,037	–1.47	12,876	155.63	14,183	10.15	16,359	15.34	29,745	81.83	33,984	14.25

B. Specially Directed Aid

1. Grants

Social Security	2,032	3,188	56.89	3,516	10.29	1,284	−59.89	820	−36.14	1,364	66.34	1,347	−1.25
Veterans' benefits	4,564	12,191	167.11	3,201	−73.74	509	35.73	445	−12.57	458	2.92	463	1.09
Military	263	282	7.22	375	32.98								
Other grants	65	184	183.08	227	23.37	100	−55.95	142	42.00	234	64.79	255	8.97
Subtotal	6,924	15,845	128.84	7,319	−53.81	1,893	−74.14	1,407	−25.67	2,056	46.13	2,065	0.44

2. Loans other

Loans and other	171	131	−23.39	116	−11.45	554	377.59	417	−24.73	340	−18.47	210	−38.24

C. Total Federal Student Aid

1. Available funds

Grants	7,594	19,304	154.20	12,600	−34.73	7,965	−36.79	7,992	0.34	8,461	5.87	9,029	6.71
Work-study	816	860	5.39	1,233	43.37	975	−20.92	879	−9.85	799	−9.10	906	13.39
Loans	5,283	5,168	−2.18	12,992	151.39	14,737	13.43	16,776	13.84	30,085	79.33	34,194	13.66
Total	13,693	25,332	85.00	26,825	5.89	23,677	−11.74	25,647	8.32	39,345	53.41	44,129	12.16

2. Composition of funds (%)

Grants	55.46	76.20		46.97		33.64		31.16		21.50		20.46	
Work-study	5.96	3.39		4.60		4.12		3.43		2.03		2.05	
Loans	38.58	20.40		48.43		62.24		65.41		76.46		77.49	
Total	100	100		100		100		100		100		100	

Sources: College Board 1998, 7, 15; 2000. 6; 200 lb, 6, Table 1.

Note: All dollar amounts in millions of constant 1997–98 dollars, converted using CPI-U.

TABLE A.3 Trends in Educational and Related Revenue per FTE in Public Institutions, 1975–96

	1975–76	1980–81	75–80 % Ch.	1985–86	80–85 % Ch.	1990–91	80–85 % Ch.	1995–96	85–90 % Ch.	Prelim. 1996–97	95–96 % Ch.
Revenue Source											
Tuition and fees	1,554	1,567	0.84	2,105	34.33	2,439	15.87	3,141	28.78	3,225	2.67
State and local funding[a]	5,804	5,761	–0.74	6,740	16.99	6,243	–7.38	6,007	–3.78	6,626	10.30
Expenditures											
Educational and related	7,562	7,614	0.69	8,996	18.15	9,173	1.97	9,749	6.28	9,817	0.70
Revenue as a percentage of Education & Related Expenditures											
Tuition and fees	20.55	20.58		23.40		26.58		32.22		32.85	
State and local	76.75	75.66		74.92		68.06		61.62		67.50	
Total	97.30	96.24		98.32		94.64		93.84		100.35	

Sources: For 1975–76, revenue calculated from NCES 1988, 259, table 224; FTE from NCES 1999a, 222, table 200. For 1980–81 through 1995–96, information from NCES 1999a: revenue from p. 349, table 325; FTE from p. 222, table 200. For 1996–97, information from NCES 2001b: FTE from p. 230, table 201; expenditures abstracted from p. 376, table 343; revenue from p. 359, table 328. For 1975–76, expenditures calculated from NCES 1988, 268, table 233. For 1980–96, expenditures calculated from NCES 1999a, 365, table 339.

Note: All dollar amounts in constant 1997–98 dollars, converted using CPI-U

a "Revenue" sums revenue from state governments and from local governments, but includes only appropriations. Restricted and unrestricted grants and contracts are excluded.

TABLE A.4 Trends in Total Student Aid from Federal, State, and Institutional Sources

	1970–71 Amt.	1975–76 Amt.	70–75 % Ch.	1980–81 Amt.	75–80 % Ch.	1985–86 Amt.	80–85 % Ch.	1990–91 Amt.	85–90 % Ch.	1995–96 Amt.	90–95 % Ch.	1999–2000 Amt.	95–99 % ch
Federal Total													
Grants	7,594	19,304	154.20	12,600	−34.73	7,965	−36.79	7,992	0.34	8,461	5.87	9,029	6.71
Work-study	816	860	5.39	1,233	43.37	975	−20.92	879	−9.85	799	−9.10	906	13.39
Loans	5,283	5,168	−2.18	12,992	151.39	14,737	13.43	16,776	13.84	30,085	79.33	34,194	13.66
Total	13,693	25,332	85.00	26,825	5.89	23,677	−11.74	25,647	8.32	39,345	53.41	44,129	12.16
State													
Grant programs	961	1,429	48.70	1,496	4.69	1,948	30.21	2,246	15.30	3,140	39.80	3,403	8.38
Non-Federal Loans										1,303		2,229	71.07
Institutional and other													
Grants	3407	3,408	0.03	3,033	−11.00	4,402	45.14	6,958	58.06	9,879	41.98	11,205	13.42
Total Student Aid	18,059	30,169	67.04	31,353	3.93	30,027	−4.23	34,852	16.07	53,668	53.99	60,966	13.60

Sources: College Board 1998, 7, 15. Data for 1997–98 from, College Board 2000, 6; 200 lb, 6.

Note: All dollar amounts in millions constant 1997–98 dollars, converted using CPI-U.

TABLE A.5 Trends in Educational Expenditures per FTE, 1975–95

	1975–76.	1980–81.	75–80 % Ch.	1985–86.	80–85 % Ch.	1990–91.	80–85 % Ch.	1995–96.	85–90 % Ch.	Prelim. 1996–97	95–96 % Ch.
A. Private Institutions											
Instruction	5,330	5,049	−5.27	5,980	18.44	7,035	17.64	7,765	10.38		
Academic support	1,053	1,068	1.42	1,290	20.79	1,552	20.31	1,740	12.11		
Student services	759	822	8.30	1,072	30.41	1,308	22.01	1,548	18.35		
Institutional support	1,863	1,896	1.77	2,407	26.95	2,837	17.86	3,058	7.79		
Operation and maintenance	1,377	1,432	3.99	1,587	10.82	1,698	6.99	1,753	3.24		
Total educational and related	10,382	10,267	−1.11	12,336	20.15	14,430	16.97	15,864	9.94		
Scholarship and fellowships[a]	611	612	0.16	1,038	69.61	1,581	52.31	2,333	47.56		
B. Public Institutions											
Instruction	4,253	4,176	−1.81	4,880	16.86	5,014	2.75	5,221	4.13	5,233	0.23
Academic support	789	852	7.98	1,047	22.89	1,208	15.38	1,216	0.66	1,246	1.02
Student services	498	548	10.04	652	18.98	703	7.82	785	11.66	807	2.80
Institutional support	1,057	1,002	−5.20	1,264	26.15	1,284	1.58	1,447	12.69	1,458	0.76
Operation and maintenance	965	1,035	7.25	1,155	11.59	1,064	−7.88	1,081	1.60	1,073	−0.74
Total education and related	7,562	7,613	0.67	8,997	18.18	9,273	3.07	9,750	5.14	9,817	0.69
Scholarship and fellowships[a]	124	103	16.94	155	50.49	203	30.97	332	63.55	354	6.63

Sources: For 1975–76 and 1980–81, expenditures derived from NCES 1988, 269, table 234; FTE derived from NCES 2001, 230, table 201. For 1985–86 through 1995–96, information abstracted from NCES 1999a: FTE derived from p. 222, table 200; expenditures derived from p. 366, table 340. For 1975–76, expenditures derived from NCES 1988, 268, table 233; FTE derived from NCES 1999, 222, table 200. For 1980–81 through 1995–96, information derived from NCES 1999a: FTE from p. 222, table 200; expenditures from p. 365, table 339. For 1996–97, information taken from NCES 2001b: FTE from p. 230, table 201; expenditures from p. 376, table 343.

Note: All dollar amounts in constant 1997–98 dollars, converted using CPI-U.

[a] Scholarships and fellowships are for unrestricted funds only.

TABLE A.6 Trends in FTE Undergraduate Enrollments

	1970	1975	1980	1985	1990	1995	1996	1997
Public four-year	3,053	3,428	3,524	3,601	4,015	3,976	3,984	4,025
Private four-year	1,407	1,486	1,585	1,603	1,729	1,822	1,856	1,892
Public two-year	1,413	2,465	2,484	2,428	2,819	2,995	3,008	3,026
Private two-year	105	114	173	221	197	168	163	138
Total	**5,978**	**7,493**	**7,766**	**7,853**	**8,760**	**8,961**	**9,011**	**9,081**

Sources: For 1970 and 1975; data from NCES 1980, 44, table 12A; 45, table 12B. For 1980 and 1985, frp, NCES 1989, 49, table 24; 50, table 25. For 1990, 1995, and 1996, from NCES 1999b, 48, table 24; 49, table 25. For 1997, NCES 2000c, tables 31 and 32.
Note: Enrollments in thousands.

TABLE A.7 High School Graduates as Percentage of Population 17 Years of Age, 1960–61 to 1999–2000

School Year	Graduates as Percentage of All 17-year-Olds
1960–61	67.9
1965–66	76.4
1970–71	75.9
1975–76	73.7
1980–81	71.7
1985–86	72.0
1990–91	73.2
1995–96	69.8
1999–2000	70.6

Source: NCES 2001b, 122, table 101.

TABLE A.8 College Enrollment Rates of All 18- to 24-Year-Old High School Graduates, by Race/Ethnicity, 1967–1999, Selected Years

| | Percentage of High School Graduates Enrolled in College | | | |
Year	Total	White	African American	Hispanic
1967	33.7	34.5	23.3	NA
1970	32.6	33.2	26.0	NA
1972[a]	31.9	32.6	27.2	25.8
1975	32.5	32.3	31.5	35.5
1980	31.8	32.1	27.6	29.9
1985	33.7	34.9	26.0	26.8
1990	39.1	40.4	32.7	28.7
1995	42.3	44.0	34.5	35.2
1999	43.7	45.3	39.2	31.6

Source: NCES 2001b, 216, table 187.

[a] First year rates were reported for Hispanic students.

TABLE A.9 Trends in Tax Expenditures per FTE

	1970–71	1975–76	1980–81	1985–86	1990–91	1995–96	1998–99
Federal							
Grants	1,127	2,276	1,428	891	801	819	901
Loans[a]	319	225	662	764	625	849	817
Subtotal	1,446	2,501	2,090	1,655	1,426	1,668	1,718
State and Local							
State grants to students	143	169	170	218	225	304	
State/local appropriations	4,315	4,522	4,393	5,078	4,770	4,592	NA
Subtotal	4,458	4,691	4,563	5,196	4,995	4,833	
Total	5,904	7,129	6,653	6,851	6,421	6,501	

Sources: FTC from NCES 2000a, 230, table 201. For federal grants and loans, dollar amounts from College Board 1998, 7, 15. For 1998–99, dollar amounts for grants and loans from College Board 2000, 6. For state and local appropriations, dollar amounts for 1980–96 from NCES 2000a; for 1975–76, from NCES 1999a; for 1970–71, from NCES 1973. State grant dollar amounts from College Board 2000, 6, 18.

Note: All dollar amounts in millions constant 1997–98 dollars, converted using CPI-U.

[a] Loan amounts calculated at fifty cents per dollar of loan.

REFERENCES

Adelman, C. 1995. *The new college course map and transcript files: Changes in course-taking and achievement, 1972–1993.* Washington, DC: National Center for Education Statistics.

———. 1999. *Answers in the tool box: Academic intensity, attendance patterns, and bachelor's degree attainment.* Washington, DC: National Center for Education Statistics.

Adkins, D. L. 1975. *The great American degree machine: An economic analysis of the human resource output of higher education.* Berkeley, CA: Carnegie Foundation for the Advancement of Teaching.

Advanced Technology and Westat. 1983. *Quality control study: Final report.* Reston, VA: Advanced Technology.

Advisory Committee on Student Financial Assistance. 2001a. *Access denied: Restoring the nation's commitment to equal educational opportunity.* Washington, DC: Advisory Committee on Student Financial Assistance.

———. 2001b. The impact of unmet need on low-income students. Staff briefing paper. Washington, DC: Advisory Committee on Student Financial Assistance.

———. 2002. *Empty promises: The myth of college access in America.* Washington, DC: Advisory Committee on Student Financial Assistance.

Alexander, K. L., and B. K. Eckland. 1974. Sex differences in the educational attainment process. *American Sociological Review* 59: 668–82.

———. 1977. High school context and college selectivity: Institutional constraints in educational stratification. *Social Forces* 56 (1): 166–88.

———. 1978. Basic attainment processes: A replication and extension, 1999. *Sociology of Education* 48: 457–95.

Allan, R. G. 1999. Taxonomy of tuition discounting. *Journal of Student Financial Aid* 29 (2): 7–20.

Allen, W. R., E. G. Epps, and N. Z. Haniff, eds. 1991. *College in black and white: African American students in predominantly white and historically black public universities.* Albany: State University of New York Press.

Andrieu, S. C. 1991. The influence of background, graduate experience, aspirations, expected earnings, and financial commitment on within-year persistence of enrolled students in graduate programs. Ph.D. diss., University of New Orleans.

Andrieu, S. C., and E. P. St. John. 1993. The influence of prices on graduate student persistence. *Research in Higher Education* 34: 399–418.

Astin, A. W. 1975. *Preventing students from dropping out.* San Francisco: Jossey-Bass.

———. 1993. *Assessments for excellence: The philosophy of assessment and evaluation in higher education.* Phoenix, AZ: Oryx.

Atwell, R. H., and A. M. Hauptman. 1986. The politics of tuition. *Educational Record* 67 (2–3): 4–6.

Balderston, F. E. 1974. *Managing today's university.* San Francisco: Jossey-Bass.

Bean, J. P. 1990. Why students leave: Insights from research. In *Strategic management of enrollment,* edited by D. Hossler, J. P. Bean, and associates. San Francisco: Jossey-Bass.

Becker, G. S. 1964. *Human capital: A theoretical and empirical analysis with special reference to education.* New York: Columbia University Press.

Bennett, W. J. 1986. Text of Secretary Bennett's speech on college costs and U.S. student aid. *Chronicle of Higher Education* 33 (13): 20.

———. 1987. Our greedy colleges. *New York Times,* 18 February, I31.

Berger, J. B. 2000. Optimizing capital, social reproduction, and undergraduate persistence. In *Reworking the student departure puzzle,* edited by J. M. Braxton. Nashville, TN: Vanderbilt University Press.

Bernal, E. M., A. F. Cabrera, and P. T. Terenzini. 1999. Class-based affirmative action admission policies: A viable alternative to race-based programs. Paper presented at the Association for the Study of Higher Education Annual Meeting, San Antonio, TX.

———. 2000. The relationship between race and socioeconomic status (SES): Implications for institutional research and admissions policies. *Removing Vestiges* 1 (3): 6–13.

Binder, M., and P. T. Ganderston. 2001. Musical chairs in higher education: Incentive effects of the NM success scholarships. Paper presented at the Civil Rights Project Forum, State Merit Aid Programs: College Access and Equity, Harvard University.

Bishop, J. H. 1992. Why U.S. students need incentives to learn. *Educational Leadership* 49 (6): 15–18.

Bishop, J. H., and S. Carter. 1991. The worsening shortage of college-graduate workers. *Educational Evaluation and Policy Analysis* 13: 221–46.

Blau, P., and O. D. Duncan. 1967. *The American occupational structure.* New York: Wiley.

Boesel, D., and E. Fredland 1999. *College for all? Is there too much emphasis on getting a four-year college degree?* Washington, DC: U.S. Department of Education.

Bourdieu, P. 1977. *The outline of a theory of practice.* Cambridge: Cambridge University Press.

———. 1990. *The logic of practice.* Stanford, CA: Stanford University Press.

Bowen, H. R. 1980. *The cost of higher education.* San Francisco: Jossey-Bass.

Bowen, H. R., and G. K. Douglass. 1971. *Efficiency in liberal education.* New York: McGraw-Hill.

Brainard, J., S. Burd, and B. Gose. 2000. The Clinton legacy. *Chronicle of Higher Education* 47 (16): A27, A29, A32.

Braxton, J. M. 2000. *Reworking the student departure puzzle.* Nashville, TN: Vanderbilt University Press.

Breneman, D. W. 1994. *Liberal arts colleges: Thriving, surviving, or endangered?* Washington, DC: Brookings Institution.

———. 2001. The outputs of higher education. In *Ford policy forum,* edited by M. E. Devlin. Cambridge, MA: Forum for the Future of Higher Education.

Breneman, D. W., C. E. Finn, and S. Nelson, eds. 1978. *Public policy and private higher education.* Washington, DC: Brookings Institution.

Brimelow, P. 1987. The untouchables. *Forbes,* 30 November, 141–50.

Cabrera, A. F. 1994. Logistic regression analysis in higher education: An applied perspective. In *Higher education: Handbook of theory and research,* vol. 10, edited by J. C. Smart. New York: Agathon Press.

Cabrera, A. F., A. Nora, and M. B. Castaneda. 1992. The role of finances in the persistence process: A structural model. *Research in Higher Education* 33: 571–93.

———. 1993. College persistence: Structural equations modeling test of an integrated model of student retention. *Journal of Higher Education* 33: 571–93.

Cabrera, A. F., J. O. Stampen, and W. L. Hansen. 1990. Exploring the effects of ability to pay on persistence in college. *Review of Higher Education* 13: 303–36.

Carlson, D. E., J. Farmer, and G. B. Weathersby. 1974. *A framework for analyzing postsecondary education finance policies.* Washington, DC: U.S. Government Printing Office.

Carnegie Commission on Higher Education. 1973. *Priorities for action: Final report.* New York: McGraw-Hill.

Carnes, B. M. 1987. The campus cost explosion: College tuitions are unnecessarily high. *Policy Review* 40: 68–71.

Carter, D. F. 1999. The impact of institutional choice and environments on African American and white students' degree expectations. *Research in Higher Education* 40: 571–93.

Cartter, A. M. 1976. *Ph.D.s and the academic labor market.* New York: McGraw-Hill.

Chaikind, S. 1987. *College enrollment by black and white students.* Prepared for the U.S. Department of Education. Washington, DC: DRC.

Chickering, A. W. 1969. *Education and identity.* San Francisco: Jossey-Bass.

———. 1976. Development as an outcome. In *Experiential learning,* edited by M. Keeton and associates. San Francisco: Jossey-Bass.

Choy, S. P. 2002. *Access and persistence: Findings from 10 years of longitudinal research on students.* Washington, DC: American Council on Education.

Clinchy, E. 2001. Needed: A new educational civil rights movement. *Phi Delta Kappan* 82 (7): 492–98.

Cofer, J. 1998. Decade of indecision: The impact of federal policy on persistence, 1987–1996. Ph.D. diss., University of Arkansas, Little Rock.

Cofer, J., and P. Somers. 2000. A comparison of the influence of debtload on the persistence of students at public and private colleges. *Journal of Student Financial Aid* 30 (2): 39–58.

Cohn, A. M., and T. Geske. 1990. *The economics of education,* 3d ed. New York: Pergamon Press.

REFERENCES   241

College Board. 1998. *Trends in student aid 1998*. Washington, DC: College Board.
———. 1999. *Trends in college pricing: 1999*. Washington, DC: College Board.
———. 2000. *Trends in student aid 2000*. Washington, DC: College Board.
———. 2001a. *Trends in college pricing*. Washington, DC: College Board.
———. 2001b. *Trends in student aid*. Washington, DC: College Board.
Committee on Economic Development. 1973. *The management and financing of colleges*. New York: Committee on Economic Development.
Cook, C. 1998. *Lobbying for higher education: How colleges and universities influence federal policy*. Nashville, TN: Vanderbilt University Press.
Cornwell, C., D. B. Mustard, and D. J. Sridhar. 2001. The enrollment effects of merit-based financial aid: Evidence from Georgia's HOPE Scholarship. Paper presented at the Civil Rights Project Forum, State Merit Aid Programs: College Access and Equity, Harvard University.
Council for Advancement and Support of Education. 1987. Tuition: The story and how to tell it. Paper presented at CASE Senior Administrators Seminar, Brown University.
Council for Aid to Education. 1997. *Breaking the social contract: The fiscal crisis in higher education*. Santa Monica, CA: RAND.
Cummings, H. 2001. The many faces of debt: A comparative study of how the prospect of debt influences student decision-making. Ph.D. diss., Indiana University.
Datnow, A. 2000. Power and politics in adoption of school reform models. *Educational Evaluation and Policy Analysis* 22: 357–74.
Davis, J. S. 1997. *College affordability: A closer look at the crisis*. Washington, DC: Sallie Mae Education Institute.
———. 2000. *College affordability: Overlooked long-term trends and recent fifty-state patterns*. USA Group Foundation New Agenda Series, vol. 3, no. 1. Indianapolis: USA Group Foundation.
DeSalvatore, K., and L. Hughes. 2000. *National Association of State Student Grant and Aid Programs NASSGAP thirtieth annual survey report, 1998–99 academic year*. Albany: New York State Higher Education Services Corporation.
DesJardins, S. L., D. A. Ahlburg, and B. P. McCall. 2002. A temporal investigation of factors related to timely degree completion. *Journal of Higher Education* 73 (5): 555–81.
Dolence, M. G., and D. M. Norris. 1995. *Transforming higher education: A vision for learning in the twenty-first century*. Ann Arbor, MI: Society for College and University Planning.
Downey, D. B. 1995. When bigger is not better: Family size, parental resources, and children's education performance. *American Sociological Review* 60: 746–61.
Dresch, S. P. 1975. A critique of planning models for postsecondary education: Current feasibility, potential relevance and a prospectus for future research. *Journal of Higher Education* 46: 246–86.
Dynarski, S. 2000. Hope for whom? Financial aid for the middle class and its impact on college attendance. National Bureau of Economic Research, working paper no. 7756. Cambridge, MA: National Bureau of Economic Research.

Eiser, L., ed. 1988. *A call for clarity: Income, loans, cost.* Washington, DC: American Association of State Colleges and Universities.

Ellison, D. G., L. Barber, T. L. Engle, and L. Kampwerth. 1965. Programmed tutoring: A teaching aid and a research tool. *Reading Research Quarterly* 1: 77–125.

Ellison, D. G., P. Harris, and L. Barber. 1968. A field test of programmed and directed tutoring. *Reading Research Quarterly* 3: 307–66.

Ellwood, D., and T. J. Kane. 2000. Who is getting a college education? Family background and the growing gaps in enrollment. In *Securing the future,* edited by S. Danziger and J. Waldfogel. New York: Russell Sage Foundation.

Finn, C. E., Jr. 1978. *Scholars, dollars, and bureaucrats.* Washington, DC: Brookings Institution.

———. 1988a. Judgment time for higher education in the court of public opinion. *Change* 20 (4): 35–38.

———. 1988b. Prepared statement and attachments. Hearing before the Subcommittee on Postsecondary Education, Committee on Education and Labor, House of Representatives, 100th Congress, 1st Session, no. 100–47, September 25. Washington, DC: U.S. Government Printing Office.

———. 1990. The biggest reform of all. *Phi Delta Kappan* 71 (8): 584–92.

———. 2001. College isn't for everyone. *USA Today,* 21 February, 14A.

Finn, C. E., Jr., and B. V. Manno. 1996. Behind the curtain. *Wilson Quarterly,* winter, 44–53.

Finn, C. E., Jr., B. V. Manno, and D. Ravitch. 2001. *Education 2001: Getting the job done.* Washington, DC: Finn, Manno, and Ravitch.

Fischer, F. G. 1990. State financing of higher education: A new look at an old problem. *Change* 22 (1): 42–56.

Flint, T. 1997. Predicting student loan defaults. *Journal of Higher Education* 68: 322–54.

Fossey, R. E. 1998. Desegregation is not enough: Facing the truth about urban schools. In *Race, the courts, and equal education: The limits of the law,* edited by R. E. Fossey. Readings on Equal Education, vol. 15. New York: AMS Press.

———. 2003. Desegregation is over in the inner cities: What do we do now? In *Reinterpreting urban school reform,* edited by L. F. Miron and E. P. St. John. Albany: State University of New York Press.

Franklin, B. M. 2003. Race, restructuring, and education reform: The mayoral takeover of the Detroit public schools. In *Reinterpreting urban school reform,* edited by L. F. Miron and E. P. St. John. Albany: State University of New York Press.

Freeman, R. B. 1976. *The overeducated American.* New York: Academic Press.

Friedman, M. 1962. *Capitalism and freedom.* Chicago: University of Chicago Press.

Garvin, D. A. 1980. *The economics of university behavior.* New York: Academic Press.

Geske, T. G. 1996. The value of investments in higher education. In *A struggle to survive: Funding higher education in the next century,* edited by D. S. Honeyman, J. L. Wattenbarger, and K. C. Westbrook. Thousand Oaks, CA: Corwin Press.

Gladieux, L. E., and T. R. Wolanin. 1976. *Congress and the colleges.* Lexington, MA: Heath.

Glenny, L. A. 1974–75. Nine myths, nine realities: Illusions of steady state. *Change* 6 (10): 24–28.

Glenny, L. A., F. M. Bowen, R. J. Meisinger, A. W. Morgan, R. A. Purves, and F. A. Schmidtlein. 1975. *State budgeting in higher education: Data digest.* Berkeley: Center for Research and Development in Higher Education, University of California, Berkeley.

Goggin, W. J. 1999. A "merit-aware" model for college admissions and affirmative action. Mortenson Research Seminar on Public Policy Analysis of Opportunity for Postsecondary Education. *Postsecondary Education Opportunity,* no. 83 (May): 6–12.

Goodwin, D. 1991. *Beyond defaults: Indicators for assessing proprietary school quality.* Washington, DC: U.S. Department of Education.

Griswold, C. P., and G. M. Marine. 1996. Political influences on state tuition-aid policy: Higher tuition/higher aid and the real world. *Review of Higher Education* 19: 361–89.

Grubb, W. N. 1993. The long-term effects of proprietary schools on wages and earnings: Implications for federal policy. *Educational Evaluation and Policy Analysis* 15: 17–33.

———. 1994. The long-term effects of proprietary schools: Corrections. *Educational Evaluation and Policy Analysis* 16: 351–56.

———. 1996a. *Learning to work.* New York: Russell Sage Foundation.

———. 1996b. *Working in the middle: Strengthening education and training for the mid-skilled labor force.* San Francisco: Jossey-Bass.

Halstead, D. K. 1974. *Statewide planning in higher education.* Washington, DC: U.S. Government Printing Office.

———. 1995. *Inflation measures for schools, colleges, and libraries.* Washington, DC: Research Associates of Washington.

Hansen, W. L. 1983. Impact of student financial aid on access. In *The crisis in higher education,* edited by J. Froomkin. New York: Academy of Political Science.

Hansen, W. L, and B. A. Weisbrod. 1969. *Benefits, costs, and finance of public higher education.* Chicago: Markham.

Hanson, S. L. 1994. Lost talent: Unrealized educational aspirations and expectations among U.S. youth. *Sociology of Education* 67: 159–83.

Hauptman, A. M. 1990. *The college tuition spiral.* New York: Macmillan.

———. 1992. *The economic prospects for American higher education.* Washington, DC: Association of Governing Boards/American Council on Education.

Hearn, J. C. 1993. The paradox of growth in federal aid for college students: 1965–1990. In *Higher education: Handbook of theory and research,* vol. 9., edited by J. C. Smart. New York: Agathon Press.

———. 2001a. Access to postsecondary education: Financing equity in an evolving context. In *The finance of higher education: Theory, research, policy, and practice,* edited by M. B. Paulsen and J. C. Smart. New York: Agathon Press.

———. 2001b. Epilogue to the paradox of growth in federal student financial aid. In *The finance of higher education: Theory, research, policy, and practice,* edited by M. B. Paulsen and J. C. Smart. New York: Agathon Press.

REFERENCES

Hearn, J. C., and M. S. Anderson. 1989. Integrating post-secondary education financing policies: The Minnesota model. In *Studying the impact of student aid on institutions,* edited by R. H. Fenske. New Directions in Institutional Research, no. 62. San Francisco: Jossey-Bass.

———. 1995. The Minnesota financing experiment. In *Rethinking tuition and student aid strategies,* edited by E. P. St. John. New Directions for Higher Education, no. 89. San Francisco: Jossey-Bass.

Hearn, J. C., and C. P. Griswold. 1994. State-level centralization and policy innovation in U.S. post-secondary education. *Educational Evaluation and Policy Analysis* 16: 161–90.

Hearn, J. C., and D. Longanecker. 1985. Enrollment effects of alternative post-secondary pricing policies. *Journal of Higher Education* 56: 485–508.

Heller, D. E. 1997. Student price response in higher education: An update to Leslie and Brinkman. *Journal of Higher Education* 68: 624–59.

Heller, D. E., and C. J. Rasmussen. 2001. Merit scholarships and college access: Evidence from two states. Paper presented at the Civil Rights Project Forum, State Merit Aid Programs: College Access and Equity, Harvard University.

Hippensteel, D. G., E. P. St. John, and J. B. Starkey. 1996. The influence of tuition and student aid on within-year persistency by adults in 2 year colleges. *Community College Journal of Research and Practice* 20: 233–42.

Honeyman, D. S., J. L. Wattenbarger, and K. C. Westbrook, eds. 1996. *Struggle to survive: Funding higher education in the next century.* Thousand Oaks, CA: Corwin Press.

Hossler, D., J. P. Bean, and associates. 1990. *The strategic management of college enrollment.* San Francisco: Jossey-Bass.

Hossler, D., and K. Gallagher. 1987. Studying student college choice: A three-phase model and the implications for policymakers. *College and University* 62: 207–21.

Hossler, D., J. P. Lund, J. Ramin, S. Westfall, and S. Irish. 1997. State funding for higher education: A Sisyphean task. *Journal of Higher Education* 68: 160–96.

Hossler, D., and J. Schmit. 1995. The Indiana postsecondary encouragement experiment. In *Rethinking tuition and student aid strategies,* edited by E. P. St. John. New Directions for Higher Education, no. 89. San Francisco: Jossey-Bass.

Hossler, D., J. Schmit, and N. Vesper. 1999. *Going to college.* Baltimore: Johns Hopkins University Press.

Hossler, D., and F. K. Stage. 1992. Family background and high school experience factors' influences on the postsecondary plans of ninth grade students: A causal model of predisposition to college. *American Educational Research Journal* 29: 425–51.

Hu, S., and E. P. St. John. 1999. Does money matter across four critical years? The effects of financial aid on student persistence in a public system of higher education. Paper presented at the Association for the Study of Higher Education Annual Meeting, San Antonio, TX.

———. 2001. Student persistence in a public higher education system: Understanding racial/ethnic differences. *Journal of Higher Education* 72: 265–86.

Hurtado, S., and D. F. Carter. 1997. Effects of college transitions and perceptions of campus racial climate on Latino students' sense of belonging. *Sociology of Education* 70: 324–45.

Jackson, G. A. 1978. Financial aid and student enrollment. *Journal of Higher Education* 49: 548–74.

———. G. A. 1988. Did college choice change during the seventies? *Economics of Education Review* 7: 15–27.

Jackson, G. A., and G. B. Weathersby. 1975. Individual demand for higher education. *Journal of Higher Education* 46: 623–52.

Jacobs, B. A. 2001. Getting tough? The impact of high school graduation exams. *Educational Evaluation and Policy Analysis* 23: 99–122.

Jencks, C., and D. Riesman. 1968. *The academic revolution.* Garden City, NJ: Doubleday.

Johnson, E. L. 1989. Misconceptions about early land-grant colleges. In *ASHE reader on the history of higher education,* edited by L. F. Goodchild and H. S. Wechsler. Needham Heights, MA: Ginn Press.

Kaltenbaugh, L. S., E. P. St. John, and J. B. Starkey. 1999. What difference does tuition make? An analysis of ethnic differences in persistence. *Journal of Student Financial Aid* 29 (2): 21–32.

Kane, T. J. 1994. College entry by Blacks since 1970: The role of college costs, family background, and returns to education. *Journal of Political Economy* 102 (5): 878–911.

———. 1995. *Rising public tuition levels and access to college.* Cambridge, MA: National Bureau of Economic Research.

———. 1999. *The price of admission: Rethinking how Americans pay for college.* Washington, DC: Brookings Institution.

———. 2001. Assessing the U.S. financial aid system: What we know, what we need to know. In *Ford Policy Forum,* edited by M. E. Devlin. Cambridge, MA: Forum on the Future of Higher Education.

Keller, G. 1983. *Academic strategy.* Baltimore: Johns Hopkins University Press.

King, J. E. 2002. *Crucial choices: How students' financial decisions affect their academic success.* Washington, DC: American Council on Education.

———, ed. 1999. *Financing a college education: How it works, how it is changing.* Phoenix, AZ: Oryx Press.

King, T., and E. Bannon. 2002. *The burden of borrowing: A report on rising rates of student debt.* Washington, DC: State PIRGs Higher Education Report.

Kipp, S. M., D. V. Price, and J. K. Wohlford. 2002. *Unequal opportunity: Disparities in college access among the fifty states.* New Agenda Series. Indianapolis, IN: Lumina Foundation for Education.

Kirshstein, R. J., D. J. Sherman, V. K. Tikoff, C. Masten, and J. Fairweather. 1990. *The escalating cost of higher education.* Prepared for the U.S. Department of Education Office of Planning, Budget, and Evaluation. Washington, DC: Pelavin Associates.

Kirshstein, R. J., V. K. Tikoff, C. Masten, and E. P. St. John. 1990. *Trends in institutional costs.* Prepared for the U.S. Department of Education Office of Planning, Budget, and Evaluation. Washington, DC: Pelavin Associates.

Knight, S. L., and J. A. Stallings. 1995. The implementation of the Accelerated School Model in an urban elementary school. In *No quick fix: Rethinking literacy programs in America's elementary schools,* edited by R. L. Allington and S. A. Walmsley. New York: Teachers College Press.

Kramer, M. A., and W. D. VanDusen. 1986. Living on credit. *Change* 18 (3): 10–19.

Kuh, G. D., and P. G. Love. 2000. A cultural perspective on student departure. In *Reworking the departure puzzle,* edited by J. Braxton. Nashville, TN: Vanderbilt University Press.

Lang, W. D. 2002. Responsibility center budgeting and management at the University of Toronto. In *Incentive-based budgeting systems in public universities,* edited by D. Priest, W. Becker, D. Hossler, and E. P. St. John. Northampton, MA: Edward Elgar.

Lee, E. C., and F. M. Bowen. 1971. *The multi-campus university: A study of academic governance.* New York: McGraw-Hill.

———. 1975. *Managing multi-campus systems: Effective administration in an unsteady state.* San Francisco: Jossey-Bass.

Lee, J. B. 2001. Access for low-income students. Paper presented at the National Governor's Association Center for Best Practices, Washington, DC.

Lee, J. B., and E. P. St. John. 1995. *Student financial aid and the persistence of recipients at Washington colleges and universities.* Prepared for the Higher Education Coordinating Board, State of Washington. Bethesda, MD: JBL Associates.

Leslie, L. L., and P. T. Brinkman. 1988. *The economic value of higher education.* New York: Macmillan.

Leslie, L. L., and G. Rhodes. 1995. Rising administrative costs. *Journal of Higher Education* 66: 187–212.

Lewis, D. R., and Dunbar, H. 2001. Costs and productivity in higher education: Theory, evidence and policy implications. In *The finance of higher education: Theory, research, policy, and practice,* edited by M. B. Paulsen and J. C. Smart. New York: Agathon Press.

Lombardi, J. V., and E. D. Capaldi. 1996. Accountability and quality evaluation in higher education. In *Struggle to survive: Funding higher education in the next century,* edited by D. S. Honeyman, J. L. Wattenbarger, and K. C. Westbrook. Thousand Oaks, CA: Corwin Press.

Madden, N. A., R. E. Slavin, N. L. Karweit, L. Donlan, and B. Wasik. 1991. *Success for All: Multi-year effects of a school restructuring program.* Report no. 18. Baltimore: Center for Research on Effective Schooling for Disadvantaged Students.

Madden, N. A., R. E. Slavin, N. L. Karweit, B. J. Livermore, and L. Donlan. 1989. *Success for All: First-year effects of a comprehensive plan for reforming urban education.* Report no. 30. Baltimore: Johns Hopkins University, Center for Research on Elementary and Middle Schools.

Manset, G., and S. Washburn. 2003. Inclusive education in high stakes, high poverty environments: The case of students with learning disabilities in Indiana's urban high schools and the graduation qualifying examination. In *Reinterpreting urban school reform,* edited by L. F. Miron and E. P. St. John. Albany: State University of New York Press.

REFERENCES

Manski, C. F., and D. A. Wise. 1983. *College choice in America.* Cambridge: Harvard University Press.

Marsden, G. M. 1994. *The soul of the American university: From Protestant establishment to established nonbelief.* New York: Oxford University Press.

McCabe, R. 2000. Underprepared students. In *Measuring up 2000: The state-by-state report card for higher education.* Washington, DC: National Center for Public Policy and Higher Education.

McDonnough, P. M. 1997. *Choosing colleges: How social class and schools structure opportunity.* Albany: State University of New York Press.

McDonnough, P. M., A. L. Antonio, and J. W. Trent. 1997. Black students, black colleges: An African-American college choice model. *Journal for a Just and Caring Education* 3: 9–36.

McKeown, M. P. 1996. State funding formulas: Promise fulfilled? In *A struggle for survival,* edited by D. S. Honeyman, J. L. Wattenbarger, and K. C. Westbrook. Thousand Oaks, CA: Corwin Press.

McPherson, M. S. 1978. The demand for higher education. In *Public policy and private higher education,* edited by D. W. Breneman and C. E. Finn, Jr. Washington, DC: Brookings Institution.

McPherson, M. S., and M. O. Schapiro. 1991. *Keeping college affordable.* Washington, DC: Brookings Institution.

———. 1993. Measuring the effects of student aid: An assessment of some methodological and empirical problems. In *Paying the piper: Productivity, incentives, and financing in U.S. higher education,* edited by M. S. McPherson, M. O. Schapiro, and G. C. Winston. Ann Arbor: University of Michigan Press.

———. 1997. *The student aid game: Meeting need and rewarding talent in American higher education.* Princeton, NJ: Princeton University Press.

Metcalf, K. K., W. J. Boone, F. K. Stage, T. L. Chilton, P. Muller, and P. Tait. 1998. *A comparative evaluation of the Cleveland scholarship and tutoring program: One year: 1996–97.* Bloomington: Junior Achievement Evaluation Project, Indiana University.

Mingle, J. R. 1987. *Focus on minorities: Trends in higher education participation and success.* Denver: Education Commission of the States / State Higher Education Executive Offices.

Miron, L. F., and E. P. St. John, eds. 2003. *Reinterpreting urban school reform.* Albany: State University of New York Press.

Mortensen, T. 1999. State tax fund appropriations for higher education, FY 2000. *Postsecondary Education Opportunity,* no. 90 (December).

———. 2001. Just and efficient college finance. *Postsecondary Education Opportunity,* no. 105 (March).

Mumper, M. 1996. *Removing college price barriers: What government has done and why it hasn't worked.* Albany: State University of New York Press.

———. 2001. State efforts to keep public colleges affordable in face of fiscal stress. In *The finance of higher education: Theory, research, policy, and practice,* edited by M. B. Paulsen and J. C. Smart. New York: Agathon Press.

National Center for Education Statistics (NCES). 1970. *Projections of education statistics to 1979–80.* Washington, DC: NCES.

———. 1973. *Digest of education statistics 1973,* by T. D. Snyder. Washington, DC: NCES.

———. 1980. *Projections of education statistics to 1988–89,* by M. M. Frankel and D. E. Gerald. Washington, DC: NCES.

———. 1987. *Digest of education statistics 1987,* by T. D. Snyder. CS 87-345. Washington, DC: NCES.

———. 1988. *Digest of education statistics 1988,* by T. D. Snyder. CS 88-600. Washington, DC: NCES.

———. 1989. *1989 Projections of education statistics 2000,* by D. E. Gerald, P. J. Horn, and W. J. Hussar. NCES 89-648. Washington, DC: NCES.

———. 1990. *1993 Projections of education statistics to 2001: An update,* by D. E. Gerald and W. J. Hussar. NCES 91–683. Washington, DC: NCES.

———. 1993a. *The condition of education 1993,* by N. Alsalam, G. E. Fischer, L. T. Ogle, G. Thompson Rogers, and T. M. Smith. NCES 93-290. Washington, DC: NCES.

———. 1993b. *Digest of education statistics 1993,* project director, T. D. Snyder; production manager, C. M. Hoffman. NCES 93-292. Washington, DC: NCES.

———. 1993c. *1993 Projections of education statistics to 2004,* by D. E. Gerald and W. J. Hussar. NCES 93-256. Washington, DC: NCES.

———. 1995a. *The condition of education 1995,* by T. M. Smith, M. Perie, N. Alsalam, R. Pratt Mahoney, Y. Bae, and B. Aronstamm Young. NCES 95-273. Washington, DC: NCES.

———. 1995b. *Projections of education statistics to 2005,* by D. E. Gerald and W. J. Hussar. NCES 95-169. Washington, DC: NCES.

———. 1996a. *National Education Longitudinal Study: 1988–1994: Descriptive summary report with an essay on access and choice in postsecondary education.* NCES 96-175. Washington, DC: NCES.

———. 1996b. *Projections of education statistics to 2006,* 25th ed., by W. J. Hussar and D. E. Gerald. NCES 96-661. Washington, DC: NCES.

———. 1996c. *The condition of education 1996,* by T. M. Smith, B. Aronstamm Young, S. P. Choy, M. Perie, N. Alsalam, M. R. Rollefson, and Y. Bae. NCES 96-304. Washington, DC: NCES.

———. 1997a. *Access to higher postsecondary education for the 1992 high school graduates,* by L. Berkner and L. Chavez; project officer, C. D. Carroll. NCES 98-105. Washington, DC: NCES.

———. 1997b. *Confronting the odds: Students at risk and the pipeline to higher education,* by L. J. Horn; project officer, C. D. Carroll. NCES 98-094. Washington, DC: NCES.

———. 1998a. *The condition of education 1998,* by J. Wirt, T. Snyder, J. Sable, S. P. Choy, Y. Bae, J. Stennett, A. Gruner, and M. Peire. Washington, DC: NCES.

———. 1998b. *Who goes to America's high ranked "national" universities?* by J. Owings, T. Madigan, and B. Daniel. NCES 98-095. Washington, DC: NCES.

————. 1999a. *Digest of education statistics, 1998.* NCES 99-036. Washington, DC: NCES.

————. 1999b. *Projections of education statistics to 2009,* 25th ed., by W. J. Hussar and D. E. Gerald. NCES 1999-038. Washington, DC: NCES.

————. 2000a. *Digest of education statistics, 1999.* NCES 2000-031. Washington, DC: NCES.

————. 2000b. *Mapping the road to college: First-generation students' math track, planning strategies, and context of support,* by L. Horn and A.-M. Nunez; project officer, L. Bobbitt. NCES 2000-153. Washington, DC: NCES.

————. 2000c. *Projections of education statistics to 2010,* 25th ed., by W. J. Hussar and D. E. Gerald. NCES 2000-071. Washington, DC: NCES.

————. 2001a. *Bridging the gap: Academic preparation and postsecondary success of first-generation students,* by E. C. Warburton and R. Bugarin; project officer, C. D. Carroll. NCES 2001-153. Washington, DC: NCES.

————. 2001b. *Digest of education statistics 2000,* by T. D. Snyder; production manager, C. M. Hoffman; program analyst, C. M. Geddes. NCES 2001-034. Washington, DC: NCES.

————. 2001c. *Students whose parents did not go to college: Postsecondary access, persistence, and attainment,* by S. Choy. Washington, DC: NCES.

————. 2001d. *Study of college costs and prices, 1988–89 to 1997–98,* vol. 1, by A. F. Cunningham, J. V. Wellman, M. E. Clinedinst, J. P. Merisotis; project officer, D. C. NCES 2002-157. Washington, DC: NCES.

National Center for Public Policy and Higher Education. 2000. *Measuring up 2000: The state-by-state report card for higher education.* Washington, DC: National Center for Public Policy and Higher Education.

National Commission on Excellence in Education. 1983. *A nation at risk.* Washington, DC: National Commission on Excellence in Education.

National Commission on the Financing of Postsecondary Education. 1973. *Financing postsecondary education in the United States.* Washington, DC: U.S. Government Printing Office.

National Commission on Responsibility for Financing Postsecondary Education. 1993. *Making colleges affordable again: Final report.* Washington, DC: NCES.

National Institute of Independent Colleges and Universities. 1987. *The truth about costs in the independent sector of higher education.* Washington, DC: NCES.

National Postsecondary Education Cooperative (NPEC). 1998. *Reconceptualizing access in postsecondary education and its ramifications for data systems: Report of the policy panel on access.* Washington, DC: U.S. Government Printing Office.

Newman, F. 1971. *U.S. task force on higher education.* Washington, DC: U.S. Government Printing Office.

————. 1985. *Higher education and the American resurgence.* Carnegie Foundation special report. Lawrenceville, NJ: Princeton University Press.

Noell, J. 1991. *Student aid and the cost of postsecondary education.* Washington, DC: Congressional Budget Office.

Orfield, G. 1992. Money, equity, and college costs. *Harvard Educational Review* 62: 337–73.

Parsons, M. D. 1997. *Power and politics: Federal higher education policy making in the 1990s.* Albany: State University of New York Press.

Pascarella, E. T., and P. T. Terenzini. 1979. Interaction effects in Spady's and Tinto's conceptual models of college drop-outs. *Sociology of Education* 52: 197–210.

———. 1980. Predicting voluntary freshmen year persistence and withdrawal behavior in a residential university: A path analytic validation of Tinto's model. *Journal of Educational Psychology* 51 (1): 60–71.

———. 1991. *How college affects students.* San Francisco: Jossey-Bass.

Paulsen, M. B. 1990. *College choice: Understanding student enrollment behavior.* ASHE-ERIC Higher Education Report no. 6. Washington, DC: George Washington University, School of Education and Human Development.

———. 1996a. Higher education and productivity: An afterword. *Thought and Action: NEA Higher Education Journal* 12 (2): 135–39.

———. 1996b. Higher education and state workforce productivity. *Thought and Action: NEA Higher Education Journal* 12 (1): 55–77.

———. 1998. Recent research on the economics of attending college: Returns on investment and responsiveness to price. *Research in Higher Education* 39: 471–89.

———. 2001a. The economics of human capital and investment in higher education. In *The finance of higher education: Theory, research, policy, and practice,* edited by M. B. Paulsen and J. C. Smart. New York: Agathon Press.

———. 2001b. The economics of the public sector: The nature of public policy in higher education finance. In *The finance of higher education: Theory, research, policy, and practice,* edited by M. B. Paulsen and J. C. Smart. New York: Agathon Press.

Paulsen, M. B., and J. C. Smart, eds. 2001. *The finance of higher education: Theory, research, policy, and practice* New York: Agathon Press.

Paulsen, M. B., and E. P. St. John. 1997. The financial nexus between college choice and persistence. In *Researching student aid: Creating an action agenda,* edited by R. A. Vorhees. New Directions for Institutional Research, no. 95. San Francisco: Jossey-Bass.

———. 2002. Social class and college costs: Examining the financial nexus between college choice and persistence. *Journal of Higher Education* 73: 189–236.

Paulsen, M. B., E. P. St. John, and D. F. Carter. 2002. *Diversity, college costs, and postsecondary opportunity: An examination of the financial nexus between college choice and persistence.* Policy research report. Bloomington: Indiana Education Policy Center.

Pelavin, S. H., and M. B. Kane. 1988. *Minority participation in higher education.* Washington, DC: Pelavin Associates.

———. 1990. *Changing the odds: Factors increasing access to college.* New York: College Board.

Peng, C. Y. J., T. S. H. So, F. K. Stage, and E. P. St. John. 2002. The use and interpretation of logistic regression in higher education journals: 1988–1999. *Research in Higher Education* 43: 259–94

Peng, S. S., and W. B. Fetters. 1978. Variables involved in withdrawal during the first two years of college: Preliminary findings from the National Longitudinal Study of the High School Class of 1972. *American Educational Research Journal* 15: 361–72.

Perna, L. W. 2000. Differences in the decisions to enroll in college among African Americans, Hispanics, and Whites. *Journal of Higher Education* 71: 117–41.

Perry, W. 1970. *Forms of intellectual and ethical development in the college years.* New York: Holt, Rinehart and Winston.

Peterson, P. 1998. School choice: A report card. In *Learning from school choice,* edited by P. E. Peterson and B. C. Hassel. Washington, DC: Brookings Institution.

Pulley, J. L. 2002. Lumina lumbers onto the higher education scene aiming to widen the road to college: New billion dollar foundation steps on toes. *Chronicle of Higher Education* 48 (22 February): A29.

Putka, G. 1987. Tracking tuition: Why college fees are rising so sharply. *Wall Street Journal,* 11 December, 1.

Rawls, J. 1971. *A theory of justice.* Cambridge: Harvard University Press.

Rendon, L. I., R. E. Jalomo, and A. Nora. 2000. Theoretical consideration in the study of minority student retention in higher education. In *Reworking the departure puzzle,* edited by J. B. Braxton. Nashville, TN: Vanderbilt University Press.

Ridenour, C., and E. P. St. John. 2002. Private scholarships and school choice: Innovation or class reproduction? In *Reinterpreting urban school reform.* Albany: State University of New York Press.

Rose, L. C., A. M. Gallup, and S. M. Elam. 1997. The 29th annual Phi Delta Kappa/Gallup poll of the public's attitudes toward the public schools. *Phi Delta Kappan* 79 (1): 41–56.

Rosenberg, B. 1989. Public school choice: Can we find the right balance? *American Education* 25: 474–99.

Ross, R. M., and L. J. Smith. 1994. Effects of Success for All model on kindergarten through second-grade reading achievement, teacher' adjustment, and classroom-school climate at an inner city school. *Elementary School Journal* 95: 121–38.

Ruppert, S. S. 1998. Reconceptualizing access: A review of the findings from the NPEC/ACE policy panel on access and its data systems ramifications. In *Reconceptualizing access in postsecondary education and its ramifications for data systems: Report of the policy panel on access,* edited by National Postsecondary Education Cooperative. Washington, DC: U.S. Government Printing Office.

Sandler, M. E. 1999. A structural model of student integration, finances, behavior, and career development: An elaborated framework of attitudes and persistence. Paper presented at the Association for the Study of Higher Education Annual Meeting, San Antonio, TX.

Schneider, W. 2001. Clinton and the Democrats. *Atlantic Monthly,* February, 65–68.

Schultz, C., 1968. *The politics of public spending.* Washington, DC: Brookings Institution.

Singha, K. W. 1997. Estimated first-time enrollment for the private, highly selective national university: A market demography application of logistic regression-based price sensitivity analysis. Ph.D. diss., Bowling Green State University.

Slaughter, S. 1991. The official "ideology" of higher education: Ironies and inconsistencies. In *Culture and ideology in higher education,* edited by W. G. Tierney. New York: Praeger.

Slaughter, S., and L. L. Leslie. 1997. *Academic capitalism: Politics, policies, and the entrepreneurial university.* Baltimore: Johns Hopkins University Press.

Slavin, R. 1991. *Education for all: Contexts for learning.* Lisse, Netherlands: Swets and Zeitlinger.

Snow, C. E., M. S. Burns, and P. Griffin, eds. 1998. *Preventing reading difficulties in young children.* Washington, DC: National Academy Press.

Somers, P. A. 1992. A dynamic analysis of student matriculation decisions in an urban public university. Ph.D. diss., University of New Orleans.

Somers, P. A., and E. P. St. John. 1997a. Analyzing the role of financial aid in student persistence. In *Student aid research: A manual for financial aid administrators,* edited by J. S. Davis. Washington, DC: National Association of Student Financial Aid Administration.

———. 1997b. Interpreting price response in institutional decisions: A comparative institutional study. *Journal of Student Financial Aid* 27 (3): 15–36.

Stage, F. K., and D. Hossler. 1989. Differences in family influences on college attendance plans for male and female ninth graders. *Research in Higher Education* 30: 301–15.

———. 2000. Where is the student? In *Reworking the departure puzzle,* edited by J. B. Braxton. Nashville, TN: Vanderbilt University Press.

Starkey, J. B. 1994. The influence of prices and price subsidies on the within-year persistence by part-time undergraduate students: A sequential analysis. Ph.D. diss., University of New Orleans.

State Higher Education Executive Officers. 1988. *Report on the cost of college to students.* Denver, CO: State Higher Education Executive Officers.

Steelman, L. C., and Powell, B. 1993. Doing the right thing: Race and parental locus of responsibility for funding college. *Sociology of Education* 66: 223–44.

St. John, E. P. 1989. The influence of student aid on persistence. *Journal of Student Financial Aid* 19 (3): 52–68.

———. 1990a. Price response in enrollment decisions: An analysis of the High School and Beyond Senior Cohort. *Research in Higher Education* 31: 161–76.

———. 1990b. Price response in persistence decisions: An analysis of the High School and Beyond Senior Cohort. *Research in Higher Education* 31: 387–403.

———. 1991a. A framework of reexamining state resource management strategies in higher education. *Journal of Higher Education* 62: 263–87.

———. 1991b. What really influences minority attendance? Sequential analyses of the High School and Beyond Sophomore Cohort. *Research in Higher Education* 32: 141–58.

———. 1992a. Changes in pricing behavior during the 1980s: An analysis of selected case studies. *Journal of Higher Education* 63: 13–26.

———. 1992b. The transformation of private liberal arts colleges. *Review of Higher Education* 15: 83–106.

———. 1993. Untangling the web: Using price-response measures in enrollment projections. *Journal of Higher Education* 64: 676–95.

———. 1994. *Prices, productivity, and investment: Assessing financial strategies in higher education.* ASHE/ERIC Higher Education Report no. 3. Washington, DC: George Washington University.

———. 1995. Rethinking tuition and student aid strategies. In *Rethinking tuition and student aid strategies,* edited by E. P. St. John. New Directions for Higher Education, no. 89. San Francisco: Jossey-Bass.

———. 1998. The effects of changes in student aid policy on persistence: A case study of a private university. *Journal of Student Financial Aid* 28 (1): 7–18.

———. 1999. Evaluating state grant programs: A study of the Washington state grant programs. *Research in Higher Education* 40: 149–70.

———. 2002. *The access challenge: Rethinking the causes of the new inequality.* Policy Issue Report no. 2002–1. Bloomington: Indiana Education Policy Center.

St. John, E. P., S. C. Andrieu, J. Oescher, and J. B. Starkey. 1994. The influence of student aid on within-year persistence by traditional college-age students in four-year colleges. *Research in Higher Education* 35: 301–34.

St. John, E. P., and J. Bardzell. 1999. *Improving early reading and literacy: A guide for developing research based-programs.* Bloomington: Indiana Education Policy Center.

St. John, E. P., and C. Byce. 1982. *The changing federal role in student financial aid: Meeting student aid needs in a period of retrenchment,* edited by M. Kramer. New Directions in Higher Education, no. 40. San Francisco: Jossey-Bass.

St. John, E. P., A. F. Cabrera, A. Nora, and E. H. Asker. 2000. Economic influences on persistence reconsidered. In *Reworking the departure puzzle,* edited by J. M. Braxton. Nashville, TN: Vanderbilt University Press.

St. John, E. P., and R. J. Elliott. 1994. Reframing policy research: A critical examination of research on federal student aid programs. In *Higher education: Handbook of theory and research,* vol. 10, edited by J. C. Smart. New York: Agathon Press.

St. John, E. P., and D. Hossler. 1998. Higher education desegregation in the post-*Fordice* legal environment: A critical-empirical perspective. In *Readings in equal education,* edited by R. Fossey. New York: AMS Press.

St. John, E. P., S. Hu, A. Simmons, and G. D. Musoba. 2001. Aptitude v. merit: What matters in persistence. *Research in Higher Education* 24: 131–52.

St. John, E. P., S. Hu, and T. Tuttle. 2000. Persistence by undergraduates in an urban public university: Understanding the effects of student aid. *Journal of Student Financial Aid* 30 (2): 23–38.

St. John, E. P., S. Hu, and J. Weber. 2000. Keeping public colleges affordable: A study of persistence in Indiana's public colleges and universities. *Journal of Student Financial Aid* 30 (1): 21–32.

———. 2001. State policy and the affordability of public higher education: The influence of state grants on persistence in Indiana. *Research in Higher Education* 42: 401–28.

St. John, E. P., R. J. Kirshstein, and J. Noell. 1991. The effects of student aid on persistence: A sequential analysis. *Review of Higher Education* 14: 383–406.

St. John, E. P., K. Kline, and E. H. Asker. 2001. The call for accountability: Rethinking the linkages to student outcomes: Affordability, access and accountability. In *Public higher education policy*, edited by D. E. Heller. Baltimore: Johns Hopkins University Press.

St. John, E. P., S. Loescher, S. Jacob, O. Cekic, and D. L. Kupersmith. 2000. *Comprehensive school reform models: A study guide for comparing CSR models (and how well they meet Minnesota's learning standards)*. Naperville, IL: North Central Regional Educational Laboratory.

St. John, E. P., G. Manset, C. G. Chung, G. D. Musoba, S. Loescher, A. B. Simmons, D. Gordon, and C. A. Hossler. 2003. Comprehensive school reform: An exploratory study. In *Reinterpreting urban school reform,* edited by L. F. Miron and E. P. St. John. Albany: State University of New York Press

St. John, E. P., G. Manset, C. G. Chung, A. B. Simmons, G. D. Musoba, K. Manoil, and K. Worthington. 2003. Research-based reading reform: The impact of state-funded interventions on educational outcomes in urban schools. In *Reinterpreting urban school reform*, edited by L. F. Miron and E. P. St. John. Albany: State University of New York Press.

St. John, E. P., and C. L. Masten. 1990. Return on the federal investment in student financial aid: An assessment of the high school class of 1972. *Journal of Student Financial Aid* 20 (3): 4–23.

St. John, E. P., and L. F. Miron. 2003. A cultural-empirical perspective on urban school reform. In *Reinterpreting urban school reform*, edited by L. F. Miron and E. P. St. John. Albany: State University of New York Press.

St. John, E. P., and G. D. Musoba. 2003. Academic access and equal opportunity: Rethinking the foundations of policy on diversity. In *Readings on equal opportunity*, edited by C. Brown and C. Freeman. New York: AMS Press.

St. John, E. P., and J. Noell. 1987. Student loans and higher education opportunities: Evidence on access, persistence, and choice of major. Paper presented at the Fourth Annual NASSGAP/NCHELP Research Network Conference, Washington University.

———. 1989. The effects of student financial aid on access to higher education: An analysis of progress with special consideration of minority enrollment. *Research in Higher Education* 30: 563–81.

St. John, E. P., D. M. Norris, and C. Byce. 1987. *Public-private enrollment in higher education: Modeling issues related to sectors of education.* Prepared for the National Center for Educational Statistics. Washington, DC: Pelavin Associates.

St. John, E. P., J. Oescher, and S. C. Andrieu. 1992. The influence of prices on within-year persistence by traditional college-age students in four-year colleges. *Journal of Student Financial Aid* 22 (1): 27–38.

St. John, E. P., and M. B. Paulsen. 2001. The finance of higher education: Implications for theory, research, policy and practice. In *The finance of higher education: Theory, research, policy, and practice,* edited by M. B. Paulsen and J. C. Smart. New York: Agathon Press.

St. John, E. P., M. B. Paulsen, and J. B. Starkey. 1996. The nexus between college choice and persistence. *Research in Higher Education* 37: 175–220.

St. John, E. P. and C. Ridenour. 2001. Market forces and strategic adaptation: The influence of private scholarships on planning in urban schools. *Urban Review* 33: 269–90.

St. John, E. P., and L. A. Robinson. 1985. Redesign of the delivery systems for federal student aid programs. *Cause/Effect* 8 (5): 46–48.

St. John, E. P., and R. Sepanic. 1982. A framework for improving management of financial aid offices. In *Meeting student aid needs in a period of retrenchment*, edited by M. Kramer. New Directions in Higher Education, no. 40. San Francisco: Jossey-Bass.

St. John, E. P., A. B. Simmons, L. D. Hoezee, and O. S. Wooden. 2002. *Trends in higher education finance in Indiana compared to peer states, and the U.S.: A changing context, critical issues, and strategic goals.* Bloomington: Indiana Education Policy Center.

St. John, E. P., A. B. Simmons, and G. D. Musoba. 2002. Merit-aware admissions in public universities: Increasing diversity. *Thought and Action: NEA Higher Education Journal* 17 (2): 35–46.

St. John, E. P., and P. A. Somers. 1997. Assessing the impact of student financial aid on first-time enrollment: A discussion. In *Student aid research: A manual for aid administration*, edited by J. S. Davis. Washington, DC: National Association for Financial Aid Administration.

St. John, E. P., and J. B. Starkey. 1994. The influence of costs on persistence by traditional college-age students in community colleges. *Community College Journal of Research and Practice* 18: 201–14.

————. 1995a. An alternative to net price: Assessing the influences of prices and subsidies on within-year persistence. *Journal of Higher Education* 66: 156–86.

————. 1995b. The influence of prices on persistence by adults. *Journal of Student Financial Aid* 25 (2): 7–18.

St. John, E. P., J. B. Starkey, M. B. Paulsen, and L. A. Mbadugha. 1995. The influence of prices and price subsidies on within-year persistence by students in proprietary schools. *Educational Evaluation and Policy Analysis* 17: 149–65.

St. John, E. P., J. G. Ward, and S. W. M. Laine. 1999. *State policy on professional development: Rethinking the linkages to student outcomes.* Oak Brook, IL: North Central Regional Educational Laboratory.

Talbet, M. 2001. Class and the classroom. *Atlantic Monthly,* February, 52–55.

Terenzini, P. T., A. F. Cabrera, and E. M. Bernal. 2001. *Swimming against the tide: The poor in American higher education.* College Board Report no. 2001–1. New York: College Entrance Examination Board.

Terkla, D. G. 1985. Does financial aid enhance undergraduate persistence? *Journal of Higher Education* 15: 11–18.

Theobald, N. 2003. The need for issue-driven school funding reform in urban schools. In *Reinterpreting urban school reform*, edited by L. F. Miron and E. P. St. John. Albany: State University of New York Press.

Tierney, M. L. 1980. The impact of student financial aid on student demand for public/private higher education. *Journal of Higher Education* 51: 527–45.

Tinto, V. 1975. Dropout from higher education: A theoretical synthesis of recent research. *Review of Educational Research* 45: 89–125.

————. 1987. *Leaving college: Rethinking the causes and cures of student attrition.* Chicago: University of Chicago Press.

————. 2000. Linking learning and leaving. In *Reworking the departure puzzle,* edited by J. B. Braxton. Nashville, TN: Vanderbilt University Press.

Torbert, W. R. 1976. *Creating a community of inquiry: Conflict, collaboration, transformation.* New York: Wiley.

Toutkoushian, R. K. 2001. Trends in revenues and expenditures for public and private higher education. In *The finance of higher education: Theory, research, policy and practice,* edited by M. B. Paulsen and J. C. Smart. New York: Agathon Press.

Trammell, M. L. 1996. An interpretive and critical analysis of Louisiana Higher Education Quality Support Fund policy construction. Ph.D. diss., University of New Orleans.

Trow, M. 1974. *Problems in the transition from elite to mass higher education.* New York: McGraw-Hill.

U.S. Department of Education. 1990. *Tough choices: A guide to administrative cost management in colleges and universities.* Washington, DC: U.S. Department of Education.

U.S. Department of Labor, Bureau of Labor Statistics. 1997. *Consumer Price Index, All Urban Consumers (city average), All Items (CPI-U).* Washington, DC: U.S. Department of Labor, Bureau of Labor Statistics

U.S. General Accounting Office. 1998. *Higher education: Restructuring student aid could reduce low-income student drop out.* GAO/HEHS. Washington, DC: U.S. General Accounting Office.

USA Today. 2001. College aid comes up short. *USA Today,* 21 February, 14A.

Voorhees, R. 2001. Community colleges. In *The finance of higher education: Theory, research, policy, and practice,* edited by M. B. Paulsen and J. C. Smart. New York: Agathon Press.

Weathersby, G. B., and F. E. Balderston. 1972. PPBS in higher education planning and management: Part I, an overview. *Higher Education* 1: 191–206.

Weathersby, G. B., G. A. Jackson, F. Jacobs, E. P. St. John, and T. Tingly. 1977. *The development of institutions of higher education: Theory and assessment of four possible areas of federal intervention.* Cambridge: Harvard Graduate School of Education.

Wells, E. D. 1996. The influence of student aid and prices on within-year persistence by undergraduates in health care professions. Ph.D. diss., University of New Orleans.

Williams, J. B. 1997. *Race discrimination in higher education.* New York: Praeger.

Wilms, W. W., R. W. Moore, and R. E. Bolus. 1987. Whose fault is default? A study of the impact of student characteristics and institutional practices on guaranteed student loan default rates in California. *Educational Evaluation and Policy Analysis* 9: 41–54.

Wilson, D. 2001. Indiana sees significant gains in students going to college. *Hoosier Times,* 11 February, A11.

Wilson, R. 1986. Overview of the issue: Minority/poverty student enrollment problems. Paper presented at the Third Annual NASSGAP/NCHELP Conference on Student Financial Aid Research, Chicago.

Witte, J. F. 1998. The Milwaukee experiment. *Educational Evaluation and Policy Analysis* 20: 229–52.

Wolanin, T. R. 2001. *Rhetoric and reality: Effects and consequences of the HOPE Scholarship.* Washington, DC: Institute for Higher Education Policies.

Wolfle, L. M. 1985. Applications of causal models in higher education. In *Higher education: Handbook of theory and research,* vol. 1. New York: Agathon Press.

Wong, K. K. 2003. Federal Title I as a reform strategy in urban schools. In *Reinterpreting urban school reform,* edited by L. F. Miron and E. P. St. John. Albany: State University of New York Press.

Zook, J. 1993. 900 institutions could be dropped from student-aid programs for high default rates: 55 are non-profit colleges. *Chronicle of Higher Education* 40 (September): A31–A32.

Zumeta, W. 1997. How did they do it? The surprising enrollment success of private nonprofit higher education from 1980 to 1995. Paper presented at the Association for the Study of Higher Education Annual Meeting, San Antonio, TX.

———. 2001 State policy and private higher education. In *The finance of higher education: Theory, research, policy, and practice,* edited by M. B. Paulsen and J. C. Smart. New York: Agathon Press.

———. Forthcoming. State higher education financing: Demand imperatives meet structural, cyclic and political constraints. In *Funding for higher education: New contexts and rationales,* edited by E. P. St. John and M. D. Parsons. Baltimore: Johns Hopkins University Press.

INDEX

GI Bill, 3, 75, 83, 177. *See also* veterans' benefits

grants, 29, 86, 108; need-based, 22, 98, 102, 142, 217. *See also* federal grants; Pell grants

Great Society, 3, 36, 50, 76–77, 86, 96–99

Guaranteed Student Loans (GSL), 76, 79–80, 102. *See also* Higher Education Act; Federal Family Education Loan Program

Higher Education Act (HEA; 1965), 3, 50, 75–78, 86, 97–98, 123, 177; amendments: —1972, 3, 50, 78, 97, 177; —1980, 100. *See also* Middle Income Student Assistance Act

Higher Education General Information Surveys (HEGIS), 225–26. *See also* Integrated Postsecondary Education Data System

high school: curriculum, 54, 58, 122; graduation rates, 57, 66; math courses, 3, 4, 9, 206

High School and Beyond (HSB), 89; senior cohort (HSB:80), 48–49, 63, 90, 92; sophomore cohort (HSB:82), 48, 63, 92

high school graduates, 15, 23, 57–58, 66–67, 85–86, 112, 123, 133–34, 147, 150, 152, 159, 171, 175, 186, 206, 210, 225, 228; college-qualified, 11

high tuition, high grant, 39, 216

Hispanics, 11, 12, 17, 27, 30, 35, 44, 61–62, 92, 123, 125–26, 141, 147, 159–60; and enrollment rates, 31, 38, 72, 88, 113–14, 136

HOPE Scholarships, 29–30, 128–30, 136, 201. *See also* Taxpayer Relief Act

human capital, 4–5, 40, 51, 155; economics of, 4, 33; individual benefits, 5; theory, 40–41, 77, 179, 221

Indiana, 138, 141–43, 147–49, 185, 207, 208, 212

Integrated Postsecondary Education Data System (IPEDS), 131, 225–26. *See also* Higher Education General Information Surveys

justice, theory of. *See* Rawls, John

K–12 (Kindergarten), 15, 45, 54, 73, 220; improvements in, 33, 43, 49, 65, 127, 150, 223; reform, 15, 23, 26–27, 33, 38, 45, 49–50, 57, 59, 122. *See also* academic preparation; school reform

labor market, 8, 54, 90, 111–14, 187, 203, 216

Land Grant Acts, 176

liberals, 21, 28, 77, 121, 128, 178–79, 182, 184, 221; analysts, 22, 182

literacy and reading reform, 207

loans, 12, 29, 31, 55, 100, 105, 108, 119, 150, 184, 198; default, 87, 128, 199, 215, 228; federally subsidized, 20, 29, 87, 202; repayment, 12, 130–31, 137, 199; state, 6

low-income students, 1, 9, 13, 27, 30, 33, 38, 95, 98, 119–20, 123, 126, 130, 138, 157, 159–60; and access, 13; and equal opportunity, 14, 204, 220; and federal grant dollars, 90; and opportunity gap, 17; and Pell grants, 18–19, 138

low-tuition philosophy, 175, 177, 180. *See also* tuition

majority, 13, 28, 30–31, 37–38, 65, 91, 123–24, 182, 184, 187, 222; access for, 9, 15, 17, 22–23, 37, 136, 145, 173, 189

Marxist theory, 44. *See also* social reproduction, social theory

math courses, 3, 4, 9, 206; and college enrollment, 4. *See also* high school

Middle Income Student Assistance Act (MISAA; 1978), 3, 79, 97, 100, 180. *See also* Higher Education Act

middle-income students, 61–62, 98, 100, 119, 222; and access, 13; and equal opportunity, 220; and loans, 150, 180; and targeted tax relief, 30

minorities, 13, 28, 63, 94, 113, 115, 119, 123–25, 143, 147, 162; and opportunity gap, 9, 17, 125, 171, 216; and enrollment rates, 25, 88, 91–92, 122, 150; impact of aid on, 13, 87. *See also* African Americans; Asian Americans; Hispanics; racial/ethnic groups

Reading Excellence Act (1998), 46

Reagan, Ronald, 104, 129, 149, 180; administration, 6, 21, 28, 63–64, 82, 100–102, 105, 109, 114, 122, 124, 180, 199; election, 3

refinancing, 12, 30, 103, 173, 185, 188, 190, 194; federal strategy, 173; higher education, 30, 70; inquiry-based approach, 188; institutional strategies, 63; in 1980s, 101, 222; states, 193–95

retention, 192, 208–10, 218. *See also* persistence

scholarships, 47, 108, 209–10. *See also* HOPE Scholarships

school choice, 35, 46–47, 209–211

school reform, 13, 28, 33, 42, 46–47, 52, 54, 65, 73, 96–97, 113, 121–24, 146–47, 171, 206–11, 218; research-based reform, 45–47, 66–67

segregation, 34, 45, 86. *See also* desegregation

situated contexts, 44–45, 49, 53, 59, 62, 65

social reproduction, 43–44, 52

Social Security Survivors Benefits Program, 3, 76, 80–81, 83, 101, 103

social theory, 33, 42–43, 52

special education referral, 47, 210, 218

state grants, 6, 55, 71, 82–83, 88, 96, 110, 113, 142, 145, 148–49, 185, 195, 202–3, 217, 220–21; merit-based, 133; need-based, 78, 88, 139, 149, 177, 220

State Student Incentive Grants (SSIG), 3, 78, 82, 102, 177. *See also* Higher Education Act

Supplemental Educational Opportunity Grant (SEOG), 76, 78–80, 101. *See also* Higher Education Act

tax credits, 12, 26, 29, 31, 70, 72, 79, 128, 130, 134, 136–37, 148–150, 178, 180–82, 184, 187, 200–201; Lifetime Learning, 129, 136; targeted, 29, 222. *See also* HOPE Scholarships

tax expenditures, 14, 28–29, 51, 138, 221; per FTE, 17, 228

tax relief, 29, 136; targeted, 21, 148, 150, 181, 201, 222. *See also* Taxpayer Relief Act; taxpayers, justice for

tax revenue, 41, 131, 200

taxation, 37, 54; tax rates, 1, 41, 222

taxpayer justice, 17, 22, 28

Taxpayer Relief Act (1997), 181. *See also* Hope Scholarships

taxpayers, 222; and college finance, 17; conservative, 23, 51, 114, 127, 149, 184, 202; costs, 1, 4, 13, 28–31, 37, 39, 84, 87–88, 98, 114, 125, 136–37, 150, 181, 218; justice for, 22, 28, 128; and spending, 28, 39; willingness to pay, 21–22, 36–37, 39, 54

theory of justice. *See* Rawls, John

Title I, 45, 65–66, 96, 99, 209. *See also* Elementary and Secondary Education Act

Title IV, 71, 77, 80, 83–84, 86, 89, 97–98, 102–3, 123–24, 130. *See also* Higher Education Act

TRIO programs (Talent Search, Upward Bound, and Special Services), 68, 97, 99, 123. *See also* Higher Education Act

tuition, 54, 131, 195, 220; charges, 2, 5–7, 9, 22, 37, 90, 96, 103–4, 115, 118–19, 124, 168, 181; discounting, 134, 188, 192; low-tuition philosophy, 175, 180. *See also* high tuition, high grant

U.S. Department of Education (ED), 100, 104, 107–9, 225. *See also* National Center for Education Statistics

U. S. Department of Health, Education and Welfare, 80

veterans, 71, 80, 130; benefits, 71, 80–81, 83, 86–87, 103. *See also* GI Bill

Washington, 138, 139, 140–42, 145, 185